UNDERSTANDING
SPIRITUAL WARFARE

UNDERSTANDING SPIRITUAL WARFARE

FOUR VIEWS

Edited by James K. Beilby & Paul Rhodes Eddy

BakerAcademic

a division of Baker Publishing Group
Grand Rapids, Michigan

Published by Baker Academic
a division of Baker Publishing Group
P.O. Box 6287, Grand Rapids, MI 49516-6287
www.bakeracademic.com

Printed in the United States of America

Library of Congress Cataloging-in-Publication Data
Understanding spiritual warfare : four views / edited by James K. Beilby & Paul Rhodes Eddy.
    p.   cm.
Includes bibliographical references and indexes.
ISBN 978-0-8010-3936-2 (pbk.)
1. Spiritual warfare. I. Beilby, James K. II. Eddy, Paul R. III. Wink, Walter.
BV4509.5.U53 2012
235'.4—dc23   2012020206

In keeping with biblical principles of creation stewardship, Baker Publishing Group advocates the responsible use of our natural resources. As a member of the Green Press Initiative, our company uses recycled paper when possible. The text paper of this book is composed in part of post-consumer waste.

12   13   14   15   16   17   18   7   6   5   4   3   2   1

Dedicated to Albert C. Bender and Judie O'Brien

Dedicated to Uncle Al, who is the definition of a "lifelong learner."
Thank you for years of wise counsel and stimulating conversations.—Jim

Dedicated to my aunt, Judie O'Brien.
Your love and encouragement mean more to me than you'll ever know.
You are to me "the aunt than which none greater can be conceived"!
Thank you, Auntie.—Paul

19.561

Contents

Acknowledgments

The list of people that have helped us bring this book to completion is long. We are thankful for the excellent work, patience, and flexibility of our contributors—Greg Boyd, David Powlison, Walter Wink, Peter Wagner, and Rebecca Greenwood. During the final stage of the editorial process, we learned with great sadness of Walter's passing. It is a high honor for us to have partnered with Walter on one of his final writing projects. We are also very thankful to Gareth Higgins and Michael Hardin for helping Walter bring his voice to this conversation during a period of failing health. Gareth edited Walter's initial essay and Michael coauthored the responses with Walter. We are also thankful for the work and encouragement of our publisher at Baker Academic, Bob Hosack, and to Bethel University for supporting this work in a variety of ways, including providing Paul with a sabbatical in the spring of 2011. In addition, Jim's teacher's assistant, Zac Bush, read portions of the manuscript and offered helpful suggestions. As always, our families have been an invaluable source of support for all of our endeavors, academic and otherwise. Words are insufficient to convey our appreciation. Finally, we would like to dedicate this book to Albert C. Bender (Jim's uncle) and Judie O'Brien (Paul's aunt). Thank you for your encouragement and love.

Introduction

Introducing Spiritual Warfare:
A Survey of Key Issues and Debates

Paul Rhodes Eddy and James K. Beilby

"Finally, be strong in the Lord and in the strength of his power. Put on the whole armour of God, so that you may be able to stand against the wiles of the devil. For our struggle is not against enemies of blood and flesh, but against the rulers, against the authorities, against the cosmic powers of this present darkness, against the spiritual forces of evil in the heavenly places" (Eph. 6:10–12 NRSV).

These words of the apostle Paul have echoed down the corridors of church history. For two millennia, they have inspired Christians toward courageous living, wise discernment, engaging prayer, and bold action. They have also served as one of the common sites of exegetical skirmish in a long-running intra-Christian dialogue and debate about the nature and extent, the biblical and theological moorings, and the rational, experiential, and practical implications of what has come to be known simply as "spiritual warfare."

Some issues of interest and dialogue within the church have their day in the sun and then, for all practical purposes, disappear. Others, however, never really leave us. They may ebb and flow; they may have seasons of higher or lower profile; they may find themselves the subject of a larger or smaller number of books published in any given year. But in one way or another they remain on the church's radar. Spiritual warfare appears to be one of these issues. From pulpit sermons to religious radio, from internet websites to conference halls to the quarterly catalogs of Christian publishers (both trade and academic; fiction and nonfiction), the topic of spiritual warfare never seems to grow old. This shouldn't really surprise us. The perpetual interest within the church regarding

1

the things of spiritual warfare is mirrored by the seemingly insatiable fascination within our wider culture(s) for things mysterious and transcendent, things otherworldly—and things even a bit frightening. But for the church, it is not simply the *interest* in this topic that is perennial. When it comes to the issue of spiritual warfare, the other realities that can be counted on are *disagreement* and *debate*.

Unfortunately, within the contemporary church, much of the disagreement and debate surrounding this topic has been characterized by more heat than light. Often, there has been more double monologue than dialogue, more talking *at* each other or *past* each other than *with* each other. This book provides a forum in which several of the important perspectives and representative voices on spiritual warfare are able to meet and interact. This essay will assist in setting the stage for conversation by offering an introduction to three of the broad issues that inform the contemporary discussion on spiritual warfare: (1) the moral objection to "spiritual warfare" language; (2) the existence and nature of spirit beings, with a focus on Satan and the demonic; and (3) Christian perspectives on the theology and practice of spiritual warfare itself. Along the way, something of a bibliographical map to the terrain will be provided (primarily in the footnotes), which will offer further avenues to those wishing to go deeper on a particular topic. This essay will end by introducing our contributors to this volume, who together offer a host of rich insights on our topic and provide a model of what honest, respectful, challenging, and fruitful dialogue on spiritual warfare can look like.

The Moral Objection to "Spiritual Warfare" Language: A Response

The first issue to be considered involves an important question that threatens to close down the discussion of spiritual warfare before it even begins. It is a question that emerges just as often from outside the church as within. It is the question of whether encouraging Christians to think about and engage in "spiritual warfare" against "evil forces" at work in the world does more harm than good. Simply put, doesn't the whole idea of "spiritual warfare" ultimately foster things like self-righteousness, intolerance, and even violence? Doesn't "spiritual warfare" language encourage people to naively imagine that everything and everyone in the world falls into one of two simplistic categories of "good" and "evil," where "good" is always linked to "us," and "evil" is always associated with "them"? Hasn't this sort of thinking and talking led to an endless stream of arrogance, judgmentalism, and suspicion—not to mention inquisitions, holy wars, witch burnings, and genocide? This is an important question, and it comes in different forms from various quarters.

For a relative few, the problem is to be found in appealing to the very idea of "evil" itself. They argue that it would be better if we stopped using this four-letter word, since it encourages us to believe in mythological monsters that do not exist (e.g., Satan) and/or to demonize certain people by categorizing them as "inhuman."[1] Taking a cue from the postmodern turn inspired by the intuitions of Friedrich Nietzsche, some see the very ideas of "good" and "evil" as "archaic categories" that simply mask bids for power to define and dominate others.[2] For most people, however, this is a position that is difficult to take seriously, let alone to hold to consistently. Even for the average postmodern materialist/atheist, recent horrors of the last hundred years alone—including two world wars, the Nazi holocaust, the human sex-trafficking industry, and other systems of exploitation and oppression—are usually enough to convince them that "evil" is a fact of human existence.[3]

And so, for most, the concern over the use of spiritual warfare language is due not to evil's nonreality but to its all-too-real presence in our world. Not surprisingly, this concern seems to have grown over the last decade. It reflects the growth of a wider concern for any and all forms of religiously motivated hate and violence that has taken place under the shadow of the 9/11 tragedy.[4] Nahi Alon and Haim Omer have recently argued for an inevitable link between use of the concept/language of the "demonic" and a host of dangerous relational attitudes and practices. They write:

> The *demonic view* is a way of experiencing an evolving attitude that begins with doubt, thrives with suspicion, ends with certainty, and aims at decisive militant action. When it seeps into a relationship, a highly negative view of the

1. Reasoning thus, Phillip Cole concludes that "we should abandon the idea of evil." *The Myth of Evil: Demonizing the Enemy* (Westport, CT: Praeger, 2006), 23. For further discussion, see David Pocock, "Unruly Evil," in *The Anthropology of Evil*, ed. David Parkin (New York: Blackwell, 1985), 42–56.

2. Fredric Jameson, *Fables of Aggression: Wyndham Lewis, the Modernist as Fascist* (Berkeley: University of California Press, 1979), 56. See Friedrich Nietzsche, *Beyond Good and Evil*, trans. Marianne Cowan (Chicago: Gateway/Regnery, 1955).

3. A point argued by the well-known Marxist/atheist Terry Eagleton in his recent book *On Evil* (New Haven: Yale University Press, 2010).

4. For a representative sampling from among the many publications on religion and violence over the last decade, see Hector Avalos, *Fighting Words: The Origins of Religious Violence* (Buffalo: Prometheus, 2005); J. Harold Ellens, ed. *The Destructive Power of Religion: Violence in Judaism, Christianity, and Islam*, 4 vols. (Westport, CT: Praeger, 2007); R. Joseph Hoffmann, ed., *The Just War and Jihad: Violence in Judaism, Christianity, and Islam* (Amherst, NY: Prometheus, 2006); Jessica Stern, *Terror in the Name of God: Why Religious Militants Kill* (New York: HarperCollins, 2003); James K. Wellmann Jr., ed., *Belief and Bloodshed: Religion and Violence across Time and Tradition* (Lanham, MD: Rowman & Littlefield, 2007); Jeremy Young, *The Violence of God and the War on Terror* (New York: Seabury, 2008).

other evolves, which in turn may lead to symmetrical counter accusations. Thus a vicious cycle arises in which both sides become more and more entrenched in their negative positions.[5]

The wider concern regarding religiously motivated violence has become a common plank among proponents of the "new atheism," who argue for an inherent relationship between religion, intolerance, and violence.[6] But in the post-9/11 world, it is usually not just "religion" in general that falls under suspicion—more particularly it is the three monotheistic, "Abrahamic" faiths of Judaism, Christianity, and Islam that are regularly charged with inciting such evils. With regard to Christianity in particular, arguments include monotheism's inherent intolerance and oppression; the long history of the church's involvement with hatred, bloodshed, and warfare; and the presence of divinely sanctioned violence throughout the Bible itself, in both the Old and New Testaments.[7]

This is not the place to offer a full-scale response to these charges, of course, but it is important to note that each line of argument here has been thoughtfully considered and convincingly answered by scholars who, although equally concerned about the misuse of religion (or Christianity in particular) to justify intolerance and violence, see the evidence quite differently.[8] For instance, a

5. Nahi Alon and Haim Omer, *The Psychology of Demonization: Promoting Acceptance and Reducing Conflict* (Mahwah, NJ: Erlbaum, 2006), 1 (emphasis in original).

6. Richard Dawkins, *The God Delusion* (Boston: Houghton Mifflin, 2006); Sam Harris, *The End of Faith: Religion, Terror and the Future of Reason* (New York: Norton, 2005); Christopher Hitchens, *God Is Not Great: How Religion Poisons Everything* (New York: Twelve, 2007). Defenders of the new atheism, however, conveniently ignore the fact that all worldviews, including atheism, have sought to justify evil and oppressive violence. The atheist writer David Steele has reminded his fellow atheists: the "history of the past one hundred years shows us that atheistic ideologies can sanctify more and bigger atrocities than Christianity or Islam ever did." *Atheism Explained: From Folly to Philosophy* (Chicago/LaSalle, IL: Open Court, 2008), xi.

7. E.g., regarding the claim of inherent intolerance within monotheism: Jan Assmann, *The Price of Monotheism*, trans. Robert Savage (Stanford: Stanford University Press, 2010); Carol Delaney, *Abraham on Trial: The Social Legacy of Biblical Myth* (Princeton: Princeton University Press, 1998). E.g., regarding intolerance and violence through church history: Toby Green, *Inquisition: The Reign of Fear* (New York: Dunne, 2009); M. Lilla, *The Stillborn God: Religion, Politics and the Modern West* (New York: Vintage, 2008). E.g., regarding the violence of the Bible: John Barton, "The Dark Side of God in the Old Testament," in *Ethical and Unethical in the Old Testament*, ed. K. J. Dell (New York: Clark, 2010), 122–34; John J. Collins, "The Zeal of Phinehas: The Bible and the Legitimation of Violence," *Journal of Biblical Literature* 122 (2003): 3–21; Gerd Lüdemann, *The Unholy in Holy Scripture: The Dark Side of the Bible*, trans. J. Bowden (Louisville: Westminster John Knox, 1997).

8. See David Martin, *Does Christianity Cause War?* (Oxford: Clarendon, 1997); J. G. McConville, *God and Earthly Power: An Old Testament Political Theology, Genesis–Kings* (New York: Clark, 2006), chap. 2; Alister McGrath, "Is Religion Evil?," in *God Is Great, God is Good: Why Believing in God Is Reasonable and Responsible*, ed. William Lane Craig and Chad V.

number of studies have demonstrated that monotheism per se is not more inherently intolerant or oppressive than any other worldview.[9] Clearly, monotheistic religions—including the Christian religion—can and have been used by people and groups over the centuries to legitimize their own political aspirations and justify violent agendas. But it is important to distinguish empirical *correlation* from *causation*—and many critics of monotheism regularly confuse the two.[10] As Miroslav Volf has argued, "Neither the character of the Christian faith (its being a religion of a monotheist type) nor its most fundamental convictions (such as that God created the world and is engaged in redeeming it) are violence inducing. The Christian faith is *misused* when it is employed to underwrite violence."[11]

With regard to the intolerance and violence that have attached to the Christian religion, no one can seriously deny the many instances of correlation through history. Many Christians themselves have regularly pointed this out and mourned the tragic pattern.[12] But, once again, careful consideration has

Meister (Downers Grove, IL: InterVarsity, 2009), 119–33; Meic Pearse, *The Gods of War: Is Religion the Primary Cause of Violent Conflict?* (Downers Grove, IL: InterVarsity, 2007); William T. Cavanaugh, *The Myth of Religious Violence: Secular Ideology and the Roots of Modern Conflict* (New York: Oxford University Press, 2009).

9. See Rainer Albertz, "Monotheism and Violence: How to Handle a Dangerous Biblical Tradition," in *The Land of Israel in Bible, History, and Theology: Studies in Honour of Ed Noort*, ed. Jacques van Ruiten and J. C. de Vos (Boston: Brill, 2009), 373–87; Miroslav Volf, "Jehovah on Trial," *Christianity Today*, April 27, 1998, 32–35. Some Christians themselves argue that "monotheism" tends toward imperialism, domination, and violence, but then go on to distance Christianity from monotheism by contrasting it with Christian "trinitarianism"; e.g., Jürgen Moltmann, *The Trinity and the Kingdom of God* (New York: Harper & Row, 1981), 197. However, others have effectively argued that, rightly understood, Christian trinitarianism is a version of monotheism and that monotheism per se is not the problem. Rather, the problem is with certain monarchical visions of monotheism, which are quite unlike the *agapē*-oriented vision of the trinitarian God offered in the New Testament. See Randall Otto, "Moltmann and the Anti-Monotheism Movement," *International Journal of Systematic Theology* 3 (2001): 293–308; Thomas H. McCall, *Which Trinity? Whose Monotheism? Philosophical and Systematic Theologians on the Metaphysics of Trinitarian Theology* (Grand Rapids: Eerdmans, 2010), 224–48. Colin Gunton has suggested that Augustine's Neoplatonically influenced approach to the Trinity helped shape Western Christianity's trinitarian speculation in a neomodalist direction, which rendered it more susceptible to political misuse, etc. See his "Trinity in Modern Theology," in *Companion Encyclopedia of Theology*, ed. P. Byrne and L. Houlden (New York: Routledge, 1995), 940–42.

10. A point emphasized in a recent article found in a notoriously antireligious journal: Benjamin G. Purzycki and Kyle Gibson, "Religion and Violence: An Anthropological Study on Religious Belief and Violent Behavior," *Skeptic* 16, no. 2 (2011): 22–27.

11. Miroslav Volf, "Christianity and Violence," in *War in the Bible and Terrorism in the Twenty-First Century*, ed. R. S. Hess and E. A. Martens (Winona Lake, IN: Eisenbrauns, 2008), 15.

12. Just to take two examples from among our contributors to this book, see Gregory A. Boyd, *The Myth of a Christian Nation: How the Quest for Political Power Is Destroying the Church* (Grand Rapids: Zondervan, 2006), 98–103; and Walter Wink's discussion of the "myth

demonstrated that this common correlation is not a sign of Christianity's inherent intolerance and proneness to violence but rather a sign of the fact that *any* religious or philosophical system can be used—and *misused*—for self-centered ends and political gains.[13] Even the vast majority of the critics of Christian violence readily acknowledge that the original vision and movement inaugurated by Jesus was one of remarkable inclusiveness, principled nonviolence, and self-giving *agapē*-love.[14]

And here is where the moral objection to spiritual warfare is most clearly seen. Some will grant that Christian monotheism is not inherently oppressive. But they will argue that it is the segments within Christian theism that traffic in spiritual warfare language that tend to become oppressive. The concern is that using the biblical language associated with "spiritual warfare" will lead Christians to embrace and imitate the whole range of biblical texts on "warfare," including the intolerance and divinely sanctioned violence in the Bible itself. Even more pressing is the concern that Christians who take spiritual warfare seriously will reframe their own human enemies as "God's enemies"— enemies who, perhaps, are today no less deserving of violent judgment than the Canaanites were in the time of the ancient Israelites.

To the ears of many, "spiritual warfare" sounds uncomfortably close to the language of "holy war." And holy war—with its "warrior God," Yahweh, and its divinely authorized violence against the "enemies" of God's people—is a common theme found throughout the Old Testament.[15] Critics remind us that the Old Testament holy war tradition always included a component of "spiritual

---

of redemptive violence" (including Christian participation) in *Engaging the Powers: Discernment and Resistance in a World of Domination* (Minneapolis: Fortress, 1992), 13–31.

13. For a cogent argument that the increasing rise of intolerance and violence within the fourth-century church was a result of ecclesiastical and governmental political ambitions, rather than the inherently violent tendencies of the early Jesus movement itself, see by H. A. Drake, "Lions into Lambs: Explaining Early Christian Intolerance," *Past and Present* 153 (1996): 3–36; H. A. Drake, *Constantine and the Bishops: The Politics of Intolerance* (Baltimore: Johns Hopkins University Press, 2002). Similarly, see John Derksen, "Why Did Early Christians Turn Violent? The Case of Early Egyptian," *Theological Review* 31 (2010): 60–91.

14. E.g., Lüdemann, *Unholy in Holy Scripture*, 48; Paul N. Anderson, "Genocide or Jesus: A God of Conquest or Pacifism?," in Ellens, ed., *Destructive Power of Religion*, 4:31–52. Thus Harold Ellens's claim of a "violent Jesus" is as rare as it is wrong; "The Violent Jesus," in Ellens, ed., *Destructive Power of Religion*, 3:15–37. On the predominance of a commitment to nonviolence within the early church in the first few centuries, see P. Brock, *Varieties of Pacifism: A Survey from Antiquity to the Outset of the Twentieth Century* (Syracuse: Syracuse University Press, 1998), 3–8.

15. For helpful introductions to the Old Testament "holy war" and/or "Yahweh as warrior" traditions, see Gerhard von Rad, *Holy War in Ancient Israel*, ed. and trans. M. J. Dawn (Grand Rapids: Eerdmans, 1991); Tremper Longman and Daniel G. Reid, *God Is a Warrior* (Grand Rapids: Zondervan, 1995); Tryggve N. D. Mettinger, "Fighting the Powers of Chaos and Hell—Towards the Biblical Portrait of God," *Studia Theologica* 39 (1985): 21–38.

warfare." As the Old Testament itself reveals, the Israelites believed that the spiritual and physical worlds were deeply interwoven, such that as they conducted war against human enemies, God and his angels led the way in the spiritual realm (2 Sam. 5:24; cf. 2 Kings 6:15–17; 1 Chron. 12:22). Both Jews and Christians have wrestled with the themes of divinely sanctioned warfare and violence in the Hebrew Bible/Old Testament for centuries.[16] Within recent scholarship, responses include the following: (1) emphasizing that Israel's role in warfare is downplayed, as God commands them to trust in him rather than in their military might;[17] (2) proposals that the depiction of Israel's violent conquest of cities in the Holy Land may represent attacks on military forts, or are instances of political propaganda and, perhaps, never really happened at all;[18] (3) reminders that Israel was itself an oppressed group and that the themes of violence are part of a "survival strategy" of a traumatized people;[19] and (4) suggestions that, for example, "divine judgment" in the Old Testament is essentially enacted through the natural consequences of sin (which can include war), or that the "final form" of the violent book of Joshua is actually a protest against war itself.[20] Some have even argued that we have simply missed the ironic "beauty" of some of the terrible and grotesque realities associated with God's warrior-like nature in the Old Testament.[21] However they explain it, most Christians see the holy war tradition in the Old Testament as one of the many things that have changed for the people of God with the coming of Jesus Christ and the new covenant.

But it is not just the Old Testament and its holy war tradition that raises concerns. As mentioned above, elements of the New Testament itself have also come under scrutiny as inspired sources of intolerance, bigotry, and violence. The most common culprits here—including the claim of being the one, true

16. For a particularly thoughtful recent treatment, see Paul Copan, *Is God a Moral Monster? Making Sense of the Old Testament God* (Grand Rapids: Baker Books, 2011). See also David T. Lamb, *God Behaving Badly: Is the God of the Old Testament Angry, Sexist and Racist?* (Downers Grove, IL: InterVarsity, 2011); Gregory Boyd, *The Crucifixion of the Warrior God: A Cruciform Reinterpretation of Divine Violence in the Old Testament* (Downers Grove, IL: Intervarsity, forthcoming).

17. Millard C. Lind, *Yahweh Is a Warrior: The Theology of Warfare in Ancient Israel* (Scottdale, PA: Herald, 1980).

18. See, respectively, Richard S. Hess, "War in the Hebrew Bible: An Overview," in *War in the Bible and Terrorism in the Twenty-First Century*, ed. R. S. Hess and E. A. Martens (Winona Lake, IN: Eisenbrauns, 2008), 29–30; and Lori L. Rowlett, *Joshua and the Rhetoric of Violence* (Sheffield: Sheffield Academic Press, 1996).

19. E.g., Kathleen M. O'Conner, "Reclaiming Jeremiah's Violence," in *The Aesthetics of Violence in the Prophets*, ed. J. M. O'Brien and C. Franke (New York: Clark, 2010), 46–49.

20. See, respectively, Terence Fretheim, "God and Violence in the Old Testament," *Word and World* 24 (2004): 23–24; Janet Tollington, "The Ethics of Warfare and the Holy War Tradition in the Book of Judges," in Dell, ed., *Ethical and Unethical in the Old Testament*, 86–87.

21. E.g., Corrine Carvalho, "The Beauty of the Bloody God: The Divine Warrior in Prophetic Literature," in O'Brien and Franke, eds., *Aesthetics of Violence in the Prophets*, 131–52.

religion and the threat of divine judgment and eternal torment in hell for all outsiders who reject the faith—often are traced back to a common villainous source: namely ancient Jewish apocalyptic eschatology, particularly its exclusivist and militant attitudes fueled by violent images of imminent divine judgment upon outsiders.[22] And here is where critics of "spiritual warfare" make the connections explicit: the Old Testament "holy war" tradition fed into the Jewish apocalyptic eschatology that developed during the intertestamental period. Next, Jesus and the early church affirmed and embraced apocalyptic eschatology with its "spiritual warfare" language.[23] It is this apocalyptically influenced "spiritual warfare" language that the church continues to use today. In this light, critics can see apocalyptic eschatology as little more than "a pathological state of the religious mind," and an impetus to a number of religious and moral ills fueled by intolerance toward, and demonization of, the "Other."[24]

Over the last two centuries, a range of scholarly reactions have emerged in response to the question of the relationship of Jewish apocalyptic eschatology to Jesus and the early church. At one end of the spectrum, some have interpreted Jesus as a full-on apocalyptic Jewish prophet in the traditional sense. That is to say, Jesus expected and preached the imminent end of the present world order through the in-breaking of God's decisive judgment. The point of debate within this perspective is whether Jesus believed that he and

22. For a well-known introduction representing the dominant contemporary North American interpretation of Jewish apocalyptic eschatology in the Second Temple period, see John J. Collins, *The Apocalyptic Imagination: An Introduction to Jewish Apocalyptic Literature*, 2nd ed. (Grand Rapids: Eerdmans, 1998). But two other contrasting perspectives—emerging from Britain and Italy—offer important correctives. See, respectively, C. C. Rowland, *The Open Heaven: A Study of Apocalyptic in Judaism and Early Christianity* (New York: Crossroad, 1982); and Gabriele Boccaccini, "Jewish Apocalyptic Tradition: The Contribution of Italian Scholarship," in *Mysteries and Revelations: Apocalyptic Studies since the Uppsa Colloquium*, ed. J. J. Collins and J. H. Charlesworth (Sheffield: JSOT, 1991), 33–50.

23. While the Jewish background is vital, it should be noted that military terminology similar to what we find in early Christian texts is also found in Greco-Roman authors of the day. See Edgar M. Krentz, "Military Language and Metaphors in Philippians," in *Origins and Method: Towards a New Understanding of Judaism and Christianity*, ed. B. H. McLean (Sheffield: Sheffield Academic Press, 1993), 105–27.

24. Randel Helms, "The Dangers of Apocalyptic Thinking," *Free Inquiry* (Summer 1984): 37. Examples of scholars who identify apocalyptic eschatology (or certain elements of it) as a primary instigator of intolerance and violence within Christianity include Warren Carter, "Constructions of Violence and Identities in Matthew's Gospel," in *Violence in the New Testament*, ed. S. Matthews and E. L. Gibson (New York: Clark, 2005), 98–102; Michel Desjardins, *Peace, Violence and the New Testament* (Sheffield: Sheffield Academic Press, 1997), 83–92; Ellens, "Violent Jesus," 30–31; John Gager, with E. Leigh Gibson, "Violent Acts and Violent Language in the Apostle Paul," in *Violence in the New Testament*, ed. S. Matthews and E. L. Gibson (New York: Clark, 2005), 17–18; Burton Mack, *A Myth of Innocence: Mark and Christian Origins* (Philadelphia: Fortress, 1988), 368–76.

his followers were to take an active (i.e., military action) or a more passive (i.e., trust and wait for God to bring the judgment) role. While a few have proposed the former view—i.e., a "zealot Jesus"—most within this broader camp have assumed the latter.[25]

At the other end of the spectrum—and at least in part to avoid associating Jesus with the attitudes of vengeance and violence connected to Jewish apocalyptic thought—some have argued that, although the Judaism he emerged from and the church he gave birth to were both apocalyptically oriented, Jesus himself was not. This has the effect of "saving" Jesus from his apocalyptic Jewish context, only to transform him into something like a Greco-Roman Cynic philosopher or a nonviolent rabble-rouser whose only real ambition was to encourage communal living while challenging the oppressive elites associated with the empire.[26] This approach also has the strange effect of removing Jesus from his historical setting and raises the question of why his early followers maintained crucial aspects of Jewish apocalyptic eschatology if Jesus himself rejected them.

However, a sizable number of scholars argues that things are far more complex than either of these first two views suggests. It appears that the most plausible interpretation of the historical and biblical data leads to the conclusion that both views are simultaneously right—and wrong! The "apocalyptic Jesus" advocates are correct that Jesus and the early church were in fact deeply shaped by much of the basic theological narrative and some of the essential features of Second Temple apocalyptic eschatology.[27] However, the "non-apocalyptic Jesus" proponents are also correct that, in a number of ways, Jesus's eschatology does not represent the common apocalyptic thinking of his day. This both/and interpretation has been articulated by a number of scholars over the years and is commonly referred to as an "inaugurated," or "already—not yet," eschatology.[28] As such, and unlike

25. E.g., see, respectively, H. S. Reimarus, *Reimarus: Fragments*, reprint ed., ed. C. H. Talbert, trans. R. S. Fraser (Chico, CA: Scholars Press, 1985); Albert Schweitzer, *The Quest of the Historical Jesus*, trans. W. Montgomery (New York: Collier/Macmillan, 1968).

26. E.g., John Dominic Crossan, *The Historical Jesus: The Life of a Mediterranean Jewish Peasant* (San Francisco: HarperSanFrancisco, 1991); Robert W. Funk, *Honest to Jesus: Jesus for a New Millennium* (San Francisco: HarperSanFrancisco, 1996).

27. See, e.g., Archie T. Wright, "Evil Spirits in Second Temple Judaism: The *Watcher Tradition* as a Background to the Demonic Pericopes in the Gospels," *Henoch* 28 (2006): 141–59.

28. For several examples of the wide range of scholars who hold to a form of this view, see J. D. G. Dunn, *Jesus Remembered* (Grand Rapids: Eerdmans, 2003), 404–65; John P. Meier, *A Marginal Jew: Rethinking the Historical Jesus*, vol. 2: *Mentor, Message, and Miracles* (New York: Doubleday, 1994), 289–454; Ben Witherington III, *The Jesus Quest: The Third Search for the Jew of Nazareth* (Downers Grove, IL: InterVarsity, 1997), 209–10; Ben Wiebe, "The Focus of Jesus' Eschatology," in *Self-Definition and Self-Discovery in Early Christianity: A Study in Changing*

typical ancient apocalyptic theology, it displays a firm conviction that God's transformative kingdom has *already broken into this world*. However, it also aligns with apocalyptic thinking in displaying an eager anticipation of future dimensions of God's eschatological kingdom *that have not yet arrived*. In other words, the "already—not yet" interpretation recognizes that, while Jesus and the early church borrowed much from apocalyptic eschatology of the times, they also modified crucial aspects of it so as to arrive at a unique, even paradoxical, vision of the kingdom of God.

This intriguing modification of Jewish apocalyptic thought not only makes the most sense of the New Testament data in general. But when considered alongside Jesus's *agapē*-love ethic, it also provides a key for understanding the distinctive, even surprising, features of the early Christian approach to apocalyptic eschatology in general, and "spiritual warfare" in particular.[29] Among other things, it provides important insights into the early Christian use of spiritual warfare categories that serve to provide answers for those who rightly are concerned about how this type of language has been used to fuel intolerance and violence throughout history. A key factor is made explicit in the apostle Paul's important statement that "our struggle is not against enemies of blood and flesh, but against the . . . cosmic powers of this present darkness, against the spiritual forces of evil in the heavenly places" (Eph. 6:12 NRSV). Unlike every other known instance of Jewish apocalyptic eschatology, the version held by Jesus and much of the early church viewed the hostile forces they struggled against as composed entirely of spiritual beings—*not fellow human beings*.[30] As N. T. Wright has correctly observed:

Horizons, ed. D. J. Hawkins and T. Robinson (Lewiston, NY: Mellen, 1990), 121–46. Even N. T. Wright, who is commonly known for his antagonism toward certain images of an apocalyptic Jesus, argues for an already—not yet eschatology that stems from Jesus into the early church; see *Jesus and the Victory of God* (Minneapolis: Fortress, 1996), 322, 467–72.

29. On this remarkable development, see William H. Brownlee, "From Holy War to Holy Martyrdom," in *The Quest for the Kingdom of God: Studies in Honor of George E. Mendenhall*, ed. H. B. Huffmon et al. (Winona Lake, IN: Eisenbrauns, 1983), 281–92. For some contemporary reflections on the benefits—ethical and otherwise—of early Christian apocalyptic thought, see J. Christiaan Beker, "The Promise of Paul's Apocalyptic for Our Times," in *The Future of Christology: Essays in Honor of Leander E. Keck*, ed. A. J. Malherbe and W. A. Meeks (Minneapolis: Fortress, 1993), 152–59; Nancy J. Duff, "The Significance of Pauline Apocalyptic for Theological Ethics," in *Apocalyptic and the New Testament: Essays in Honor of J. Louis Martyn*, ed. J. Marcus and M. L. Soards (Sheffield: JSOT Press, 1989), 279–96; David N. Scholar, " 'The God of Peace Will Shortly Crush Satan under Your Feet' (Romans 16:20a): The Function of Apocalyptic Eschatology in Paul," *Ex Auditu* 6 (1990): 53–61.

30. On fellow human "gentiles," in one way or another, as the primary eschatological enemy within all other forms of Jewish apocalyptic eschatology, see Lawrence H. Schiffman, "War in Jewish Apocalyptic Thought," in *War and Peace in the Jewish Tradition*, ed. L. Schiffman and J. B. Wolowelsky (New York: Yeshiva University Press, 2007), 477–95.

One of the key elements in Jesus' perception of his task was therefore his *re-definition* of who the real enemy was. . . . The pagan hordes surrounding Israel [including Rome] were not the actual foe of the people of YHWH. Standing behind the whole problem of Israel's exile was the dark power known in some Old Testament traditions as the satan, the accuser. The struggle that was coming to a head was therefore cosmic.[31]

This fact explains a number of otherwise mysterious features of Jesus and the early Christian faith, including the fact that, on one hand, Jesus presented himself in terms of a "messianic" warrior-king, and yet, on the other hand, he refused the use of the sword and both modeled and taught *agapē*-love and forgiveness toward human "enemies."[32] As Paul Middleton has recently demonstrated, unlike other forms of Jewish apocalyptic eschatology, "[early] Christianity had no temporal outlet [i.e., they refused to identify human enemies and/or participate in earthly war and violence] . . . and so Christian apocalyptic war was conceived in wholly cosmic terms, with a cosmic enemy, a cosmic outcome and a cosmic stage on which martyrs lived and died: nothing less than cosmic conflict."[33] In fact, especially prior to its post-Constantinian affiliation with the Roman Empire, the early church was commonly known not for inciting intolerance and violence but for its spirit of inclusiveness, principled nonviolence, and what Middleton refers to as "radical martyrdom"—a willingness to die rather than do violence to others.[34] Importantly, even the practice of *spiritual* warfare, as exemplified by Jesus and his early followers, was characterized not by self-righteous and aggressive bravado toward the demonic in the spirit realm (e.g., Jude 8–10) but by humility of spirit, trust

31. Wright, *Jesus and the Victory of God*, 450–51 (emphasis in original).

32. On the complete reidentification of "enemy" from the human to the spiritual realm as a key to understanding Jesus's self-understanding as "messiah," see Paul Rhodes Eddy, "Remembering Jesus' Self-Understanding: James D. G. Dunn on Jesus' Sense of Role and Identity," in *Memories of Jesus: A Critical Appraisal of James D. G. Dunn's Jesus Remembered*, ed. R. B. Stewart and G. R. Habermas (Nashville: B&H Academic, 2010), esp. 249–53. On this unexpected twist to the Jewish "divine warrior" motif, see Thomas R. Yoder Neufeld, *"Put on the Armour of God": The Divine Warrior from Isaiah to Ephesians* (Sheffield: Sheffield Academic Press, 1997). Relatedly, see Thomas R. Yoder Neufeld, *Killing Enmity: Violence and the New Testament* (Grand Rapids: Baker Academic, 2011).

33. Paul Middleton, *Radical Martyrdom and Cosmic Conflict in Early Christianity* (New York: T&T Clark, 2006), 134. In light of this observation, contemporary American Christians are called to avoid the all-too-easy comparison of early Christian martyrs with fallen national warriors. On this comparison, see Jon Davies, *The Christian Warrior in the Twentieth Century* (Lewiston, NY: Mellen, 1995).

34. See Rodney Stark, *The Rise of Christianity: A Sociologist Reconsiders History* (Princeton: Princeton University Press, 1996), chaps. 4 and 5; Brock, *Varieties of Pacifism*, 3–8; Middleton, *Radical Martyrdom and Cosmic Conflict*.

in the liberating power of God, and the giving of one's own life for the sake of others on earth.

The moral objection to spiritual warfare language is motivated by very important concerns regarding the propagation of intolerance and violence in the world. But as it turns out, the New Testament concept of spiritual warfare—rightly understood—not only does not contribute to these evils but goes even further by offering a vision of reality where, ultimately, no fellow human is recognized as "enemy" when viewed from a kingdom perspective. Of course, Christians can agree on this broad perspective of spiritual warfare while still disagreeing on whether, with regard to the human geopolitical realm, war and violence are ever justified in the face of certain evils. And although the "just war" and "pacifist" traditions within the Christian family diverge here, members of both traditions can be found embracing the language of spiritual warfare.

Of course, one might still object that, while this is all well and good on a theoretical level, when real people begin to consistently resort to such language, problems follow. A recent study by David Durst of six contemporary American churches where the language of spiritual warfare is used consciously and freely is helpful here. At least with regard to the six churches under investigation, Durst found that

> the use of militant language does not determine how believers participate militarily or politically, how they imagine eschatological events, or how they attempt to influence society. . . . The language of conflict is an integrated rhetorical type in each of these churches, but does not overshadow other types of speech. In human-divine and interpersonal relationships, as well as in approaches to organizational leadership, the language of love and family are more prominent, and many participants are concerned with what the militant language communicates to outsiders.
>
> Observations of these churches do not validate the worst fears of those who advocate the elimination of exclusive salvation claims and belief in cosmic conflict. . . . These churches have many beliefs and values that reflect a warfare worldview, but also display great love and compassion, both for one another and for their communities and the entire human family. They are missional without being imperialistic.[35]

However, as Durst also reminds us, it is absolutely crucial that Christians who employ spiritual warfare language take responsibility both for explicating

---

35. David M. Durst, "Fighting the Good Fight: Missional Use of Militant Language" (PhD diss., Asbury Theological Seminary, 2010), 243.

its meaning and for maintaining constant sensitivity to situations and contexts wherein the use of such language can be easily misunderstood.[36] Again, Christians must remain vigilant lest they subtly—even unconsciously—shift New Testament spiritual warfare language from its original context of the spirit realm to the world of fellow humans. For example, as Rick Love observes:

> In contrast to modern missions literature and strategy, the New Testament does not use military metaphors to describe the task of evangelism. Missions in the New Testament is not portrayed in military terms. Paul does not put on "crusades," "mobilize," "establish beachheads," or "target" a people. In other words, evangelicals have "extended" the meaning of military metaphors beyond the intent of New Testament authors.[37]

The Existence and Nature of Angels and Demons

The Biblical Data and the Christian Tradition

The existence of spirit beings, both benevolent and malicious, has been accepted in the vast majority of human cultures and religions across time and place.[38] This was clearly the case for the ancient Near Eastern world of the

36. Ibid., 244.

37. Rick Love, "Muslims and Military Metaphors," *Evangelical Missions Quarterly* 37 (January 2001): 67. For similar words of caution, see Richard Beaton, "New Testament Metaphors and the Christian Mission," *Evangelical Missions Quarterly* 37 (January 2001): 60–64; John Gilchrist, *Our Approach to Islam: Charity or Militancy?* (Benoni, South Africa: Jesus to the Muslim, 1990). Similar warnings appear in the statements from the Consultation on Mission Language and Metaphors (held at Fuller Theological Seminary, June 1–3, 2000, available at http://www.ad2000.org/re00620.htm) and the Lausanne-related "Deliver Us From Evil" Consultation (held in Nairobi, August 16–22, 2000, available in *Deliver Us from Evil: An Uneasy Frontier in Christian Mission*, ed. A. Scott Moreau et al. [Monrovia, CA: MARC, 2002], xxiv, 312). Clearly the question of metaphor is central to this discussion. There is strong evidence concerning the inherently metaphorical nature of human conceptual systems; see George Lakoff and Mark Johnson, *Metaphors We Live By* (Chicago: University of Chicago Press, 1980). Some critics of the Christian use of the concept and language of spiritual warfare use this observation to suggest that the notion of a cosmic conflict in the spiritual realm is *merely metaphor*—i.e., as simply a phenomenon of language, lacking any objective reality. But as even Lakoff and Johnson (who are themselves wary of a strong objectivist definition of truth) make clear, identifying something as a "metaphor" does not mean it is removed from the world of "real things, existing independently of us, which constrain both how we interact with them and how we comprehend them" (226). For Christians, this is an important point to remember if we are to talk of spiritual warfare as a "metaphor"—i.e., "metaphor" does not mean "mere metaphor."

38. While this volume focuses on perspectives within the Christian tradition regarding spirit beings and spiritual warfare, it should be noted that parallel considerations are found in a wide range of human religious systems. See, e.g., Umar Sulaiman Al-Ashqar, *The World of the Jinn and Devils*, trans. Jamaah al-Din M. Zarabozo (Boulder, CO: Al-Basheer, 1998);

Old Testament.[39] Intriguingly, when it comes to the Old Testament itself, while mention is occasionally made of "demons" and "evil spirits" (e.g., Lev. 17:7; Deut. 32:17; Judg. 9:22–25; 1 Sam. 16:14; 1 Kings 22:21–23; 2 Chron. 11:15; Ps. 106:37), they are comparatively rare.[40] Similarly, "(the) Satan" (i.e., "the adversary") is mentioned by name/role in only three passages of the Old Testament (Job 1–2; Zech. 3:1–10; 1 Chron. 21:1).[41] However, many scholars have highlighted other, more common themes in the Old Testament that point to a cosmic conflict in the spiritual world between forces of good and evil, including the sinister, chaos-related themes of hostile waters (e.g., Job 7:12; 9:8; 38:8–11; Ps. 29:3–4, 10; 74:10, 13; 77:16; 104:6; Prov. 8:29; Isa. 51:9–11; Nah. 1:4; Hab. 3:8, 15) and sea monsters such as Leviathan and Rahab (e.g., Job 3:8; 9:13; 26:12–13; 41:1–34; Ps. 74:13–14; 89:9–10; Isa. 27:1; 30:7; 51:9–10; Ezek. 29:3–5), the themes of Yahweh's divine council, the "angels of the nations," and the

---

Winston Davis, *Dojo: Magic and Exorcism in Modern Japan* (Stanford: Stanford University Press, 1980); Graham Dwyer, *The Divine and the Demonic: Supernatural Affliction and Its Treatment in Northern India* (New York: RoutledgeCurzon, 2003); Amira El-Zein, *Islam, Arabs, and the Intelligent World of the Jinn* (Syracuse: Syracuse University Press, 2009); Peter G. Riddell and Beverly Smith Riddell, eds., *Angels and Demons: Perspectives and Practice in Diverse Religious Traditions* (Nottingham: Apollos, 2007); Gail H. Sutherland, *The Disguises of the Demon: The Development of the Yaksa in Hinduism and Buddhism* (Albany: SUNY Press, 1991); Richard von Glahn, *The Sinister Way: The Divine and the Demonic in Chinese Religious Culture* (Berkeley: University of California Press, 2004).

39. On views of the demonic, etc., in the ancient Near East, see Neil Forsyth, *The Old Enemy: Satan and the Combat Myth* (Princeton: Princeton University Press, 1987), chaps. 1–2; Jeremy Black and Anthony Green, *Gods, Demons and Symbols of Ancient Mesopotamia: An Illustrated Dictionary* (Austin: University of Texas Press, 1992); Otto Böcher, *Dämonenfurcht und Dämonen-abwehr: Ein Beitrag zur Vorgeschichte der christlichen Taufe* (Stuttgart: Kohlhammer, 1970); Armin Lange, Hermann Lichtenberger, and K. F. Diethard Römheld, eds., *Die Dämonen: Die Dämonologie der israelitisch-jüdischen und frühchristlichen Literatur im Kontext ihrer Umwelt* (Tübingen: Mohr Siebeck, 2003); Jeffrey Burton Russell, *The Devil: Perceptions of Evil from Antiquity to Primitive Christianity* (Ithaca, NY: Cornell University Press, 1977); and the numerous relevant entries in Karel van der Toorn, Pieter W. van der Horst, and Bob Becking, eds., *Dictionary of Deities and Demons in the Bible* (*DDD*), 2nd ed. (New York: Brill, 1999).

40. Michael J. Gruenthaner, "The Demonology of the Old Testament," *Catholic Biblical Quarterly* 6 (1944): 6–27; Dennis F. Kinlaw, "The Demythologization of the Demonic in the Old Testament," in *Demon Possession*, ed. John Warwick Montgomery (Minneapolis: Bethany, 1976), 29–35; Robin Routledge, "'An Evil Spirit from the Lord'—Demonic Influence or Divine Instrument?," *Evangelical Quarterly* 70 (1998): 3–22; Edwin Yamauchi, "Magic or Miracle? Diseases, Demons and Exorcisms," in *Gospel Perspectives*, vol. 6: *The Miracles of Jesus*, ed. David Wenham and Craig Blomberg (Sheffield: JSOT Press, 1986), 115–20.

41. For several perspectives on (the) Satan in the Old Testament, see Gregory A. Boyd, *God at War: The Bible and Spiritual Conflict* (Downers Grove, IL: InterVarsity, 1997), 143–67; Derek R. Brown, "The Devil in the Details: A Survey of Research on Satan in Biblical Studies," *Currents in Biblical Research 9* (2011): 203–5; Peggy L. Day, *An Adversary in Heaven: Satan in the Hebrew Bible* (Atlanta: Scholars Press, 1988); Marvin E. Tate, "Satan in the Old Testament," *Review and Expositor* 89 (1992): 461–74.

motif of the rebellious gods/fallen angels (e.g., Exod. 32:8; Ps. 82:1–7; 89:5–10; Isa. 24:21; Dan. 10:3–20), including the sinful "sons of God" in Genesis 6:1–4.[42]

The various cultures of the Greco-Roman period also commonly held to convictions about a well-populated spiritual world.[43] Theological developments within Second Temple Judaism, including the rise and growth of apocalyptic eschatology, led to an increasing emphasis on angelic and demonic forces, including Satan.[44] This set the context for the significant role played by these spiritual entities in the thought of Jesus and the early Christian movement, as witnessed by the New Testament documents.[45]

42. On hostile waters/sea monsters themes, see Boyd, *God at War*, 73–113; John Day, *God's Conflict with the Dragon and the Sea: Echoes of a Canaanite Myth in the Old Testament* (New York: Cambridge University Press, 1985); John Day, "God and Leviathan in Isaiah 27:1," *Bibliotheca Sacra* 155 (1998): 423–36; Mary K. Wakeman, *God's Battle with the Monster: A Study in Biblical Imagery* (Leiden: Brill, 1973). On divine council and/or rebellious gods/fallen angels, see Boyd, *God at War*, 114–42; Lowell K. Handy, *Among the Host of Heaven: The Syro-Palestinian Pantheon as Bureaucracy* (Winona Lake, IN: Eisenbrauns, 1994); Michael Heiser, "The Divine Council in Second Temple Literature" (PhD diss., University of Wisconsin-Madison, 2004); R. A. Johnson, "The Old Testament Background for Paul's Use of 'Principalities and Powers'" (PhD diss., Dallas Theological Seminary, 2004); Christoph Auffarth and Loren T. Stuckenbruck, eds., *The Fall of the Angels* (New York: Brill, 2004); Hugh Rowland Page, *The Myth of Cosmic Rebellion: A Study of Its Reflexes in Ugaritic and Biblical Literature* (New York: Brill, 1996). On the "sons of God" in Genesis 6:1–4 as rebellious angels, see Rick Marrs, "The Sons of God (Gen. 6:1–4)," *Restoration Quarterly* 23 (1980): 218–24; Robert C. Newman, "Ancient Exegesis of Genesis 6:2, 4," *Grace Theological Journal* 5 (1984): 13–36; Loren T. Stuckenbruck, "The 'Angels' and 'Giants' of Genesis 6.1–4 in Second and Third Century BCE Jewish Interpretation: Reflections on the Posture of Early Apocalyptic Traditions," *Dead Sea Discoveries* 7 (2000): 354–77.

43. Frederick E. Brenk, "In the Light of the Moon: Demonology in the Early Imperial Period," in *Aufstieg und Niedergang der Römischen Welt*, ed. H. Temporini and W. Haase (New York: de Gruyter, 1986), II. 16. 3, 2068–145; Everett Ferguson, *Demonology of the Early Christian World* (Lewiston, NY: Mellen, 1984), chap. 2; Soren Skovgaard Jensen, *Dualism and Demonology: The Function of Demonology in Pythagorean and Platonic Thought* (Copenhagen: Munksgaard, 1966); Yamauchi, "Magic or Miracle?"

44. Maxwell J. Davidson, *Angels at Qumran: A Comparative Study of I Enoch 1–36, 72–108 and Sectarian Writings from Qumran* (Sheffield: JSOT Press, 1992); Annette Yoshiko Reed, *Fallen Angels and the History of Judaism and Christianity: The Reception of Enochic Literature* (New York: Cambridge University Press, 2005); Archie T. Wright, *The Origins of the Evil Spirits: The Reception of Genesis 6.1–4 in Early Jewish Literature* (Tübingen: Mohr Siebeck, 2005).

45. For various perspectives on the New Testament concepts of "principalities and powers," demons, and/or Satan, see Clinton Arnold, *Powers of Darkness: Principalities and Powers in Paul's Letters* (Downers Grove, IL: InterVarsity, 1992); Otto Böcher, *Christus Exorcista: Dämonismus und Taufe im Neuen Testament* (Stuttgart: Kohlhammer, 1972); Boyd, *God at War*, chaps. 6–10; Brown, "Devil in the Details," 209–14; Susan R. Garrett, *The Demise of the Devil: Magic and the Demonic in Luke's Writings* (Minneapolis: Fortress, 1989); Kabiro wa Gatumu, *The Pauline Concept of Supernatural Powers: A Reading from the African Worldview* (Colorado Springs: Paternoster, 2008); James Kallas, *The Satanward View: A Study in Pauline Theology* (Philadelphia: Westminster, 1966); Graham H. Twelftree, *Jesus the Exorcist: A Contribution to the Study of the Historical Jesus* (Tübingen: Mohr-Siebeck, 1993); Walter Wink, *Naming the Powers: The Language of Power in the New Testament* (Philadelphia: Fortress, 1984).

Prior to the modern era, the Christian tradition by and large interpreted the New Testament as representing angels and demons as personal spiritual agents. From the early church through the Middle Ages to the Reformation era, leading scholars and writers of the various streams of the Christian tradition continued to affirm, speculate on, and significantly develop the general New Testament conceptions of Satan and the demonic.[46]

Skepticism toward Spirit Beings in the Modern Era

Since the rise of the modern era, the question of the existence of angels and demons has provoked a wide range of responses in the Western world. In the eyes of many modern scholars—and reflective of a deistic or naturalistic worldview—the very idea of such creatures is commonly linked to such things as "mythology," "superstition," and a "primitive" mind-set.[47] From this perspective, it is believed that modern science has put to rest any notion of taking such things seriously. This view is well captured by the title of Carl Sagan's last book to be published before his death, *The Demon-Haunted World: Science as a Candle in the Dark*.[48]

Following in the train of this skeptical thought, much of modern, liberal Christianity has tended to see angels and demons as outdated ideas that are

46. Regarding the early church, see Gerald Bonner, *The Warfare of Christ* (London: Faith, 1962); Ferguson, *Demonology of the Early Christian World*, chaps. 4–5; Francis X. Gokey, *The Terminology for the Devil and Evil Spirits in the Apostolic Fathers* (Washington, DC: Catholic University of America Press, 1961); Archbishop Basil Krivocheine, "Angels and Demons in the Eastern Orthodox Spiritual Tradition," *Sourozh* 20 (May 1985): 32–41, and 21 (August 1985): 28–41; Elizabeth Ann Leeper, "Exorcism in Early Christianity" (PhD diss., Duke University, 1991); Jeffrey Burton Russell, *Satan: The Early Christian Tradition* (Ithaca, NY: Cornell University Press, 1981). Regarding the medieval world, see Alain Boureau, *Satan the Heretic: The Birth of Demonology in the Medieval West*, trans. Teresa Lavender Fagan (Chicago: University of Chicago Press, 2006); R. P. H. Greenfield, *Traditions of Belief in Late Byzantine Demonology* (Amsterdam: Hakkert, 1988); Antonio Moreno, "Demons According to St. Teresa and St. John of the Cross," *Spirituality Today* 43 (1991): 258–70; Paul M. Quay, "Angels and Demons: The Teaching of IV Lateran," *Theological Studies* 42 (1981): 20–45; Jeffrey Burton Russell, *Lucifer: The Devil in the Middle Ages* (Ithaca, NY: Cornell University Press, 1984). Regarding the Reformation era, see Adrian Hallett, "The Theology of John Calvin. Part Three: The Christian's Conflict with the Devil," *Churchman* 105 (1991): 293–325; Heiko A. Oberman, "Luther and the Devil," *Lutheran Theological Seminary Bulletin* 69 (Winter 1989): 4–15; Jeffrey Burton Russell, "The Reformed Devil," in *Mephistopheles: The Devil in the Modern World* (Ithaca, NY: Cornell University Press, 1986), 25–76.

47. On the progressive growth of skepticism regarding Satan and the demonic in seventeenth- and eighteenth-century European thought, see Jonathan I. Israel, "The Death of the Devil," in *Radical Enlightenment: Philosophy and the Making of Modernity 1650–1750* (New York: Oxford University Press, 2001), 375–405; Russell, *Mephistopheles*, 128–67.

48. Carl Sagan, *The Demon-Haunted World: Science as a Candle in the Dark* (New York: Ballantine, 1996).

best left behind (except, perhaps, as poetic metaphors for expressing the idea of evil).[49] This sentiment was famously captured by Rudolf Bultmann: "It is impossible to use electric light and the wireless and to avail ourselves of modern medical and surgical discoveries, and at the same time to believe in the New Testament world of spirits and miracles."[50] Naturalistic explanations of human belief in and/or experience of spirit beings appeal to a range of purely natural phenomena, including sociological, psychological, and even nutritional factors.[51] Commonly, Western academics dismiss contemporary belief in angels and demons as an unfortunate idiosyncrasy associated with such questionable belief systems as the New Age movement or religious "fundamentalism."[52] Some, while retaining a place for the linguistic categories of "Satan" and/or the "demonic," do so only in a thoroughly reinterpreted form, reducing them without remainder to metaphors for purely naturalistic forces.[53] For others, study of the development of the concepts of Satan and/or the demonic over time is a matter of purely historical interest, or can actually serve an ethical purpose today by exposing the dangers of framing the Other as diabolical.[54]

Beyond Skepticism: Entertaining Angels in the Modern World

For a sizable number of scholars in modern times, however, the naturalistic approach has not been the final word on the subject. Their motives for taking

49. E.g., Friedrich Schleiermacher, *The Christian Faith*, ed. H. R. MacKintosh and J. S. Stewart (Edinburgh: Clark, 1928), 161–70; Don Cupitt, "Four Arguments against the Devil," *Theology* 64 (1961): 413–15.

50. Rudolf Bultmann, "New Testament and Mythology," in *Kerygma and Myth*, ed. H. W. Bartsch, trans. R. H. Fuller (London: SPCK, 1953), 5.

51. E.g., Mansell Pattison, "Psychosocial Interpretations of Exorcism," *Operational Psychiatry* 8 (1977): 5–19; Pow Meng Yap, "The Possession Syndrome: A Comparison of Hong Kong and French Findings," *Journal of Mental Science* 106 (1960): 114–37; Alice B. Kehoe and Dody H. Giletti, "Women's Preponderance in Possession Cults: The Calcium-Deficiency Hypothesis Extended," *American Anthropologist* 83 (1981): 549–61.

52. E.g., Stephen Hunt, "The Devil's Advocates: The Function of Demonology in the World View of Fundamentalist Christianity," in *Fundamentalism: Church and Society*, ed. M. Percy and I. Jones (London: SPCK, 2002), 66–91.

53. E.g., Howard K. Bloom, *The Lucifer Principle: A Scientific Expedition into the Forces of History* (New York: Atlantic Monthly Press, 1995); Andrew Delbanco, *The Death of Satan* (New York: Farrar, Strauss & Giroux, 1995).

54. Paul Carus, *The History of the Devil and the Idea of Evil* (New York: Bell, 1969); William A. Glasser, *The Autobiography of Satan (Authorized Edition)* (n.p.: CreateSpace, 2011); Henry Ansgar Kelly, *Satan: A Biography* (New York: Cambridge University Press, 2006); Christopher Nugent, *Masks of Satan: The Demonic in History* (London: Sheed and Ward, 1983); Elaine Pagels, *The Origin of Satan* (New York: Random, 1995); Miguel A. De La Torre and Albert Hernandez, *The Quest for the Historical Satan* (Minneapolis: Fortress, 2011); William Tremmel, *Dark Side: The Satan Story* (St. Louis: CBP, 1987); T. J. Wray and Gregory Mobley, *The Birth of Satan: Tracing the Devil's Biblical Roots* (New York: Palgrave Macmillan, 2005).

seriously the concept of the angelic or demonic, not surprisingly, range widely. Some reject a naturalistic stance based on their suspicions that a reductive naturalism obscures as much as it explains. For example, in the early twentieth century, William James raised a question about the closed-mindedness of the "enlightened" worldview of his day and anticipated a time when Westerners would once again be open to the reality of such things as spirits:

> The refusal of modern "enlightenment" to treat "possession" as a hypothesis to be spoken of as even a possibility, in spite of the massive human tradition based on concrete experience in its favor, has always seemed to me a curious example of the power of fashion in things scientific. That the demon-theory . . . will have its innings again is to my mind absolutely certain. One has to be "scientific" indeed to be blind and ignorant enough to suspect no such possibility.[55]

More recently, the effects of such things as sociology-of-knowledge studies, postmodern epistemologies, and convictions of cultural relativism have led to a relativizing of the naturalistic assumptions of the Western academy. Peter Berger, a leading voice for sociology-of-knowledge theory, clearly states the implications for the question of the existence of spirits:

> We may agree, say, that contemporary consciousness is incapable of conceiving of either angels or demons. We are still left with the question of whether, possibly, both angels and demons go on existing despite this incapacity of our contemporaries to conceive of them.
>
> One (perhaps literally) redeeming feature of sociological perspective is that relativizing analysis, in being pushed to its final consequence, bends back on itself. The relativizers are relativized, the debunkers are debunked—indeed, relativization itself is somehow liquidated. What follows is *not*, as some of the early sociologists of knowledge feared, a total paralysis of thought. Rather, it is a new freedom and flexibility in asking questions of truth.[56]

In light of this turn, it becomes an important datum for social scientists that belief in the existence of spirit beings appears to be ubiquitous among humans both through history and across cultures.[57] Erika Bourguignon has

---

55. William James, "Report on Mrs. Piper's Hodgson-Control," *Proceedings of the English Society for Psychical Research* 23 (1909): 118. Some of the data and bibliography in this section are drawn from Paul Rhodes Eddy and Gregory A. Boyd, *Apology for the Devil: A Case for the Reality of Spirits*, unpublished manuscript, 2004.

56. Peter L. Berger, *A Rumor of Angels: Modern Society and the Rediscovery of the Supernatural* (Garden City, NY: Doubleday, 1969), 52–53.

57. On belief in spirit beings in various cultures/religions, see Felicitas D. Goodman, *How about Demons? Possession and Exorcism in the Modern World* (Bloomington: Indiana University

reported the "striking finding" that of 488 societies sampled, drawn from all of the "six major ethnographic regions into which the *Ethnographic Atlas* divides the world," spirit-possession beliefs appeared in no less than 74 percent (i.e., 360 of the 488).[58] And so, in the last few decades, it has become increasingly common for social scientists and other scholars to tread lightly when discussing spirits and possession/exorcism, often deferring judgment on the ontological status of such phenomena.[59] Interestingly, a number of scholars operating within a naturalistically oriented model of psychology have found that using exorcistic practices with those who resonate culturally with the idea of spirit possession often provides an effective treatment for such phenomena.[60]

Still others within the ranks of contemporary academics and professionals take a further step and make a positive case for the existence of spirits.[61] In doing so, they join a significant majority of the American populace today who, despite enjoying the sort of advancements in science and technology mentioned by Bultmann above, continue to find the existence of spirit beings (i.e., angels and/

Press, 1988); F. V. Reiterer, T. Nicklas, and K. Schöpflin, eds., *Angels: The Concept of Celestial Beings—Origins, Development, and Reception* (New York: de Gruyter, 2007); Riddell and Riddell, eds., *Angels and Demons*. Craig Keener has recently collected a good amount of evidence for the transcultural phenomenon of "spirit possession." See Keener, "Spirit Possession as a Cross-cultural Experience," *Bulletin for Biblical Research* 20 (2010): 215–36; Keener, *Miracles: The Credibility of the New Testament Accounts* (Grand Rapids: Baker Academic, 2011), esp. appendix A and B. Keener's book on miracles is a truly impressive work and now appears to represent the most exhaustive treatment of spirit-possession phenomena from a scholarly Christian perspective.

58. Erika Bourguignon, "Spirit Possession Belief and Social Structure," in *The Realm of the Extra-Human: Ideas and Actions*, ed. A. Bharatic (Paris: Mouton, 1976), 19.

59. E.g., Graham Dwyer, *The Divine and the Demonic: Supernatural Affliction and Its Treatment in North India* (New York: RoutledgeCurzon, 2003); Carl Goldberg, *Speaking with the Devil: A Dialogue with Evil* (New York: Viking, 1996), xii; Goodman, *How about Demons?* 123–26; Gavin Ivey, "Diabolical Discourses: Demonic Possession and Evil in Modern Psychopathology," *South African Journal of Psychology* 32 (2002): 54–59; Jeffrey Burton Russell, "The Evil One," in *Facing Evil: Light at the Core of Darkness*, ed. P. Woodruff and H. A. Wilmer (LaSalle, IL: Open Court, 1988), 58, 61.

60. Jaime Bulatao, "Local Cases of Possession and their Cure," *Philippine Studies* 30 (1982): 415–25; S. C. Cappannari et al., "Voodoo in the General Hospital: A Case of Hexing and Regional Enteritis," *Journal of the American Medical Association* 232 (1975): 938–40; M. G. Kenny, "Multiple Personality and Spirit Possession," *Psychiatry* 44 (1981): 338; E. Schendel and R. F. C. Kourany, "Cacodemonomaina and Exorcism in Children," *Journal of Clinical Psychiatry* 41 (1980): 119–23.

61. E.g., Stafford Betty, "The Growing Evidence for 'Demonic Possession': What Should Psychiatry's Response Be?" *Journal of Religion and Health* 44 (2005): 13–30; Terry D. Cooper and Cindy K. Epperson, *Evil: Satan, Sin, and Psychology* (New York: Paulist Press, 2008); Richard E. Gallagher, "A Case of Demonic Possession," *New Oxford Review* 75 (March 2008): 22–32; W. O. Mundia Jr., "The Existence of the Devil" (PhD diss., Boston University School of Theology, 1994); Phillip H. Wiebe, *God and Other Spirits: Intimations of Transcendence in Christian Experience* (New York: Oxford University Press, 2004).

or demons) quite plausible.[62] Now and then, unexpected personal experiences
have led members of the naturalistically inclined academic guild to undergo a
paradigm shift with regard to belief in spirits. Noteworthy examples in recent
years include psychologist Scott Peck's personal involvement with two exorcisms
and anthropologist Edith Turner's experience of visibly witnessing a spirit
entity in Africa.[63] Naturally, within this group of scholars, there are substantial
differences of opinion on how best to conceive of these spiritual phenomena.

A Personal Devil: The Traditional Christian Perspective in Contemporary Context

Many contemporary scholars who work from within a worldview indebted
to historic, orthodox Christianity have had no trouble believing in angels—
both good and evil—as real, personal spirit beings who have influence within
creation.[64] Here, they find themselves in continuity with much of the Christian

62. The 2005 Baylor Religion Survey found that 75 percent of Americans believe in Satan,
while 73 percent believe in demons. See Joseph Baker, "Who Believes in Religious Evil? An In-
vestigation of Sociological Patterns of Belief in Satan, Hell, and Demons," *Review of Religious
Research* 50 (2008): 211. This remarkable level of belief in spirit beings among contemporary
Americans was reflected in the "angel craze" of the 1990s. See Kenneth L. Woodward, "Angels,"
Newsweek, December 27, 1993, 52–57.

63. M. Scott Peck, *Glimpses of the Devil: A Psychiatrist's Personal Accounts of Possession,
Exorcism, and Redemption* (New York: Free Press, 2005); Edith Turner, "A Visible Spirit Form in
Zambia," in *Being Changed: The Anthropology of Extraordinary Experience*, ed. D. E. Young and
J.-G. Goulet (Orchard Park, NY: Broadview, 1994), 71–95; Edith Turner, "The Reality of Spirits:
A Tabooed or Permitted Field of Study?," *Anthropology of Consciousness* 4 (1993): 9–12. (We
are grateful to Edith Turner for her personal correspondence and for sharing with us a substantial
bibliography of related anthropological sources.)

64. This view is commonly held within both evangelical Protestantism and the Roman
Catholic Church. Representative of evangelicalism, see Clinton E. Arnold, *3 Crucial Questions
about Spiritual Warfare* (Grand Rapids: Baker, 1997); Ed Murphy, *The Handbook for Spiritual
Warfare* (Nashville: Nelson, 1992); Sydney H. T. Page, *Powers of Evil: A Biblical Study of Satan
and Demons* (Grand Rapids: Baker, 1995); Robert V. Rakestraw, "New Dimensions in the Study of
Angels and Demons," in *New Dimensions of Evangelical Thought: Essays in Honor of Millard
J. Erickson*, ed. D. S. Dockery (Downers Grove, IL: InterVarsity, 1998), 270–86; C. Peter Wagner
and F. Douglas Pennoyer, eds., *Wrestling with Dark Angels: Toward a Deeper Understanding of
the Supernatural Forces in Spiritual Warfare* (Ventura, CA: Regal, 1990); Peter S. Williams, *The
Case for Angels* (Waynesboro, GA: Paternoster, 2002). For examples of more traditional Roman
Catholic approaches, see "Christian Faith and Demonology," in *Vatican Council II: Postconciliar
Documents*, ed. A. Flannery (Northport, NY: Costello, 1982), 456–85; Fr. Gabriele Amorth, *An
Exorcist Tells His Story*, trans. N. V. MacKenzie (San Francisco: Ignatius, 1999); James McManus,
The Ministry of Deliverance in the Catholic Tradition (London: National Service Committee for
Catholic Charismatic Renewal, 1980). Some who espouse a traditional view of Satan and demons
as real spiritual agents also warn that these evil creatures have chosen a path that renders them
subpersonal in some sense, and that, while they do possess independent consciousness and will,
they should not be dignified with the unqualified title of "personal" in the full and positive sense
of the term. See, e.g., Thomas N. Finger, *Christian Theology: An Eschatological Approach*,

tradition going back to the earliest church, as reflected in the theology and/or preaching of those such as Tertullian, Origen, Augustine, Thomas Aquinas, Martin Luther, John Calvin, John Wesley, William and Catherine Booth, C. S. Lewis, and Pope Benedict XVI.

From this traditional Christian perspective, Satan and the other fallen angels/powers are understood as having been originally created by God as good creatures, designed for fellowship. But, similar to the first humans, Satan and his cohorts chose the path of self-assertion and rebellion. With regard to the nature of "demons" per se, most who hold to a traditional view today understand demons as equivalent to fallen angels. However, in both ancient Judaism and the early church, this was only one of two perspectives on this question. Other ancient Jews and Christians held that demons are the spirits of the deceased "giants" (the *Nephilim*) mentioned in Genesis 6:1–4, who were the hybrid children produced by sexual liaisons between evil angels (the "sons of God") and human women.[65] In either case, in the traditional view demons are understood to be personal spirit beings intent on fostering evil throughout the earth. In this present volume, three of the four viewpoints under consideration affirm and build on this traditional understanding of angels and demons (Boyd, Powlison, and Wagner and Greenwood).

Those who hold to this sort of traditional Christian view today usually do so for reasons beyond "tradition" alone. First and foremost, appeal is made to the Christian Scriptures, where both angels and demons are interpreted as personal spiritual agents possessing self-consciousness, intelligence, and will, as well as the ability to influence/interact with the physical creation (e.g., 1 Kings 22:19–21; Dan. 10:5–21; Matt. 4:3–11; Mark 5:6–13).[66] Theological coherence is a second factor. In the words of Carl Braaten:

> True Christianity is stuck with the Devil, like it or not. . . . The decision for or against the Devil is a decision for or against the integrity of Christianity as such. We simply cannot subtract the Devil, along with demons, angels, principalities, powers, and elemental spirits, without doing violence to the shape of the Christian faith, as transmitted by Scripture and tradition, our primary sources.[67]

---

2 vols. (Scottdale, PA: Herald, 1985, 1989), 2:163; Nigel Wright, *The Satan Syndrome: Putting the Power of Darkness in Its Place* (Grand Rapids: Academie, 1990), 28–31.

65. Interestingly, the book of *1 Enoch* can serve as the basis for both of these understandings of demons (compare *1 Enoch* 15:8–16:1; 19:1–2). For an example of the "giants" interpretation of demons in early Christianity, see Justin Martyr, *Second Apology* 5.2.

66. E.g., Stephen F. Noll, *Angels of Light, Powers of Darkness: Thinking Biblically about Angels, Satan and Principalities* (Downers Grove, IL: InterVarsity, 1998); Page, *Powers of Evil*.

67. Carl E. Braaten, *That All May Believe: A Theology of the Gospel and the Mission of the Church* (Grand Rapids: Eerdmans, 2008), 109–10.

Considerations of theodicy—especially with regard to natural evil—often come into play here.[68] It is in this light that Wallace Murphy argues that "any view which would affirm the orthodox concept of a theistic God and yet deny the existence of the devil is inherently untenable."[69] Finally, human experiences of actual spirit beings—whether witnessed firsthand or via the testimony of others—is often viewed as corroborating the traditional view of these things.

While there appears to be a broad agreement among most evangelical scholars today regarding the existence and nature of angelic beings, including Satan and demons, perspectives vary on questions such as how much authority and influence these powers of darkness exert in the world on this side of the victorious death and resurrection of Jesus, how this influence relates to the sovereignty and providence of God, and the degree to which explicit attention should be given to these creatures within a contemporary theological system. When dealing with Satan and the demonic, it is common to find evangelical theologians emphasizing the importance of maintaining a "balance," famously articulated by C. S. Lewis:

> There are two equal and opposite errors into which our race can fall about the devils. One is to disbelieve in their existence. The other is to believe, and to feel an excessive and unhealthy interest in them. They themselves are equally pleased by both errors and hail a materialist or a magician with the same delight.[70]

That "balance" is important in this area is a widely shared conviction among evangelicals.[71] However, this unity quickly gives way to diversity when it comes to the questions of just *how* this balance should be achieved and what constitutes the appropriate degree of attention.

On the one hand, for those whose theology of divine sovereignty and providence is shaped by the Augustinian-Calvinist tradition, everything that transpires within creation—including every specific thing done by Satan and demons—is divinely ordained and thus is ultimately attributable to

68. A notable example is Alvin Plantinga's "Free Will Defense." See his *God, Freedom, and Evil* (Grand Rapids: Eerdmans, 1977); Alvin Plantinga, *The Nature of Necessity* (Oxford: Clarendon, 1974), 191–93. Others who appeal to a more traditional view of Satan/the demonic as a response to natural evil include Gregory A. Boyd, *Satan and the Problem of Evil: Constructing a Trinitarian Warfare Theodicy* (Downers Grove, IL: InterVarsity, 2001), chaps. 8–10; C. S. Lewis, *The Problem of Pain* (New York: Macmillan, 1945), 121–23.

69. Wallace A. Murphy, "Can Theism Survive without the Devil?" *Religious Studies* 21 (1985): 231.

70. C. S. Lewis, *The Screwtape Letters* (New York: Macmillan, 1962), 3.

71. E.g., Arnold, *3 Crucial Questions about Spiritual Warfare*, 32–37; Millard Erickson, *Christian Theology* (Grand Rapids: Baker, 1983–85), 451; Andrew Walker, "The Devil You Think You Know: Demonology and the Charismatic Movement," in T. Smail, A. Walker, and N. Wright, *Charismatic Renewal: The Search for a Theology* (London: SPCK, 1993), 86.

God's all-encompassing sovereign will.[72] On the other hand, for those who hold to the "Arminian" view that angels and humans were created by God with libertarian freedom (i.e., the ability to choose between alternatives) for the purpose of love, this very freedom has allowed Satan and the demonic to choose a path of evil and rebellion that God never intended for them.[73] One might think that the Augustinian-Calvinist approach to Satan and the sovereignty of God would naturally lead scholars within this tradition to downplay both the role of Satan/demons and the importance of spiritual warfare. However, while such tendencies are visible among some Calvinist thinkers, many retain a prominent role for these things within their theological worldview.[74]

One's sense of influence and power exercised by Satan and demons in the world is also affected by eschatological convictions. For example, for those with a more strongly "realized" eschatology, the influence of Satan can be almost entirely eclipsed by the victorious death and resurrection of Christ.[75] It is commonly assumed that those within Pentecostal/charismatic circles are predisposed to placing an inordinately strong emphasis on the role of Satan and the demonic within the daily Christian life. However, while this is certainly the case within certain sectors of these movements, one also finds others within these traditions providing both warnings against imbalance and examples of a cautious approach to these matters.[76]

Similarly, there are differences of opinion among evangelicals regarding the place that should be given to spiritual warfare within the Christian life. Some see a "spiritual-warfare worldview" at the center of the early Christian worldview, calling on the New Testament documents themselves as a

72. E.g., Greg L. Bahnsen, "The Person, Work and Present Status of Satan," *Journal of Christian Reconstruction* 1 (1974): 17–18, 30–33; Erickson, *Christian Theology*, 398; Erwin W. Lutzer, *The Serpent of Paradise: The Incredible Story of How Satan's Rebellion Serves God's Purposes* (Chicago: Moody, 1996). See also Henri Blocher, *Evil and the Cross: Christian Thought and the Problem of Evil* (Downers Grove, IL: InterVarsity, 1994), 84–104.

73. E.g., Carolyn Denise Baker and Frank D. Macchia, "Created Spirit Beings," in *Systematic Theology: A Pentecostal Perspective*, ed. S. M. Horton (Springfield, MO: Logion, 1994), 205–6; Boyd, *God at War*; Boyd, *Satan and the Problem of Evil*.

74. E.g., David Powlison, *Power Encounters: Reclaiming Spiritual Warfare* (Grand Rapids: Baker, 1995); John Piper, "Cosmic-Level Spiritual Warfare," *The Standard* (March 1990): 28–29. It is true, however, that those influenced by the Augustinian/Reformed/Calvinist tradition are particularly sensitive to approaches to spiritual warfare that can be read as overplaying Satan's influence to the detriment of God's sovereignty. The title of an article by Tim Meadowcroft nicely captures this concern: "Sovereign Lord or Paranoid Universe? The Lord of Hosts Is His Name," *Evangelical Review of Theology* 27 (2003): 113–27.

75. E.g., Bahnsen, "Person, Work and Present Status of Satan," 37, 39.

76. E.g., Baker and Macchia, "Created Spirit Beings," 194–212; Walker, "The Devil You Think You Know."

witness.[77] Others challenge this notion. Robert Guelich has made the case that the contemporary Christian fascination with spiritual warfare owes more to the imagination of Frank Peretti than it does to Jesus or the apostle Paul.[78] One common concern here is that an overemphasis on Satan and spiritual warfare can lead to a "devil made me do it" attitude, thus fostering the loss of a sense of personal responsibility for sin.[79]

Rethinking Satan: Contemporary Christian Reinterpretations of Angels and Demons

A number of contemporary theologies, while rejecting certain aspects of the more traditional views of angels and Satan/demons, nonetheless retain a place of significance for these categories, if in modified forms.[80] In this section, we will consider three contemporary reinterpretations of angels and Satan/ the demonic: those of Karl Barth, Walter Wink, and Amos Yong.[81]

KARL BARTH

Barth devotes more than 160 pages of his *Church Dogmatics* to angelology and related matters.[82] Of this, only a few pages are devoted to the demonic.

77. E.g., Boyd, *God at War*, chaps. 6–10; Will Brooks, "Pauline Spiritual Warfare: How a Warfare Mentality Shaped Paul's Approach to Missions," *Great Commission Research Journal* 3 (Summer 2011): 97–113.

78. Robert A. Guelich, "Spiritual Warfare: Jesus, Paul, and Peretti," *Pneuma* 13 (1991): 33–64. It is noteworthy how many critics of the contemporary evangelical fascination with spiritual warfare attribute the problem, to one degree or another, to Frank Peretti's novel *This Present Darkness* (Ventura, CA: Regal, 1986). E.g., John Bolt, "Satan Is Alive and Well in Contemporary Imagination: A Bibliographic Essay with Notes on 'Hell' and 'Spiritual Warfare,' " *Calvin Theological Journal* 29 (1994): 506; Walker, "The Devil You Think You Know," 101.

79. Baker and Macchia, "Created Spirit Beings," 209; Christian B. Breuninger, "Where Angels Fear to Tread: Appraising the Current Fascination with Spiritual Warfare," *Covenant Quarterly* 53 (1995): 40; Paul M. Miller, *The Devil Did Not Make Me Do It* (Scottdale, PA: Herald, 1977).

80. On various interpretations and/or reinterpretations of the demonic in twentieth-century theology, see Vernon R. Mallow, *The Demonic: A Selected Theological Study: An Examination into the Theology of Edwin Lewis, Karl Barth, and Paul Tillich* (Lanham, MD: University Press of America, 1983); Howard Vann Pendley, "Views of the Demonic in Recent Religious Thought" (PhD diss., Southern Baptist Theological Seminary, 1976); Donald E. Roulet, "Identifying and Interpreting the Demonic: A Critical Study of the Demonic in Contemporary Theology with Implications for Managing Forces Which are Destructive to the Life and Ministry of the Congregation" (DMin thesis, San Francisco Theological Seminary, 1982); Amos Yong, "Pentecostal Salvation as Deliverance from the Powers: The Political Dimensions," in *In the Days of Caesar: Pentecostalism and Political Theology* (Grand Rapids: Eerdmans, 2010), 121–65.

81. A more comprehensive survey would add others to this list, including Paul Tillich and Edwin Lewis. See Tillich, *The Interpretation of History*, trans. E. L. Talmey (New York: Scribner's Sons, 1936), 77–122; Lewis, *The Creator and the Adversary* (New York: Abingdon-Cokesbury, 1948).

82. Karl Barth, *Church Dogmatics* III/3, trans. G. W. Bromiley and R. J. Ehrlich (Edinburgh: Clark, 1960), 369–531.

In Barth's words, when it comes to consideration of demons, nothing more than a "quick, sharp glance" is appropriate.[83] In his short section on demons, several features immediately stand out.

First, Barth contrasts angels and demons to such a degree that he rejects the traditional idea that demons represent fallen angels.[84] Rather, Barth proposes that with regard to Satan and demons, "their origin and nature lie in nothingness."[85] The concept of "nothingness" (a translation of the German phrase *das Nichtige*) is crucial to Barth's theology of creation and evil.[86] It is also one of the most complex—and contested—elements of his thought. According to Barth, "nothingness" has "no substantive existence within creation," and yet this does not mean that "nothingness is nothing."[87] On one hand, nothingness is "in opposition primarily and supremely to God himself," yet, on the other, "God himself comprehends, envisages, and controls it."[88] Barth explains:

> That which God renounces and abandons in virtue of his decision [i.e., to freely elect what he will] is not merely nothing. It is nothingness. . . . Nothingness is that which God does not will. It lives only by the fact that it is that which God does not will. But it does live by this fact. For not only what God wills, but what he does not will, is potent, and must have a real correspondence. What really corresponds to that which God does not will is nothingness.[89]

At one point, Barth notes that "nothingness is really privation."[90] In making this connection, Barth taps into a well-known stream of Augustinian Christian tradition that defines evil in terms of privation and the absence of good/being.

For Barth, then, it is out of this nothingness that Satan and demons derive their origin, nature, and—in some sense—"reality." But, according to Barth, one must be very careful here. On the one hand, Satan and the demonic are not to be ignored or dismissed as outmoded figments of primitive imagination. Yet, on the other hand, Barth immediately contrasts Christian "belief" in angels with the "radical unbelief" that is appropriate toward the demons.[91] He writes:

83. Ibid., 519.
84. Ibid., 520–21.
85. Ibid., 522.
86. For Barth's extensive discussion of "nothingness," see ibid., 289–368. For discussion, see Sung Min Jeong, *Nothingness in the Theology of Paul Tillich and Karl Barth* (Lanham, MD: University Press of America, 2003).
87. Barth, *Church Dogmatics* III/3, 302, 349.
88. Ibid., 302.
89. Ibid., 352.
90. Ibid., 353.
91. Ibid., 521.

They are null and void, but they are not nothing. . . . Their being is neither that of God nor that of the creature, neither that of heavenly creatures nor that of earthly, for they are neither the one nor the other. They are not divine but non-divine and anti-divine. On the other hand, God has not created them, and therefore they are not creaturely. . . . This is all to be said of demons as of nothingness.[92]

In this sense, for Barth, Satan and the demonic "are *the* myth, the myth of all mythologies."[93] And yet, at the same time, they—like the nothingness they emerge from—are always at work "in, with, and under" the things of our world, "like the tentacles of an octopus."[94] Barth's view has been characterized as engaging in "mental gymnastics"[95] and has been criticized for failing to do justice to a full-orbed biblical demonology at several points.[96] However, his move to relegate Satan and the demonic to the edges of existence, and particularly his refusal to believe *in* them—as opposed to believing *against* them—clearly resonates with the inclinations of a number of contemporary thinkers.[97]

WALTER WINK

A second highly influential reinterpretation of Satan and the demonic has been proposed by Walter Wink, a contributor to this present volume. Wink was originally inspired by previous twentieth-century postwar writers who were working to reinterpret, and so rehabilitate, the New Testament notion of "principalities and powers" in the modern world. Among such scholars,

92. Ibid., 523.
93. Ibid., 521.
94. Ibid., 528.
95. Wright, *Satan Syndrome*, 40.
96. E.g., Gabriel Fackre, "Angels Heard and Demons Seen," *Theology Today* 51 (1994): 348; Russell, *Mephistopheles*, 265–66; Howard Van Pendley, "Views of the Demonic in Recent Religious Thought" (PhD diss., Southern Baptist Theological Seminary, 1976), 199–203; Wright, *Satan Syndrome*, 41–42. For a review and critique of Barth's angelology, see Lawrence Osborn, "Angels: Barth and Beyond," in *The Unseen World: Christian Reflections on Angels, Demons, and the Heavenly Realm*, ed. A. N. S. Lane (Grand Rapids: Baker, 1996), 29–48.
97. E.g., Thomas A. Noble, "The Spirit World: A Theological Approach," in Lane, ed., *Unseen World*, 218–19; Wright, *Satan Syndrome*, 24–25, 41–42. Even those who criticize much of Barth's demonology and who defend the notion of Satan and demons as personal, disembodied evil spirits can be drawn to Barthian-like language at this point; e.g., Richard H. Bell, *Deliver Us from Evil: Interpreting the Redemption from the Power of Satan in the New Testament* (Tübingen: Mohr Siebeck, 2007), 352. Of course, a similar language and rationale can be proposed by those who ultimately reduce Satan and/or the demonic to purely human categories, e.g., Darrell J. Fasching, *Narrative Theology after Auschwitz: From Alienation to Ethics* (Minneapolis: Fortress, 1992), 143–48; René Girard, *I Saw Satan Fall Like Lightning*, trans. J. G. Williams (Maryknoll, NY: Orbis, 2001), 44–46.

there was a common tendency to reinterpret the "powers" in terms of human corporate/structural categories of power, dominance, and oppression.[98] For some, this reinterpretation of the powers allowed for both spiritual and human realities; for others the powers were ultimately reduced to human structures without remainder.[99] Wink went on to produce his famous *Powers* trilogy, which has profoundly shaped the conversation on spiritual warfare over the last few decades.[100] At the heart of Wink's approach to these matters is what he has come to call the "Integral" worldview.[101] While admitting that the "Traditional" worldview of the ancient world is now outmoded in various ways, Wink is just as quick to critique the modern "Materialist" worldview that dominates the hard sciences today. But rather than embracing the contemporary, reactionary "Supernatural" worldview in response—that is, a "schizoid" view that saves the "spiritual realm" only by rendering it completely "immune to confirmation or refutation" and thus sacrifices a unified view of reality—Wink proposes the "Integral Worldview" as the way through.[102] Drawing inspiration and insights from the "new physics," modern psychology (particularly Carl Jung), religious

98. Among those twentieth-century thinkers who contributed to this broad trajectory, see Hendrikus Berkhof, *Christ and the Powers*, trans. J. H. Yoder (Scottdale, PA: Herald, 1962); G. B. Caird, *Principalities and Powers: A Study in Pauline Theology* (Oxford: Clarendon, 1956); Jacques Ellul, *The Ethics of Freedom*, trans. Geoffrey W. Bromiley (Grand Rapids: Eerdmans, 1976); Jacques Ellul, *The New Demons*, trans. C. Edward Hopkin (New York: Crossroad/Seabury, 1975); Heinrich Schlier, *Principalities and Powers in the New Testament* (New York: Herder & Herder, 1961); William Stringfellow, *Free in Obedience* (New York: Seabury, 1964); John Howard Yoder, *The Politics of Jesus* (Grand Rapids: Eerdmans, 1972), 135–214. While expressing significant disagreement, Wink was also inspired early on by the work of Wesley Carr, *Angels and Principalities: The Background, Meaning and Development of the Pauline Phrase hai archai kai hai exousiai* (New York: Cambridge University Press, 1981).

99. Three options regarding the nature of the "powers"—spiritual beings, human structures, or a both/and approach—continue to characterize the interpretive field today. Reductionist theories that demythologize the "powers" remain attractive to many, e.g., Richard A. Horsely, *Jesus and the Powers: Conflict, Covenant, and the Hope for the Poor* (Minneapolis: Fortress, 2011). For a brief survey and critique of various reductive approaches, see Peter O'Brien, "Principalities and Powers and their Relationship to Structures," *Evangelical Review of Theology* 6 (1982): 50–61.

100. Wink, *Naming the Powers*; Wink, *Unmasking the Powers: The Invisible Forces that Determine Human Existence* (Philadelphia: Fortress, 1986); Wink, *Engaging the Powers*. Wink's book *The Powers That Be: Theology for a New Millennium* (New York: Doubleday, 1998) offers something of a summary digest of his three larger volumes. For two collections of essays engaging Wink's proposals, see Raby Gingerich and Ted Grimsrud, eds., *Transforming the Powers: Peace, Justice, and the Domination System* (Minneapolis: Fortress, 2006); D. Seiple and Frederick W. Weidmann, eds., *Enigmas and Powers: Engaging the Work of Walter Wink for Classroom, Church, and World* (Eugene, OR: Wipf & Stock, 2008).

101. Wink, *Powers That Be*, 19–22; Wink, "The New Worldview: Spirit at the Core of Everything," in Gingerich and Grimsrud, eds., *Transforming the Powers*, 21–24.

102. Wink, "New Worldview," 21.

mysticism, process philosophy/theology, and "maverick" theologians such as Teilhard de Chardin, Morton Kelsey, and Matthew Fox, Wink espouses a view of reality where everything has "an inner and an outer aspect."[103] He explains: "In the Integral Worldview, soul permeates the universe. God is not just within us but within everything. The universe is suffused with the divine. This is not pantheism, where everything is God, but panentheism . . . , where everything is in God and God is in everything."[104]

When it comes to the question of the nature of the "powers," Wink refuses to fully reduce them to human institutions and social structures. Rather, in concert with the integral worldview, he proposes a both/and model. In Wink's words:

> The "principalities and powers" are the inner and outer aspects of any given manifestation of power. As the inner aspect they are the spirituality of institutions, the "within" of corporate structures and systems, the inner essence of outer organizations of power. As the outer aspect, they are political systems, appointed officials, the "chair" of an organization, laws—in short, all the tangible manifestations which power takes.[105]

Wink goes on:

> Every Power tends to have a visible pole, and outer form—be it a church, a nation, or an economy—and an invisible pole, an inner spirit or driving force that animates, legitimates, and regulates its physical manifestation in the world. Neither pole is the cause of the other. Both come into existence together and cease to exist together. When a particular Power becomes idolatrous, placing itself above God's purposes for the good of the whole, then that Power becomes demonic.[106]

And so, for Wink, while the principalities and powers have a spiritual dimension, they are not to be viewed as personal spiritual beings. Rather, they are the spiritual dimension of earthly, human institutions and structures. Thus, in Wink's view, these spiritual powers cannot exist apart from their corresponding human institutions and structures. They are the spiritual interiority of human social structures and, in this sense, are comparable to Jung's archetypes. With further inspiration from Jung, Wink understands these "powers"—including Satan and the demonic—as ultimately destined for eternal reconciliation with God, as humans resist the all-too-natural "psychological repression" of the

---

103. Ibid.
104. Ibid., 22.
105. Wink, *Naming the Powers*, 5.
106. Ibid.

demonic powers, and instead strive toward "individuation" and the eventual "sublimation of evil into the godhead."[107] While some evangelical scholars have recognized significant value in Wink's proposal, others have concluded that it represents an unwarranted deviation from the biblical teaching by rejecting the independent reality of personal spirit beings, both angelic and demonic.[108]

AMOS YONG

In his book *The Spirit of Creation*, the Pentecostal scholar Amos Yong proposes a fascinating reinterpretation of the angelic and demonic.[109] He does so in the context of developing a comprehensive "pneumatological cosmology," one that is indebted to "an emergentist cosmology that provides nonreductionistic accounts for pneumatic or spiritual realities while, at the same time, challenging dualistic construals about the relationship between the spiritual and material world."[110] In fleshing out his proposal concerning angelic and demonic spirits, Yong draws upon an interesting range of disciplines and perspectives, including the contemporary theology-and-science dialogue, process philosophy and cosmology (though he expressly rejects dipolar theism), parapsychological and anomalistic studies, and, of course, Pentecostal/charismatic experience and theology. Along the way, he finds inspiration from two thinkers in particular: the renowned process theologian David Ray Griffin and Walter Wink.[111] Yong explains:

> What I want to take from Wink, in combination with Griffin's contributions, are the basic building blocks for an emergentist cosmology, one that features emergent spiritual dimensions rather than a merely materialistic world. On the one hand, Griffin's nondualistic and nonsupernaturalistic defense of the survival hypothesis is suggestive for an ontology of disembodied spiritual realities. On the other hand, Wink's reinterpretation of the biblical materials regarding

---

107. Wink, *Unmasking the Powers*, 39. Those who approach Satan and the demonic in a manner broadly similar to Wink include A. Roy Eckardt, "Between the Angelic and the Demonic," *Theology Today* 51 (1994): 405–15; David Ray Griffin, "Why Demonic Power Exists: Understanding the Church's Enemy," *Lexington Theological Quarterly* 28 (1993): 223–39.

108. For generally positive assessments, see Osborn, "Angels"; Yong, "Pentecostal Salvation as Deliverance from the Powers." For more critical perspectives, see Clinton Arnold, *Ephesians: Power and Magic* (New York: Cambridge University Press, 1989), 48–51; Chloe Lynch, "How Convincing Is Walter Wink's Interpretation of Paul's Language of the Powers?" *Evangelical Quarterly* 83 (2011): 251–66.

109. Amos Yong, *The Spirit of Creation: Modern Science and Divine Action in the Pentecostal-Charismatic Imagination* (Grand Rapids: Eerdmans, 2011), 173–225. Yong has further developed his thoughts on the political dimensions of a Pentecostal approach to spiritual warfare in *In the Days of Caesar*, 121–65.

110. Yong, *Spirit of Creation*, 31.

111. Ibid., 199–207.

principalities, powers, and the demonic is also suggestive of the reality of emergent spiritual forces. Put together, the spirit-filled cosmos of the pentecostal-
charismatic imagination can be understood within an emergentist framework.[112]

Yong presents his proposal in the form of a series of "ten theses for consideration"—he is clear that this is "a piece of speculative theology" that will
require further fleshing out.[113] One can gain a sense of Yong's "emergentist"
approach to the angelic and demonic by touching on several of his theses.[114]
First, Yong proposes, as "an article of faith," that the "triune God is the only
necessary, transcendent, and purely spiritual reality."[115] A key to understanding
Yong's novel emergentist approach is found in the claim that God is the only
"purely spiritual reality." Unlike the more traditional understanding, in Yong's
model angels and demons are not disembodied spirit beings created by God in
an autonomous spiritual realm that is separate from the physical world. This
is because there is no autonomous created spiritual realm that is dualistically
separate from the physical. Rather, created spirits—whether angelic spirits,
demonic spirits, human spirits, and even animal spirits—always emerge from,
and then supervene upon, the complex material world that, itself, is always-
already an "interrelational cosmos."[116] Here, one sees the shaping influence of a
process metaphysics on Yong's pneumatological (i.e., Spirit-focused) cosmology.
Yong goes on further to explain the nature of angels within his model:

> Angelic spirits, then, are emergent benevolent realities that minister the salvific
> grace of God to human lives. . . . Just as the human spirit emerges from and
> supervenes upon the embodied relationships that constitute our existence [i.e.,
> the material body/brain], so also, I suggest, do benevolent spiritual realities
> emerge from the complex material and personal relationships through which
> God's redemption is at work.[117]

It is important to note here that, while Yong draws upon Wink's work at
certain points, he disagrees with Wink at a crucial juncture. For Yong, while

112. Ibid., 207.
113. Ibid., 208. Yong notes that he is currently working on an edited volume, tentatively
titled *Loosing the Spirits: Interdisciplinary Perspectives on a Spirit-Filled World*, that will further
explore these issues. One of Yong's doctoral students, David Bradnick, is currently working on
a dissertation that develops the thesis of an emergentist theology of the demonic, tentatively
titled "Loosing and Binding the Spirits: Towards an Emergentist Theology of the Demonic."
114. Here, the term "emergentist" refers to the idea that created "spirits" always emerge
out of physical matter.
115. Yong, *Spirit of Creation*, 208.
116. Ibid., 211.
117. Ibid., 213.

angels are "emergent from their material substrates," they are, in fact, "personal realities." And yet, Yong can also say that "what we call angels are higher-level transpersonal or suprapersonal realities, constituted by and supervening upon the human relationships from which they derive."[118] Before leaving his discussion of angels, Yong clarifies the implications of his emergentist theory of the angelic, and here one clearly sees the parallel between his thought and that of Wink:

> Therefore, I am also saying that without the various underlying material—that is, human and relational—substrates, there are no angels; yet I am also strongly insistent against reducing angelic spirits to their constituent members.[119]

In turning to the demonic, Yong simply applies his emergentist theory to the dark side of things. He writes:

> Demonic spirits, then, are divergent (as opposed to *emergent*) malevolent realities that oppose the salvific grace of God in human lives. . . . But just as the human spirit emerges from socially and environmentally embedded brain and body, and just as angelic spirits emerge as supervenient upon the concreteness and complexity of our interpersonal, social, and cosmic relations, so also, I suggest, do demonic spirits emerge from and supervene upon the human experience of alienation that disintegrates personal lives and destroys human relationships in general and human well-being as a whole.[120]

But whereas Yong is quite willing to recognize the personal dimensions of angels, he is reluctant to do so when it comes to demons. In fact, in good Augustinian fashion (i.e., evil as privation), he is hesitant to confer upon them the status of robust ontological reality. He writes:

> Insofar as demonic realities are emergent from and supervenient upon origi-nally good things, they lack their own being or onticity and thus emerge only parasitically in and through moral behaviors, actions, and intentions of free creatures. . . . As parasitic and privative—ultimately nothingness in comparison to the goodness and reality of God—the reality of the demonic, like sin, escapes rational definition. . . . The demonic's irrationality means that it can never exist as authentically personal entities; rather, that which is demonic opposes, distorts, and destroys the integrity of personhood.[121]

118. Ibid., 216.
119. Ibid., 217.
120. Ibid., 217–18.
121. Ibid., 219–20.

The Nature and Practice of Spiritual Warfare

Among those who agree that spiritual warfare holds an important place in the Christian life, there remains significant diversity of perspective regarding the nature and practice of spiritual warfare. This section will briefly address several of the many issues that can arise when conversation turns to the actual practice of spiritual warfare.

In the Book of Common Prayer, the Lord is asked to spare his people from "all the deceits of the world, the flesh, and the devil." This triumvirate has become one common way of expressing the primary foci of spiritual warfare. We will use these three categories to summarize three different approaches to spiritual warfare in the church today. It must be clearly stated that these three foci themselves are not mutually exclusive. All three themes are clearly found in Scripture, and one regularly finds a wide range of spiritual warfare proponents affirming that each of these—the world, the flesh, and the devil—must be addressed in one way or another. Here, however, these three themes will be used to highlight three distinct models of spiritual warfare with their corresponding emphases.[122]

"The World": The "World Systems" Model of Spiritual Warfare

As noted above, Walter Wink has become famous for his understanding of "principalities and powers" as naming the spiritual dimension of this-worldly institutions and structures. For Wink, when these world structures become oppressive, demonic systems of domination, it becomes the responsibility of the church to name, unmask, and engage them. A key to this calling is emulating the "third way" modeled for us by Jesus—namely, the way of nonviolent resistance (thus avoiding the two ditches of violent resistance on one hand, and passive nonresistance on the other).[123] In this present volume, Wink, with assistance from Higgins and Hardin, ably represents this approach to spiritual warfare.

While more traditional Christians will disagree with Wink regarding the ontological status of Satan and the demonic, nonetheless many of them have come to appreciate central features of this world systems model of spiritual warfare. Andrew Walker provides one such example. He writes:

> While not needing to deny the reality, we need to understand the dark powers
> as interpenetrating the power structures of society, so that we fight evil not in

122. For helpful surveys of approaches to spiritual warfare in recent times, see Charles H. Kraft, "Contemporary Trends in the Treatment of Spiritual Warfare," in Moreau et al., eds., *Deliver Us from Evil*, 177–202; A. Scott Moreau, "A Survey of North American Spiritual Warfare Thinking," in Moreau et al., eds., *Deliver Us from Evil*, 117–26.

123. Wink, *Engaging the Powers*, 175–93; Wink, *Powers That Be*, 98–111.

the realm of fantasy or the heavenlies, but in the public world of politics and economics. Hence I have suggested that we must fight collective evil wherever it is to be found, whether this be organized crime or racism. . . . I am persuaded that the essence of spiritual warfare is not taking on demonic forces by binding strong men, destroying amulets and charms and banning Halloween. . . . I believe that genuine spiritual warfare means quite simply refusing to play the war game: we can only overcome evil with good, for if we appropriate the enemy's weapons we are lost. . . . Paradoxically, there is a more powerful way to dispel the gloom of demonic fear: lifting high the burning torch of God's love.[124]

And so, even for those who embrace significant elements of the two remaining models, confronting such idolatrous systemic evils as racism, sexism, classism, and violence (in its manifold forms and spheres) can be seen as a vital aspect of the church's call to spiritual battle.[125] J. Nelson Kraybill, for example, urges that this sort of "macroexorcism" (i.e., "naming and confronting the powers of evil on a systemic and political level") is a necessary partner to "microexorcism" (i.e., the confronting of evil powers on a "personal level") and that both should work together in complementary fashion.[126]

"The Flesh": The "Classic" Model of Spiritual Warfare

While the classic model of spiritual warfare certainly recognizes the importance of addressing each aspect of the world-flesh-devil triumvirate, many within this camp today express concern with models that focus on confronting sociopolitical structures, or, alternatively, on identifying and casting out personal demonic entities. Instead, the classic model calls for a focus on fighting the temptation and sin that arises so easily from our fleshly, sinful nature. In his book *Power Encounters: Reclaiming Spiritual Warfare*—one of the most

124. Walker, "The Devil You Think You Know," 99–100, 103–4.
125. E.g., Gregory A. Boyd, "The Kingdom as a Socio-Political Spiritual Revolution," *Criswell Theological Review* 6 (2008): 23–42; Gregory A. Boyd, *The Myth of a Christian Religion: Losing Your Religion for the Beauty of a Revolution* (Grand Rapids: Zondervan, 2009); Knud Jorgensen, "Spiritual Conflict in Socio-political Context," in Moreau et al., eds., *Deliver Us from Evil*, 213–30; Robert Linthicum, *City of God, City of Satan: A Biblical Theology of the Urban Church* (Grand Rapids: Zondervan, 1991). With regard to dysfunctional family systems, see Ronald E. Hammer, "The Systemic Spirit of the Family: Reframing Intergenerational Sin in a Therapeutic Culture," in *Even the Demons Submit: Continuing Jesus' Ministry of Deliverance*, ed. L. L. Johns and J. R. Kraybill (Elkhart, IN: Institute of Mennonite Studies, 2006), 55–65. For a helpful survey of various approaches to dealing with the "principalities and power," especially in regard to missions, see Thomas H. McAlpine, *Facing the Powers: What Are the Options?* (Monrovia, CA: MARC, 1991).
126. J. Nelson Kraybill, "Where from Here?," in Johns and Kraybill, eds., *Even the Demons Submit*, 133.

sustained cases for the classic model available today—David Powlison forcefully argues this point:

> Not only do the world, the flesh and the devil appear in concert, but the Bible
> consistently presents them in a carefully crafted balance. Of the three, God
> primarily focuses on the flesh—the human heart and its vulnerability to evil.
> Humans stand center stage. We are called to a radical self-knowledge in relation
> to the gospel of Christ's grace. We are called to search out all the corruption,
> deceit, and depravity of our hearts, hands, and tongues. We are called to know
> God in fellowship with our blood-bought brothers and sisters. Scripture ad-
> dresses people, not demons.[127]

In the course of providing an appreciative summary of Powlison's book,
well-known Christian blogger Justin Taylor (whose blog is titled *Between Two
Worlds*) offers a succinct description of the classic model as primarily involving "evangelism, discipleship, and personal growth. . . . [The classic model]
follows the pattern of Jesus facing Satan in the desert," when he simply and
effectively dealt with temptation by using the sword of the Spirit, the Word
of God (Eph. 6:17; cf. Heb. 4:12).[128] In the classic model, with its focus on the
"weapons" of repentance, truth, prayer, obedience, worship, and study of
the Scriptures, spiritual warfare and Christian growth/discipleship are seen
as virtually one and the same.

Proponents of the classic model, of course, acknowledge that Jesus and
his early followers practiced more direct forms of spiritual warfare—namely,
the casting out of demons—in the early days of the church. However, they
argue that this served a very particular purpose in the establishment of the
church—namely, "to attest to the identity and authority of the one bringing
the message"—but that there is no indication that this form of spiritual warfare was meant to continue on through the centuries.[129] Powlison explains:

> [The model of spiritual warfare that focuses on the casting out of demons]
> offers an extremely graphic *metaphor* for sin's moral invasion and the sinner's
> moral decline into servitude. But they take their metaphor as reality, proceeding
> to cast out demons that are actually deeply entrenched sins. This moral slavery,
> listening to the deceits Satan whispers, is exactly what classic-mode spiritual
> warfare addresses.[130]

127. Powlison, *Power Encounters*, 110.
128. Justin Taylor, "Spiritual Warfare 101," available at http://thegospelcoalition.org/blogs
/justintaylor/2007/09/10/spiritual-warfare-101/.
129. Powlison, *Power Encounters*, 95.
130. Ibid., 127, emphasis in original.

In this light, it is not surprising that most proponents of the classic model reject the idea that Christians can be personally demonized.[131] Many contemporary proponents of the classic model are united by their commitment to the Calvinist-Reformed soteriological tradition, and by the affinity of their approach to earlier Reformed classics on spiritual warfare such as William Gurnall's seventeenth-century work *The Christian in Complete Armour*.[132]

"The Devil" and His Demons: The "Deliverance" Model of Spiritual Warfare

The third model of spiritual warfare—which we will refer to as the deliverance model—recognizes, among other things, the importance of dealing directly with personal demonic agents.[133] Within this broad model, one finds an array of methods and practices by which the demonic powers are to be confronted. Central to this model is the conviction that demonic entities can take up residence in people's lives and that exorcism—or "deliverance" ministry—in one form or another is frequently required for their liberation and healing. In the contemporary conversation about spiritual warfare, most of the questions and debates seem to center on various aspects of the deliverance model. We will now consider several of these.

131. E.g., Bahnsen, "Person, Work and Present Status of Satan," 39; Baker and Macchia, "Created Spirit Beings," 207–9; Thomas Ice and Robert Dean, *A Holy Rebellion: Strategy for Spiritual Warfare* (Eugene, OR: Harvest House, 1990), 119–20. This book has been republished as *Overrun by Demons: The Church's New Preoccupation with the Demonic* (Eugene, OR: Harvest House, 1993).

132. William Gurnall, *The Christian in Complete Armour* (Carlisle, UK: Banner of Truth, 1979). For other proponents of a classic model, see James M. Boice, "A Better Way: The Power of Word and Spirit," in *Power Religion: The Selling Out of the Evangelical Church*, ed. M. S. Horton (Chicago: Moody, 1992), 122–23; Ice and Dean, *Overrun by Demons*; John MacArthur, *How to Meet the Enemy: Arming Yourself for Spiritual Warfare* (Wheaton: Victor, 1992).

133. For several helpful historical surveys of this model (with a focus on more recent times), see Kraft, "Contemporary Trends in the Treatment of Spiritual Warfare"; Moreau, "A Survey of North American Spiritual Warfare Thinking"; Stephen Hunt, "Deliverance: The Evolution of a Doctrine," *Themelios* 21, no. 1 (1995): 10–13; C. Peter Wagner, "Missiology and Spiritual Power," in *Paradigm Shifts in Christian Witness: Insights from Anthropology, Communication, and Spiritual Power, Essays in Honor of Charles H. Kraft*, ed. C. E. Van Engen et al. (Maryknoll, NY: Orbis, 2008), 91–97. See also James M. Collins, *Exorcism and Deliverance Ministry in the Twentieth Century: An Analysis of the Practice and Theology of Exorcism in Modern Western Christianity* (Colorado Springs: Paternoster, 2009), who—whether or not one agrees with his thesis that "religious enthusiasm" is its common ground—provides a very helpful survey of deliverance ministry in the contemporary Western Christian context. The journalist Michael Cuneo offers a chronicle of exorcism/deliverance ministry in twentieth-century America from an outsider's perspective, proposing that the Hollywood entertainment industry (e.g., the film *The Exorcist*) has had a profound effect upon its views and practices. See *American Exorcism: Expelling Demons in the Land of Plenty* (New York: Doubleday, 2001).

The Nature of Deliverance (Exorcism)

Within the deliverance model, one can find a dizzying array of theories of, and approaches to, deliverance ministry, or the casting out of demons.[134] Terminology becomes important here. While some within this model are comfortable with the term "exorcism," others equate exorcism with non-Christian methods of demon expulsion and so prefer the term "deliverance." Many within this model tend to distinguish between various levels of demonic influence within a person's life. Common terms within this continuum approach include "temptation," "oppression," "obsession," "demonization," and "possession."[135]

Those who would locate themselves primarily within one of the other two models frequently charge proponents of the deliverance model with an unhealthy focus on demons, demonization, and deliverance. Common concerns here include offering people an excuse to avoid personal responsibility for sin, unintentionally encouraging an undue magnification of Satan and the demonic, and fostering a paranoia that leads to seeing a "demon behind every bush." However, adherents of the deliverance model commonly counter this by pointing out that they encourage people to find a biblical balance in these things. They state, for example, that people are urged to consider the possibility of demonic activity as only one potential source of their troubles. It is

134. For a sampling of the stunning array of diversity within this broad model (with a focus on some of the more well-known names/works), see Amorth, *An Exorcist Tells His Story*; Neal T. Anderson, *The Bondage Breaker* (Eugene, OR: Harvest House, 2000); Arnold, *3 Crucial Questions about Spiritual Warfare*; Don Basham, *Deliver Us from Evil* (Old Tappan, NJ: Revell, 1980); Rebecca Brown, *He Came to Set the Captives Free* (Chino, CA: Chick, 1986); Fred Dickason, *Demon Possession and the Christian: A New Perspective* (Chicago: Moody, 1989); Francis Frangipane, *The Three Battlegrounds* (Cedar Rapids, IA: Arrow, 1989); Rebecca Greenwood, *Breaking the Bonds of Evil: How to Set People Free from Demonic Oppression* (Grand Rapids: Chosen, 2006); Frank and Ida Mae Hammond, *Pigs in the Parlor* (Kirkwood, MO: Impact, 1973); Kurt Koch, *Demonology, Past and Present* (Grand Rapids: Kregel, 1973); Charles H. Kraft, *Defeating Dark Angels: Breaking Demonic Oppression in the Believer's Life* (Ann Arbor, MI: Servant, 1992); Francis MacNutt, *Deliverance from Evil Spirits: A Practical Manual* (Grand Rapids: Chosen, 1995); Ed Murphy, *The Handbook for Spiritual Warfare*, rev. ed. (Nashville: Nelson, 1996); John R. Nevius, *Demon Possession* (Grand Rapids: Kregel, 1968); Jessie Penn-Lewis, with Evan Roberts, *War on the Saints*, abridged ed. (Fort Washington, PA: Christian Literature Crusade, 1977); John Sandford and Mark Sandford, *A Comprehensive Guide to Deliverance and Inner Healing* (Grand Rapids: Chosen, 1992); Charles R. Swindoll, *Demonism: How to Win against the Devil* (Portland: Multnomah, 1981); Wagner and Pennoyer, eds., *Wrestling with Dark Angels*; Timothy Warner, *Spiritual Warfare* (Westchester, IL: Crossway, 1991); John White, "Problems and Procedures in Exorcism," in *Demon Possession*, ed. J. Warwick Montgomery (Minneapolis: Bethany, 1976), 281–99; Tom White, *The Believer's Guide to Spiritual Warfare* (Ann Arbor, MI: Servant, 1990).

135. E.g., Arnold, *3 Crucial Questions about Spiritual Warfare*, 101; L. Grant McClung, "Pentecostal/Charismatic Understanding of Exorcism," in Wagner and Pennoyer, eds., *Wrestling with Dark Angels*, 206–7; White, *Believer's Guide to Spiritual Warfare*, 42–43.

common for deliverance ministry to be seen as but one tool among many—to be used alongside traditional counseling methods and the therapeutic use of prescription medication—within a holistic, integrated approach to human health and healing.[136]

Again, the actual methods of deliverance within this model can differ significantly. Commonly, a potentially demonized person will meet with a team of people who proceed to pray and eventually take authority over the demonic entity, commanding it to leave in the name of Jesus. Those who practice this model offer the many examples of Jesus casting out demons in the Synoptic Gospels as the basic template for their own method. Among those who practice this basic approach, there is quite a bit of diversity as to whether—and, if so, which—additional techniques should be used so as to most effectively liberate people from demonic oppression.[137] Some, like Gregory Boyd, emphasize the importance of following the simple, straightforward deliverance method of Jesus:

> It was Jesus' reliance on the Holy Spirit, activated through faith and prayer, that more than anything else set his [deliverance] ministry apart. Indeed, the only weapons we ever see employed by Jesus in his deliverance ministry are faith and prayer.[138]

Others take a more elaborate approach to Christian deliverance ministry. Common issues of disagreement include: Is it helpful/necessary to ascertain

136. For a range of Christian perspectives on the use of deliverance ministry within the traditional counseling setting, etc., see Jay E. Adams, "Demon Possession and Counseling," in *The Big Umbrella, and Other Essays on Christian Counseling* (Grand Rapids: Baker, 1972), 115–21; J. T. de Jongh van Arkel, "Pastoral Counselling and Demonology," in *Like a Roaring Lion: Essays on the Bible, the Church and Demonic Powers*, ed. P. G. R. de Villiers (Pretoria: University of South Africa, 1987), 141–46; Rodger K. Bufford, *Counseling and the Demonic* (Dallas: Word, 1988); Grayson Ensign and Edward Howe, *Counseling and Demonization: The Missing Link* (Amarillo: Recovery Publications, 1989); Thomas Miegs, "Pastoral Care Methods and Demonology in Selected Writings," *Journal of Psychology and Theology* 5 (1977): 234–46; Millard J. Sall, "Demon Possession or Psychopathology? A Clinical Differentiation," *Journal of Psychology and Theology* 4 (1976): 286–90; S. Southard, "Demonizing and Mental Illness (II): The Problem of Assessment, Los Angeles," *Pastoral Psychology* 34 (1986): 264–87; S. Southard and M. Southard, "Demonizing and Mental Illness (III): Explanations and Treatment, Seoul," *Pastoral Psychology* 35 (1986): 132–51; H. A. Virkler, "Demonic Influence and Psychopathology," in *Baker Encyclopedia of Psychology*, ed. D. G. Benner (Grand Rapids: Baker, 1985), 293–99; Paul J. Yoder, "Demonization and the Therapeutic Community," in Johns and Kraybill, eds., *Even the Demons Submit*, 119–32.

137. For a statement representing a more conservative, minimalist approach to deliverance technique, see Gerry Breshears, "Deliverance Ministry: A Consensus Statement from Pentecostals, Charismatics, and Historic Evangelicals" (paper presented at the Annual Meeting of the Evangelical Theological Society, New Orleans, November 17, 1990), 1–5. Revised version available at http://www.epm.org/resources/2010/Jul/5/deliverance-ministry/.

138. Boyd, *God at War*, 203.

the name and/or rank of the demonic entity? Are there demons associated with particular sins? Is it helpful to allow the demonic entities to "manifest" during a deliverance session or should they be commanded not to? Should one ever directly question a demon for informational purposes? Does "binding and loosing" play a significant role in deliverance ministry?[139] Can buildings and/or physical objects be demonized and so require spiritual cleansing? Should the deliverance minister explore the possibility of generational sins/curses—or, even more controversially, satanic ritual abuse?[140]

With his well-known book *The Bondage Breaker*, Neal Anderson introduced many people to a unique approach to the deliverance model: the "truth encounter."[141] This approach urges that the most effective forms of deliverance ministry focus on cognitive apprehension of the truth of one's position and identity in Christ. In this sense, the truth encounter strategy can be seen as something of a bridging effort between "power encounter" versions of the deliverance model and the classic model.[142] Anderson offers a guided prayer exercise—what he calls "Steps to Freedom in Christ"—designed to facilitate the breaking of demonic bondages.[143] This approach focuses on prayerful renunciation of, and repentance from, prior occultic involvement, demonic deception, unforgiveness, a rebellious spirit, self-glorifying pride, sinful bondages, and

139. On this concept, see K. Neill Foster with Paul L. King, *Binding and Loosing: Exercising Authority over Powers of Darkness* (Camp Hill, PA: Christian, 1998).

140. Fueled by books such as Michelle Smith and Lawrence Pazder's *Michelle Remembers* (New York: Pocket, 1980), the controversy surrounding the question of satanic ritual abuse (SRA) reached its zenith in the early 1990s, and served to split the ranks of those within the broader deliverance model. Those who take the SRA phenomenon seriously include Ken Olson, *Exorcism: Fact or Fiction?* (Nashville: Nelson, 1992); Carl A. Raschke, *Painted Black* (New York: Harper, 1990), chap. 10. Those who have expressed skepticism concerning a wide-ranging SRA conspiracy phenomenon include Arnold, *3 Crucial Questions about Spiritual Warfare*, 133–38; B. J. Oropeza, *99 Answers to Questions about Angels, Demons, and Spiritual Warfare* (Downers Grove, IL: InterVarsity, 1997), 171–72. The question of SRA phenomena has also been debated within wider cultural circles. See, e.g., David K. Sakheim and Susan E. Devine, eds., *Out of Darkness: Exploring Satanism and Ritual Abuse* (New York: Lexington, 1992); Jeffrey S. Victor, *Satanic Panic: The Creation of a Contemporary Legend* (Chicago and LaSalle, IL: Open Court, 1993).

141. Anderson, *Bondage Breaker*. See also Neil T. Anderson, *Victory over the Darkness: Realizing the Power of Your Identity in Christ* (Ventura, CA: Regal, 1990); Neal Anderson and Pete and Sue Vander Hook, *Spiritual Protection for Your Children: Helping Your Children and Family Find their Identity, Freedom, and Security in Christ* (Ventura, CA: Regal, 1996).

142. Others who advocate for a more "truth encounter" approach include Jim Logan, *Reclaiming Surrendered Ground* (Chicago: Moody, 1995); and A. Scott Moreau, *Essentials of Spiritual Warfare* (Wheaton: Shaw, 1997). Kraft ("Contemporary Trends in the Treatment of Spiritual Conflict," 190–91) also classifies Ed Smith's "theophostic" approach to prayer counseling as a form of the truth-oriented model. See Ed M. Smith, *Beyond Tolerable Recovery*, rev. ed. (Campbellsville, KY: Theophostic Ministries, 2000).

143. Anderson, *Bondage Breaker*, 199–252.

generational sins and curses from the past. When engaging in deliverance ministry, Anderson suggests that one begin with a prayer that "Satan and all his demons be bound to silence and commanded not to interfere with the process." The counselee then takes the proper steps to renounce and take authority over the demonic powers. As they take these steps of faith, "they will command the demons to leave."[144]

CAN A CHRISTIAN BE DEMONIZED?

With the consideration of the deliverance model, one particularly contentious question perennially arises: Can a Christian have a demon? As noted above, staunch adherents of the classic model commonly reject this possibility. Most proponents of the deliverance model, however, believe that Christians can, in fact, have a demon. Here, terminology once again becomes important. More specifically, terminological equivocation and lack of precision can quickly lead to misunderstanding and talking past each other on this prickly subject. Many holding to the deliverance model argue that we should not confuse "demon possession" with "demonization" and that the latter, or something like it, is a far more accurate rendering of the idea behind the New Testament's Greek word *daimonizomai* (the biblical term commonly translated into English as "demon possessed").[145] Given this terminological distinction, many who affirm this model argue that, while a Christian cannot be "demon possessed" (i.e., they cannot be "owned" or fully controlled by a demon), they can be "demonized," or significantly influenced by a demon to one degree or another, and thus stand in need of deliverance ministry.[146]

Those who hold that a Christian can, in fact, come under the direct influence of a demon point not infrequently to a remarkable reversal of opinion on this matter by the well-known evangelical Old Testament scholar Merrill Unger. Unger wrote a book in 1952 on the topic of demonology.[147] In this book he concluded that a true Christian cannot have a demon. Almost twenty years later, Unger wrote a second book on the topic.[148] He notes that in the

144. Neal T. Anderson, "Finding Freedom in Christ," in Wagner and Pennoyer, eds., *Wrestling with Dark Angels*, 138.

145. Arnold, *3 Crucial Questions about Spiritual Warfare*, 78–93; Dickason, *Demon Possession and the Christian*, 37–39.

146. Arnold, *3 Crucial Questions about Spiritual Warfare*, chap. 2; Don Basham, *Can a Christian Have a Demon?* (Monroeville, PA: Whitaker, 1971); Dickason, *Demon Possession and the Christian*; Murphy, *Handbook for Spiritual Warfare*, 429–36.

147. Merrill F. Unger, *Biblical Demonology: A Study of the Spiritual Forces behind the Present World Unrest* (Wheaton: Van Kampen, 1952).

148. Merrill F. Unger, *Demons in the World Today: A Study of Occultism in the Light of God's Word* (Wheaton: Tyndale, 1971).

intervening years he received numerous letters in response to his first book—mostly from fellow believers on the mission field outside of America—that gave testimony of genuine Christians who, nonetheless, gave unavoidable evidence of being demonized and in need of deliverance. In light of this evidence, Unger changed his position on this question.[149] Several years later, Unger wrote a third book that more directly addressed the issue: *What Demons Can Do to Saints*.[150]

A final area of debate that arises among those who hold to the deliverance model involves the question of which "level(s)" of the demonic realm the Christian is called to do warfare against. The more traditional forms of the deliverance model see spiritual warfare as relegated solely to what can be called the "ground-level" realm—that is, freeing individual people from demonic influences that foster areas of bondage in their personal lives. In recent years, what has come to be known as "strategic-level"—or "cosmic-level"—spiritual warfare has emerged as an alternative approach within the deliverance model. We now turn to a consideration of this new approach.

Cosmic Deliverance: Territorial Spirits and Strategic-Level Spiritual Warfare

A final topic of consideration has provoked intense debate in recent years and centers on the ideas of territorial spirits, spiritual mapping, and identificational repentance. This approach to spiritual warfare—commonly known as strategic- or cosmic-level spiritual warfare—can be seen as emerging from, and thus sharing the basic convictions of, the deliverance model, while further developing it in significant ways. It also shares some intriguing elements with the world systems model. A growing interest in this approach within certain sectors of evangelical Christianity can be traced back to the Lausanne II Congress on World Evangelization held in Manila, Philippines, in 1989. The remarkable interest in workshops on the Holy Spirit, spiritual warfare, and prayer offered at Lausanne II eventually led to the birth of the AD 2000 Movement and its United Prayer Track, as well as the Spiritual Warfare Network.[151] At the intersection of these groups was a man who has become the most widely recognized advocate for strategic-level spiritual warfare today, C. Peter Wagner. Wagner, along with Rebecca Greenwood, advocates for the practice of strategic-level spiritual warfare (henceforth SLSW) in their contribution to this present volume.[152]

---

149. Ibid., 116–17.

150. Merrill F. Unger, *What Demons Can Do to Saints* (Chicago: Moody, 1977).

151. For the 1993 Lausanne Statement on Spiritual Warfare, see http://www.lausanne.org/en/documents/all/consultation-statements/206--statement-on-spiritual-warfare-1993.html.

152. C. Peter Wagner's most important books on this subject include: Wagner, *Confronting the Powers: How the New Testament Church Experienced the Power of Strategic-Level Spiritual*

SLSW is indebted to the notion of territorial spirits—that is, powerful, high-ranking spirit beings that have authority over particular geographical regions of the earth. Proponents of SLSW point to a number of biblical texts and themes in their defense of territorial spirits, including the ideas that there are angelic authorities over the nations (Deut. 32:8; Ps. 82) and that the gods/idols of the nations are actually demonic entities (Deut. 32:17; Ps. 96:5; 106:37–38). The most important text here is Daniel 10, which apparently depicts two evil spiritual beings—the "prince of Greece" and the "prince of Persia"—in battle against God's angelic forces of good, including the angel Michael. In addition to these Old Testament texts, several passages in the New Testament are cited in support of this concept (i.e., Luke 10:19; 11:20–22; John 12:31; 14:30; 16:11; 1 Cor. 2:6–8; 2 Cor. 4:4; Eph. 6:12; 1 John 5:19; Rev. 2:12; 12:7–9; 18:2).

Building on the concept of demonic territorial spirits, proponents argue for the importance of several things that, together, compose the primary foci and activities of the SLSW model. First is the concept of "strategic-level" spiritual warfare itself. Wagner coined this phrase in the process of distinguishing between three levels of activity in the practice of spiritual warfare: "ground-level" (i.e., casting demons out of individual people), "occult-level" (i.e., dealing with demonic forces within Satanism, witchcraft, and other forms of "structured occultism"), and finally "strategic-level" (i.e., direct confrontation of territorial spirits that hold "cities, nations, neighborhoods, people groups, religious alliances, industries, or any other form of human society in spiritual captivity").[153] SLSW commonly involves "spiritual mapping," a process by which the specific territorial spirit(s) of an area is discerned and named.[154]

Warfare (Ventura, CA: Regal, 1996); Wagner, *Confronting the Queen of Heaven* (Colorado Springs: Wagner Institute for Practical Ministry, 1998); Wagner, ed., *Breaking Strongholds in Your City: How to Use Spiritual Mapping to Make Your Prayers More Strategic, Effective, and Targeted* (Ventura, CA: Regal, 1993); Wagner, ed., *Engaging the Enemy: How to Fight and Defeat Territorial Spirits* (Ventura, CA: Regal, 1991); Wagner, ed., *Territorial Spirits: Practical Strategies for How to Crush the Enemy through Spiritual Warfare* (Shippensburg, PA: Destiny Image, 2012). Rebecca Greenwood focuses on SLSW in her book *Authority to Tread: A Practical Guide for Strategic-Level Spiritual Warfare* (Grand Rapids: Chosen, 2005). See also Cindy Jacobs, *Taking Our Cities for God* (Altamonte Springs, FL: Creation House, 1991); George Otis Jr., *The Last of the Giants* (Tarrytown, NY: Chosen, 1991); Ed Silvoso, *That None Should Perish: How to Reach Entire Cities for Christ through Prayer Evangelism* (Ventura, CA: Regal, 1994).

153. Wagner, *Confronting the Powers*, 21–22.

154. Art Moore, "Spiritual Mapping Gains Credibility among Leaders," *Christianity Today*, January 12, 1998, 55. It is interesting to note that the concept of "spiritual mapping" of cities is capable of being transformed and used by proponents of the world systems model of spiritual warfare, wherein various systems of structural evil and injustice in a given locale are clearly named and engaged. See Tai M. Yip, "Spiritual Mapping: Another Approach," *Evangelical Missions Quarterly* 31 (1995): 166–70; Bill Wylie-Kellermann, "Discerning the Angel of Detroit," *Sojourners* 18 (October 1989): 16–21.

"Identificational repentance" is also a common component. This involves Christians investigating the past sins of a particular city and then identifying with those sins through confession and repentance on behalf of the city. The goal is effectively to break the authority of territorial spirits over the city and facilitate reconciliation, healing, and conversion to Christ among its people.[155] Finally, SLSW involves focused, aggressive prayer against the territorial spirits themselves. Cindy Jacobs, cofounder of Generals International, an intercessory and prophetic alliance, explains the relationship between identificational repentance and prayer against the territorial spirits of a city: "Once sin has been repented of, I usually ask the local pastors who have strong anointings and authority to lead in the actual prayer against the territorial spirits and command their power to be broken. This must not be done until the sins have been remitted or the power of the strongholds will not be broken."[156]

Some critics of SLSW grant that the biblical evidence for territorial spirits is worthy of consideration—or even persuasive—but that biblical warrant for practicing SLSW itself is lacking.[157] Others argue that even the biblical texts used to support claims about territorial spirits are ambiguous at best and are better interpreted in other ways.[158] As a consequence, they fear that SLSW proponents have unwittingly given territorial spirits "more 'territory' than they deserve."[159] Some critics go so far as to charge SLSW proponents with unwittingly succumbing to a syncretistic mixing of Christianity with an "animist" worldview.[160] Proponents of SLSW have responded by suggesting

155. The concept of identificational repentance is developed most thoroughly in John Dawson, *Taking Our Cities for God: How to Break Spiritual Strongholds* (Mary Lake, FL: Creation House, 1989); John Dawson, *Healing America's Wounds* (Ventura, CA: Regal, 1994).

156. Cindy Jacobs, *Possessing the Gates of the Enemy: A Training Manual for Militant Intercession*, 2nd ed. (Grand Rapids: Chosen, 1994), 245–46.

157. Arnold, *3 Crucial Questions about Spiritual Warfare*, 143–99; Oropeza, 99 *Answers to Questions about Angels, Demons, and Spiritual Warfare*, 125–26.

158. Chuck Lowe, *Territorial Spirits and World Evangelization? A Biblical, Historical, and Missiological Critique of Strategic-Level Spiritual Warfare* (Kent, UK: Mentor/OMF, 1998), 29–73. Lowe's book is the most thorough critique of SLSW to date. For several other critiques of territorial spirits and/or SLSW, see David Greenlee, "Territorial Spirits Reconsidered," *Missiology* 22 (1994): 507–14; Charles R. A. Hoole, "Territorial Spirits: An Indian Perspective," *Stulos Theological Journal* 5 (1997): 59–68; Bob Priest, Thomas Campbell, and Bradford A. Mullen, "Missiological Syncretism: The New Animistic Paradigm," in *Spiritual Power and Missions: Raising the Issues*, ed. E. Rommen (Pasadena: William Carey Library, 1995), 9–87; Mike Wakely, "A Critical Look at a New 'Key' to Evangelization," *Evangelical Missions Quarterly* 31 (1995): 152–62.

159. Greenlee, "Territorial Spirits Reconsidered," 507.

160. See esp. Priest, Campbell, and Mullen, "Missiological Syncretism: The New Animistic Paradigm." See also Lowe, *Territorial Spirits and World Evangelization?*, 103–12; Scott Moreau, "Religious Borrowing as a Two-Way Street: An Introduction to Animistic Tendencies in the Euro-North American Context," in *Christianity and the Religions: A Biblical Theology of World*

that the animist worldview happens to share some important aspects with the biblical worldview. They in turn fear that the critics of their approach to spiritual warfare have drunk too deeply at the wells of the modern naturalistic worldview, and in the process have fallen victim to what missiologist Paul Hiebert has called "the flaw of the excluded middle"—namely, a systematic neglect of the spiritual world of angelic and demonic powers.[161]

Competing Models of Spiritual Warfare and the Question of Balance

The foregoing discussion on the nature of spiritual warfare has focused on some of the many diverse perspectives within the church today. For purposes of clarity, different models and methods have been defined heuristically and set over against each other. But as we end this section, it is important to note that a number of proponents of spiritual warfare approach these options with a both/and rather than an either/or perspective. For example, in his book *Spiritual Warfare for Every Christian*, Dean Sherman writes:

> Some think spiritual warfare is only deliverance. Others emphasize pulling down strongholds in the heavenlies. Still others say spiritual warfare is doing the works of Jesus—preaching, teaching, and living the truth. Yet another group says all this is impractical. They claim we should focus on feeding the hungry, resisting racism, and speaking out against social injustice. I believe we have to do it all. Pulling down strongholds is only important if people are led to Christ as a result. However, some are deaf to the preaching of the Gospel until we deal with hindering powers. And some can't break through into victory until bondage is broken in their lives. We must do it all as appropriate, and as God leads.[162]

Religions, ed. Edward Rommen and Harold Netland (Pasadena: William Carey Library, 1995), 166–182; Hoole, "Territorial Spirits," 66–67.

161. Paul G. Hiebert, "The Flaw of the Excluded Middle," *Missiology* 10 (1982): 35–47. For two responses to the "animist" charge, see Charles Kraft, "'Christian Animism' or God-Given Authority?," in Rommen, ed., *Spiritual Power and Missions*, 88–136; Wagner, *Confronting the Powers*, 64–71. This debate raises the broader question of the role one's worldview plays in how one approaches questions about spiritual warfare. For further reflections on this issue, see Paul Hiebert, "Spiritual Warfare and Worldview," *Evangelical Review of Theology* 24 (2000): 240–54; Charles Kraft, *Christianity with Power: Your Worldview and Your Experience of the Supernatural* (Ann Arbor, MI: Servant, 1989); Marguerite Kraft, "Spiritual Conflict and the Mission of the Church: Contextualization," in Moreau et al., eds., *Deliver Us from Evil*, 267–89; Wink, "New Worldview."

162. Dean Sherman, *Spiritual Warfare for Every Christian* (Seattle: YWAM, 1990), 187. In a similar vein, the renowned Reformed pastor John Piper, while clearly having theological sympathies with the classic model, nonetheless expresses an appreciation for the deliverance model, and even calls for an openness to territorial spirits and SLSW. See John Piper, "Cosmic-Level Spiritual Warfare"; John Piper, "Putting the Gods in their Place," at http://www.desiringgod .org/resource-library/taste-see-articles/putting-the-gods-in-their-place; John Piper, "Do You

Introducing Our Contributors

It is with great pleasure and confidence that we introduce our contributors to this volume and then turn the conversation over to them. Walter Wink will start things out, with assistance from Gareth Higgins and Michael Hardin along the way. As noted above, Wink has been a leading voice in the discussion on spiritual warfare for several decades, most notably in the form of his *Powers* trilogy: *Naming the Powers* (1984), *Unmasking the Powers* (1986), and *Engaging the Powers* (1992). Within this volume, Wink's view is distinguished by its grounding in a panentheistic "Integral worldview," its understanding of the principalities and powers as the spiritual interiority of human social structures (and thus its rejection of angelic/demonic spirits as autonomous, personal agents), and its deep indebtedness to what we have called a world systems model of spiritual warfare. Gareth Higgins, who provides editorial support for Wink's opening essay, is a cofounder of the zero28 Project, a faith-based peace and justice initiative in Northern Ireland, and has written various articles on religion and conflict. Michael Hardin, who collaborates with Wink on his responses to the other contributors, is the executive director of Preaching Peace and has recently written a book that touches on our topic at hand, *The Jesus Driven Life: Reconnecting Humanity with Jesus* (2010), for which Wink wrote the afterword.

David Powlison is our next contributor. Powlison became a significant voice in the spiritual warfare conversation with the publication of his 1995 book *Power Encounters: Reclaiming Spiritual Warfare*. Powlison champions the classic model of spiritual warfare in this volume. Contrary to Wink (and in agreement with Boyd, and Wagner and Greenwood), he argues that demons are personal, spiritual agents. But against Boyd, and Wagner and Greenwood, and in defense of the classic model, he holds that spiritual warfare is best accomplished through things like repentance, prayer, Scripture reading, and discipleship rather than by direct power encounters with the demonic.

Gregory Boyd is our third contributor. In his major writings on spiritual warfare to date—*God at War* (1997), *Satan and the Problem of Evil* (2001), and *The Myth of a Christian Religion* (2009)—Boyd has approached the topic from the standpoints of biblical theology, theodicy, and Christian lifestyle respectively. In this volume, Boyd articulates and defends a form of the ground-level deliverance model, one that includes an emphasis on emulating Jesus's lifestyle as key to the practice of a biblically informed approach to spiritual warfare.

Believe We Should Cast Out Demons Today?," at http://www.desiringgod.org/resource-library/ask-pastor-john/do-you-believe-we-should-cast-out-demons-today.

Finally, the team of C. Peter Wagner and Rebecca Greenwood provide the fourth view in this volume. As noted above, Wagner has been a leading advocate of SLSW for over two decades. His most thorough articulation and defense of this approach is *Confronting the Powers* (1996). Greenwood, a faculty member at Wagner's Leadership Institute, has also taught and written extensively on SLSW. Her books include *Authority to Tread* (2005) and *Let Our Children Go: Steps to Free Your Child from Evil Influences and Demonic Harassment* (2011). Together in this volume, they offer a view of the deliverance model that uniquely situates territorial spirits and strategic-level activity at the center of the practice of spiritual warfare.

And now—let the dialogue begin!

1

The World Systems Model

WALTER WINK, EDITED BY GARETH HIGGINS

Nothing commends Satan to the modern mind. It is bad enough that Satan is spirit, when our worldview has banned spirit from discourse and belief. But worse, he is evil, and our culture resolutely refuses to believe in the real existence of evil, preferring to regard it as a matter of systems break-down that can be fixed with enough tinkering. Worse yet, Satan is not a very good intellectual idea. Once theology lost its character as reflection on the experience of knowing God and became a second-level exercise in "knowing about," the experiential ground of theology began to erode away. "Although mythologically true," Morton Kelsey writes, "the devil is intellectually inde-fensible, and once it was realized that the conception of the powers of evil was 'only' a representation of peoples' experience, no matter how accurate, the devil began to fade."[1]

The Satan image, even where it lingers on, has been whittled down to the stature of a personal being whose sole obsessions seem to be with sexuality, adolescent rebellion, crime, passion, and greed. While not themselves trivial, these preoccupations altogether obscure the massive satanic evils that plunge

1. Morton Kelsey, "The Mythology of Evil," *Journal of Religion and Health* 13, no. 1 (January 1974): 16.

and drive our times like a trawler before an angry sea. Not that we have progressed beyond evil. On the contrary, the evil of our time has become so gigantic that it has virtually outstripped the symbol and become autonomous, unrepresentable, beyond comprehension.

While the symbol may have fallen on hard times, the reality to which it gave expression has become all the more virulent. Satan did not begin life as an idea but as an experience. The issue is not whether one "believes" in Satan but whether one is able to identify the actual events of life in that dimension of experience the ancients called "Satan." Nor is the metaphysical question, does Satan really exist?, of any real urgency, unless the question is asked in the context of an actual encounter with something or someone that leads one to posit Satan's existence.

Without a means of symbolization, however, evil cannot come to conscious awareness and thus be consciously resisted. Like an undiagnosed disease, it rages through society, and we are helpless to produce a cure. Evil must be symbolized precisely because it cannot be thought. Is there any way we can resymbolize evil? Thought cannot resuscitate Satan, but only committed persons consciously making choices for God, as we will see. But thought can perhaps roll away the stone. Then, perhaps, if we can live through that dark interval between Satan's death and resurrection, we may yet see Satan functioning again—as a servant of the living God!

Satan as a Servant of God

We are not accustomed to thinking of Satan as God's servant. But when Satan makes his late appearance in the Old Testament, that is precisely who he is—a servant of the Lord.

The faith of early Israel actually had no place for Satan. God alone was Lord, and thus whatever happened, for good or ill, was ascribed to God. "I kill and I make alive," says the Lord, "I wound and I heal" (Deut. 32:39 NRSV).

So it was not inconsistent to believe that Yahweh might call Moses to deliver Israel from Egypt and then, on the way, attempt to murder him. The text, much neglected by preachers, is Exodus 4:24–26a. "On the journey, when Moses had halted for the night, Yahweh came to meet him and tried to kill him. At once Zipporah, taking up a flint, cut off her son's foreskin and with it she touched the genitals of Moses. 'Truly, you are the bridegroom of blood to me!' she said. And Yahweh let him live" (Jerusalem Bible). Perhaps Moses had fallen critically ill; or had almost been killed by an attack, fall, or avalanche; or had somatized his terror at the enormity of his task. In any case, the attack was ascribed not to natural causes but to God.

The God who led Israel out of Egypt, however, was a God of justice. How then could God demand justice, be just, and still cause evil? Had not Abraham challenged God with the question, "Shall not the judge of all the earth do right?" (Gen. 18:25 KJV). This problem was the terrible price Israel had been forced to pay for its belief that Yahweh was the primary cause of all that happens. Morally, the cost was unbearable. Gradually Yahweh became differentiated into a "light" and a "dark" side, both integral to the Godhead, with Yahweh transcending both as the unity that encompasses multiplicity. The bright side came to be represented by the angels, the dark side by Satan and his demons. Yet this process of differentiation was completed so late that Satan makes only three appearances in the Old Testament.

In 2 Samuel 24:1 Yahweh, in anger against Israel, had incited David to carry out a census (the basis of taxation and military conscription). But in Chronicles, a postcaptivity revision of Samuel and Kings, this same passage is changed to read, "Satan stood up against Israel, and incited David to number Israel" (1 Chron. 21:1 RSV). The adversary has assumed the function of executor of God's wrath. He does not represent disorder, chaos, or rebellion here, but rather the imposition of a suffocating bureaucratic order (the census). Satan furthers God's will by visiting wrath on disobedient mortals, and in so doing carries out the will of God.

In Zechariah 3:1–5 (RSV) we find a second appearance of Satan; here "the satan" is in the role of accuser or prosecuting attorney.

> Then he showed me Joshua the high priest standing before the angel of the LORD, and Satan [ha satan] standing at his right hand to accuse him. And the LORD said to Satan, "The LORD rebuke you, O Satan! The LORD who has chosen Jerusalem rebuke you! Is not this a brand plucked from the fire?" Now Joshua was standing before the angel clothed in filthy garments. And the angel said to those who were standing before him, "Remove the filthy garments from him." And to him he said, "Behold, I have taken your iniquity away from you, and I will clothe you with rich apparel." And I said, "Let them put a clean turban on his head." So they put a clean turban on his head and clothed him with garments; and the angel of the LORD was standing by.

The scene is set in the heavenly council, with the accuser at the right of the accused, Joshua. The high priest (Joshua), representing the whole people of Israel, is dressed in filthy garments, symbolic of the sins that Israel's prophets had identified as the cause of Israel's exile in Babylon. The vision is dated around 520 BCE; this means that upward of three generations of Jews had lived with the belief that they had gone into captivity in 585 as punishment for their infidelity to Yahweh. Joshua bears all that collective guilt. The adversary merely reiterates what the accusing conscience of the people has been affirming all along. The guilt is real, and it is deserved. Only God's undeserved grace causes the case to be quashed.

Satan is clearly not demonic here. If anything, Satan echoes what everyone knows to be the attitude of God toward Israel, prior to God's unexpected reversal of the judgment. Satan merely repeats what the prophets had been saying all along! Nevertheless God intervenes. Israel is "a brand plucked from the fire" and will be consumed by guilt and succumb to hopelessness unless it experiences forgiveness soon. Satan is thus not merely a mythological character invented out of whole cloth; the "adversary" is that actual inner or collective voice of condemnation that any sensitive person hears tirelessly repeating accusations of guilt or inferiority. And indeed, there is a degree of truth in the charges. But Satan's demand for strict justice, untempered by mercy, can crush the spirit of a person or a people. This "voice" is a phenomenological fact; its mythic conceptualization allows the people of Israel to isolate it, lift it to consciousness, and ask whether it is indeed the voice of God in a judgmental mode.

The final Old Testament reference to Satan is in the prologue to Job: "Now there was a day when the sons of God [bene elohim] came to present themselves before the LORD, and Satan [ha satan] also came among them." Here again, Satan is not a fallen angel but a fully credentialed member of the heavenly court. "The LORD said to Satan, 'Whence have you come?' Satan answered the LORD, 'From going to and fro on the earth, and from walking up and down on it.'" His role is somewhat like that of a district attorney, zealously seeking out lawbreakers to bring before the bar of divine justice. "And the LORD said to Satan, 'Have you considered my servant Job, that there is none like him on the earth, a blameless and upright man, who fears God and turns away from evil?'" Satan has indeed considered him well: "Then Satan answered the LORD, 'Does Job fear God for naught? Hast thou not put a hedge about him and his house and all that he has, on every side? Thou hast blessed the work of his hands, and his possessions have increased in the land. But put forth thy hand now, and touch all that he has and he will curse thee to thy face.' And the LORD said to Satan, 'Behold, all that he has is in your power; only upon himself do not put forth your hand.' So Satan went forth from the presence of the LORD" (Job 1:6–12 RSV). This is more than simply prosecution, however. It is entrapment. Not content merely to uncover injustice, Satan is here, as in 1 Chronicles 21:1, an agent provocateur, actively striving to coax people into crimes for which they can then be punished. Excessive zeal for justice always becomes satanic. All Job's oxen, asses, camels, sheep, and servants are slain; then finally all his sons and daughters. Yet Job holds piously to his faith (1:21).

When next they meet, God chides Satan for his failure: Job "still holds fast his integrity, although you moved me against him, to destroy him without cause" (2:3 RSV). What kind of God is this, that trifles with the lives and flesh of humans in order to win a bet? This God seems too bent on sheer power to mark the sufferings of mere people. The author seems to deliberately ridicule the God of a degenerate Deuteronomic theology. That God (represented by Job's three "comforters"), who rewards the wealthy, landed aristocrats with riches and long life and who curses the poor, is mercilessly lampooned by an outraged writer who has acutely observed the oppressed and infirm suffer undeserved evil at the hands of the powerful and rich. Those listeners, whom God had not blessed and who had no such vast herds and spacious houses but who barely subsisted on the land, must have relished seeing this rich man stripped of his props and reduced to their level. And they must have chuckled with delight at the storyteller's artful repetition in 2:1–3, where God behaves like a forgetful potentate unable to recall the job description of his own appointee!

Job's Satan, in short, is no friend of Job's, but he is in fact humanity's best friend because he lures God into a contest that will end by stripping God of the projections of the oppressors. Satan has already persuaded God to act arbitrarily ("to destroy him without cause," 2:3 RSV). Now Satan compounds the murder of Job's children with the torture of Job's own body: " 'Put forth thy hand now, and touch his bone and his flesh, and he will curse thee to thy face.' And the LORD said to Satan, 'Behold, he is in your power; only spare his life' " (2:5–6 RSV). In all this Satan manifests no power independent of God. Even when Satan slays, it is not Satan who does so, but God who slays through Satan ("the fire of God," 1:16; "you moved me against him," 2:3; "put forth thy hand," 2:5 RSV). God alone is supreme; Satan is thoroughly integrated into the Godhead in a wholly nondualistic fashion. Satan is not evil, or demonic, or fallen, or God's enemy. This adversary is merely a faithful, if overzealous, servant of God, entrusted with quality control and testing. Satan in fact prompts God and humanity (in the person of Job) to explore the problem of evil and righteousness at a depth never before plumbed—and seldom since.

These three passages exhaust the references to Satan in the Old Testament, and even in these passages Satan is more a function ("the adversary") than a personality. It is only in the period between the Testaments, and even more in the period of the New Testament and early church, that Satan gains recognition. Soon he will become known as the enemy of God, the father of lies, the black one, the archfiend, and assume the stature of a virtual rival to God. We will come to all that. But first we must do justice to those passages in the New Testament where Satan continues to function as a servant of God. So accustomed are most of us to thinking of Satan as purely evil that we tend to read this interpretation into passages where it does not exist. If we suspend that bias, the evidence points to a strikingly different picture that Jesus presents.

Luke 22:31–34. Jesus is speaking: " 'Simon, Simon, behold, Satan demanded to have you [plural], that he might sift you [plural] like wheat, but I have prayed for you [singular] that your [singular] faith may not fail; and when you [singular] have turned again, strengthen our brethren.' And he said to him, 'Lord, I am ready to go with you to prison and to death.' He said, 'I tell you, Peter, the cock will not crow this day, until you three times deny that you know me' " (RSV). Satan is God's sifter, the left hand of God, whose task is to strain out the impurities in the disciples' commitment to God. Had Peter been fully conscious of his frailty and flightiness, he never would have responded with such bravado. Had he been able to say, "Yes, Lord, I am weak and impulsive; pray for me to stand through this trial," perhaps such sifting would not have been necessary. But it is clear that nothing Jesus has been able to do has weaned him or the rest from egocentricity. Satan has made a legitimate request; they deserve to be put to the test. Jesus has to grant Satan's request. He does not pray that they will be delivered from the test but only that their faith will not fail through it. Satan is depicted here as able to accomplish something that Jesus had himself been unable to achieve during his ministry. If we refuse to face our own evil, but take refuge, like Peter, in claims to righteousness, our own evil will meet us in the events triggered by our very own unconsciousness. Satan is not then a mere idea invented to "explain" the problem of evil but is rather the distillate precipitated by the actual existential experience of being sifted. When God cannot reach us through our conscious commitment, sometimes there is no other way to get our attention than to use the momentum of our unconsciousness to slam us up against the wall. This is heavenly jujitsu practiced by God's "enforcer," this meat-fisted, soul-sifting Satan—servant of the living God!

1 Corinthians 5:1–5. A man in the Corinthian church is sleeping with his stepmother. Paul writes:

> Let him who has done this be removed from among you. For though absent in body I am present in spirit, and as if present, I have already pronounced judgment in the name of the Lord Jesus on the man who has done such a thing. When you are assembled, and my spirit is present, with the power of our Lord Jesus, you are to deliver this man to Satan for the destruction of the flesh, that his spirit may be saved in the day of the Lord Jesus. (RSV)

This reads uncomfortably like a text from the Spanish Inquisition. Is the man to be ritually murdered? The language is extreme, but apparently Paul means only that he should be excommunicated (5:2, 13), thus forcing him to choose between his sexual preoccupation and his faith in Christ. Destruction of the "flesh" would then refer, not to his body, but, as is usual in Paul, to the spirit: a shrunken spirit focused only on sensual gratification. Satan is to punish him through ceremonial exclusion (and possibly shunning), "that his spirit might be saved"—at least on Christ's return, but possibly immediately, through Satan's good offices.

Apparently the man did repent, for 2 Corinthians 2:5–11 seems to relate the outcome of the punishment. Ironically, however, the very congregation that had tolerated his sin as an expression of Christian freedom from the law now refuses to forgive him and receive him back. And the same Paul who chastised them with the full force of his spiritual authority now must plead with the congregation to forgive and comfort him lest he be overwhelmed with excessive sorrow.

Such self-righteous, judgmental behavior manifests the very qualities we saw associated with Satan in Zechariah 3:1–5. Their newfound zeal for justice is as overweening and one-sided as their previous indifference. Paul wants to "keep Satan from gaining the advantage over" them (2 Cor. 2:11 RSV), an advantage that would be won, not through their tolerance of sin, but by their refusal to forgive!

Satan's role here is remarkably fluid. Satan is again God's holy sifter. Using the momentum of the man's sin, Satan casts him into the annealing fire of solitude in which he is given precisely what he thought he wanted—and absolutely nothing else. But the choice could have gone either way. Had the man chosen the woman and not the church, Satan would have appeared to be the instrument of his damnation.

Again, if the church had refused to tender its forgiveness to the man, Satan would have caught them in a charade of self-righteousness, thus "gaining the advantage over us" (2 Cor. 2:11 RSV). By refusing to forgive, the church plays the role of Satan in Zechariah 3, who reiterates an accusation that God is prepared to drop. Satan is thus not an independent operative but rather the inner and actual spirit of the congregation itself when it falls into the accusatory mode. So Satan cannot be described as "good" or "evil." It is our choices that cause him to crystallize as the one or the other. And most astonishing of all, Paul does not say that Satan enticed this man to sin; rather, Satan is the means of his deliverance! This understanding of Satan has little in common with the irremediably evil Satan of popular Christian thought.

1 Timothy 1:20. The writer of 1 Timothy says (in the name of Paul) that he has delivered the heretics Hymanaeus and Alexander "to Satan that they may learn not to blaspheme." Apparently the writer does not mean that he has damned them to hell for eternal punishment. He really seems to expect them to learn to stop blaspheming and return to the fold. Once we acknowledge that Satan is a devoted servant of God, the meaning is transparent: these men, like the fellow in 1 Corinthians 5, are to be excommunicated in order to force them to recover a sense of "conscience" (1:19) and abandon their libertine ways.

Matthew 4:1–13 (Luke 4:1–13). Jesus has just left his baptism, where he has heard God declare him his beloved Son. The dovelike Spirit that came upon him there now leads him out into the wilderness "to be tempted by the devil" (Matt. 4:1 RSV). What kind of collusion is this? Why, if he needs testing, does the Spirit not provide it? Why place him in ultimate jeopardy by throwing him into the hands of Satan? It makes no sense at all if Satan is evil personified. But if he is the heavenly sifter, the setter of choice, then we have a different story altogether.

"And the tempter came and said unto him, 'If you are the Son of God, command these stones to become loaves of bread'" (4:3 RSV). What is so wrong about that? Later Jesus will feed the five thousand. The fast of forty days has ended ("afterward he was hungry," v. 2 RSV); now he must eat or die. If he could demonstrate such power to meet the basic needs of the masses, surely he could generate an instant following. Moses had cried to God and God had sent manna to the people of Israel; how much more ready should God be to perform mighty works on behalf of Jesus? People would recognize Jesus as the New Moses, the prophet of the end of time, the deliverer of Israel, and flock to his banner.

Jesus refuses. Is it because such acts violate the nature of the "Father" revealed to him at his baptism? Or is it because of that sticky "if you are the Son of God," with its taunt to prove his sonship by a miracle?—an act that could only prove his mistrust in God. For whatever reason, he turns the temptation aside by means of Deuteronomy 8:3. He will not live by bread alone but "by every word that proceeds from the mouth of God" (Matt. 4:4 RSV). He will live by what God says, and God said at his baptism, "Thou art my beloved son" (Mark 1:11; Luke 3:22 RSV).

Nothing exposes one to temptation more than a successful rebuff of temptation. Satan seizes upon the very answer as the next temptation: You mean to live by every word that proceeds from the mouth of God? Very well then here is one such word, taken from Psalm 91:11–12 (NRSV): "It is written, 'He will give his angels charge of you' and 'on their hands they will bear you up, lest you strike your foot against a stone.'" Put God to the test. Trust God's promises. "If you are the son of God, throw yourself down" from the pinnacle of the temple in Jerusalem. Surely the courtyard will be teeming with people. They will instantly recognize in such an amazing rescue God's stamp of approval on the Chosen One of God.

What would be appealing to Jesus in such a suicidal fantasy? He is being tempted to prove himself invulnerable and indestructible, a superhuman immune from the threat of death. Having just foresworn the shortcut of feeding the masses, what guarantee has he that God will protect his life on the more difficult path of making disciples? He has received an immense calling; what will become of his mission if he is prematurely killed? Will God intervene to guarantee his survival until he has accomplished his task?

This temptation takes place at the temple, where Malachi had prophesied that the Lord would suddenly appear to cleanse it of pollution and purify the priesthood (Mal. 3:1–4). Is he perhaps called to be the priestly Messiah who would restore true worship in Israel?

Jesus again refuses. "Again it is written, 'You shall not tempt the Lord your God'" (Matt. 4:7 RSV). To live by what one has heard from God does not mean biblical proof texting. It means listening to what God says to us about the specific life-tasks we are called to. The Word of God must be found and heard among all the welter of voices of Scripture, tradition, creed, doctrine, experience, science, intuition, the community; but God's Word is none of these alone, or even all of them together. Jesus is being nudged by God toward a new, unprecedented thing, for which no models existed. No one else could have helped advise him. Scripture itself seemed loaded in the opposite direction—toward messianic models of power, might, and empire. The dominant image was—but let Satan say it: "Again, the devil took him to a high mountain, and showed him all the kingdoms of the world and the glory of them; and he said to him, 'All these I will give you, if you will fall down and worship me'" (Matt. 4:8–9 RSV).

Satan is offering him the kingdom of David, grown to the size of world empire. Scripture was rife with this hope. Israel seethed with longing for some form of fulfillment. Jesus could not but have internalized that desire: freedom from Roman oppression, restoration of God's nation, the vindication of Yahweh's honor. This is no bald seduction. What is Satan tempting him with here and in each of these "temptations" if not what everyone knew to be the will of God? Mosaic prophet, priestly Messiah, Davidic king—theses are the images of redemption that everyone believed God had given in Scripture. (And in no time at all they would be titles given to Jesus by the church: Prophet, Priest, and King.) What irony: everyone in Israel knew the will of God for redemption—except Jesus. He was straining to hear what it was as if he alone did not know.

And Satan's function in all this? He is no archfiend seducing Jesus with offers of love, wealth, and carnal pleasures. Satan's task is far more subtle. He presents Jesus with well-attested scriptural expectations that everyone assumed were God's chosen means of redeeming Israel. Satan presents to Jesus the collective messianic hopes and by doing so brings them for the first time to consciousness as options to be chosen rather than as a fate to be accepted. Tested against his own sense of calling, they did not fit. Jesus could perceive them to be "yesterday's will of God," not what was proceeding out of the mouth of God.

Am I belaboring the point? I shall labor even more, to rectify two millennia in which Satan has been so persistently maligned.

This aspect of Satan as God's servant is stated with wonderful simplicity in the following exchange between Sidney Harris and his daughter.

> My little nine year old girl said to me, "Daddy, there's something peculiar about the whole story of God and the devil and hell. It just doesn't hold together." "Oh," I said, "and why doesn't it hold together?" "Well," she continued, "God is supposed to love good people, and the devil is supposed to favor bad people. Right? The good people go to God, but the bad people go to hell, where the devil punishes them forever. Isn't that the story?" When I agreed it was, she continued, "It doesn't make sense. In that case, the devil couldn't be the enemy of God. I mean, if the devil really was on the side of the bad people, he wouldn't punish them in hell, would he? He'd treat them nicely and be kind to them for coming over to his side. He'd give them candy and presents and not burn them up." "You've got a point," I said. "So how do you work it out?" She thought for a moment, and then she asserted, "It seems to me that if the whole story is true, then the devil is secretly on the side of God, and is just pretending to be wicked. He works for God as a kind of secret agent, testing people to find out who's good or bad, but not really fighting against God." "That's remarkable!" I exclaimed. "Do you think there's any proof?" "Well," she concluded, "here's another thing. If God is really all-powerful, no devil would have a chance against him. So if a devil really exists, it must be because he's secretly in cahoots with God!"[2]

It would be difficult to develop a systematic picture from all this. Some of it is plainly repugnant: there is a straight line from John 8:44 (you Jews "are of your father the devil," RSV) to the persecutions and pogroms directed at Jews by Christians; and the scorn with which the "pagan" religion is regarded in these passages will haunt us into the future.

There is a terrible split in these images of Satan as evil. Satan appears to have virtually no relationship with God, serves no redemptive functions, not even negatively, and strains the outer limits of the notion that there is but one benevolent Reality in the world. But there is also something existentially accurate

---

2. Sidney Harris, *Word and Witness*, May 25, 1980.

here. For Satan's fall did in fact take place, not in time or in the universe, but in the human psyche. Satan's fall was an archetypal movement of momentous proportions, and it did indeed happen every bit as much as the Peloponnesian War, but it happened in the collective symbolization of evil. "The whole world is given over to the evil one" (1 John 5:19, author's translation): Satan has become the world's corporate personality, the symbolic repository of the entire complex of evil existing in the present order. Satan has assumed the aspect of a suprapersonal, nonphysical, spiritual agency, the collective shadow, the sum total of all the individual darkness, evil, unredeemed anger, and fear of the whole race, and all the echoes and reverberations through time from those who have chosen evil before us.

The image of Satan is the archetypal representation of the collective weight of human fallenness, which constrains us toward evil without our even being aware of it. It is a field of negative forces that envelops us long before we learn to think or even speak, and it fills us with racial, sexual, and role stereotypes as if they were indubitable reality itself. Satan is "the god of this world" (2 Cor. 4:4 RSV) because we humans have made him a god as a consequence of will-fully seeking out our own good without reference to any higher good, thus aligning our narcissistic anxiety with the spirit of malignant narcissism itself. But since narcissism is antithetical to the needs of a harmonious and ecological universe, Satan has become, by our own practice of constantly giving the world over to him, the principle of our own self-destruction.

When in Luke 4:6 Satan declares that he can give Jesus all the kingdoms of the world and their glory, he is not lying; "for it has been delivered to me, and I give it to whom I will" (RSV). God permits Satan such power but has not handed it over to him; we have delivered it, as a consequence of all the consciously or unconsciously evil choices we have individually and collectively made against the long-range good of the whole. Satan thus becomes the symbol of the spirit of an entire society alienated from God, the great system of mutual support in evil, the spirit of persistent self-deification blown large, the image of unredeemed humanity's collective life.

All this runs the risk of personifying Satan, however, and personification was the subtle poison by which Satan's theological assassins did him in. Personification is too rationalistic to deal with archetypal realities. It merely uses the word "Satan" as a shorthand for a cluster of ideas—ideas that could fare quite well without the name.

If Satan has any reality at all, it is not as a sign or even an explanation, but as a profound experience of numinous, uncanny power in the psychic and historic lives of real people. Satan is the real interiority of a society that idolatrously pursues its own enhancement as the highest good. Satan is the spirituality of an epoch, the peculiar constellation of alienation, greed, inhumanity, oppression, and entropy that characterizes a specific period of history as a consequence of human decisions to tolerate and even further such a state of affairs.

We are not dealing here with the literal "person" of popular Christian fantasy, who materializes in human form as a seducer and fiend. The Satan of the Bible is more akin to an archetypal reality, a visionary or imaginal presence or event experienced within. But it is more than inner, because the social sedimentation of human choices for evil has formed a veritable layer of sludge that spans the world. Satan is both an outer and an inner reality.

It is not then a question of whether we "believe" in Satan or not, but of how the archetypal and/or reality of evil is currently manifesting itself in persons and in society. Perhaps we should distinguish between the archetypal images of Satan that are served up in actual encounters with primordial evil (what M. Scott Peck calls the extraordinarily willful spirit of "malignant narcissism"[3]) and the theological use of the term "Satan" for speaking about such experiences and reflecting on their meaning. "Belief" in Satan serves only to provide a grid that one can superimpose on the actual experiential phenomenon in order to comprehend it, and even then the wrong kind of belief in Satan may do more harm than good, since it is usually so one-sided.

But the phenomenon itself is there, named or unnamed. We wake up screaming, terrified by an image in a dream. We watch our feet walking straight into acts that we consciously know risk everything we most value. We encounter a landlord who deliberately attempts to blow up an apartment building full of tenants by opening a gas main in order to end their rent strike. Or we hear of a teenager trying to stop using drugs whose friends spike her candy with a fatal dose. Here the issue is not whether there is a metaphysical entity called Satan but how we are to make sense of our actual experiences of evil. In that sense, Satan is an archetypal image of the universal human experience of evil and is capable of an infinite variety of representations. The archetype itself is unfathomable; the primordial power of evil is as much more than our images of it as God is more than our images of God.

If some literal-minded person were to conclude from the jargon of transactional analysis that there really exists a being designated by the term "the negative parent," that would parallel what has happened to Satan: the name given to the personal reality that functions as an accuser, slanderer, and inner critic has been granted metaphysical status as an actual being. This worked fine as long as the metaphysical entity was still experienced as an aspect of the

---

3. M. Scott Peck, *People of the Lie: The Hope for Healing Human Evil*, 2nd ed. (New York: Touchstone, 1998), 79.

process of living. Once the experiential dimension was lost, however, Satan became a "being" in whom one was free to believe or disbelieve, quite apart from the phenomenology of everyday life. That is why in this study I am relatively uninterested in the metaphysical question, is there a Satan? If we do not encounter the experience that came to be named "Satan," we really have no further need for the word.

Beliefs about Satan are a matter of debate, but the experience of Satan is a brute and terrifying fact. A couple very dear to us lost their ten-year-old son to cancer after a heroic and utterly devastating nine-month fight. Some time after the death they went to the beach for restoration. One night, on the ninth floor of the hotel, the husband had this dream: He was standing by a great bog. He knew it was his own inner evil and that he could not run from it, so he just jumped in. With that he woke up. As he lay there at two o'clock in the morning, a voice said to him, "Why don't you go to the balcony and jump?" My friend said no, thinking he must still be dreaming. But the voice insisted, "Go ahead, you won't hurt yourself. You'll land in the trees; they'll break your fall." He got up, went to the bathroom, splashed water in his face, trying to break out of the dream. He went back and sat on the edge of the bed. The voice assailed him again: "You can jump to the swimming pool." No, I'd never make it, and anyway, the nearest part is the shallow end. "But if you jumped, you would see your son." At that moment a vision of his dead son seemed to hang in the room. For the first time the idea of jumping became appealing. He resisted, and the voice began to scream: "Jump! Jump! Jump!" relentlessly. Then it got very quiet. "Why don't you go out and sit on the balcony?" This went on for more than two hours. Finally he woke his wife and asked her to hold him. The moment she did, the assault ceased.

No doubt such an experience is susceptible to a variety of explanations. The satanic voice could be interpreted as the "voice" of a part of this man that felt defeated and desperate after the long and futile struggle for his child's life. Or the voice could be considered an external, malevolent power attempting to exploit a father's grief as a way of destroying him. The problem is that this question cannot in principle be settled, and from a phenomenological point of view need not be. Whether Satan is located inside or outside, what matters is that the experience actually happened and could have led to suicide. What this man experienced as "Satan" was an actual force of evil, however it be conceived, craving his annihilation. This force of evil is far more pervasive in human experience than most people are aware.

I am oppressively aware of the hazards involved in labeling things satanic; yet there are some evils too horrendous to be named otherwise. And naming something correctly can sometimes help us see it in the right light. When we label the nuclear arms race "satanic," for example, we realize that the struggle is not between the administrations in Washington and Moscow, but that both were on the same side.

Whether we call it "death" or "evil," "Satan" or "the satanic," there seems to exist some irreducible power that cannot be finally humanized, cured, or integrated, but only held at bay. And this power is never more diabolical than when it has become linked in a pact with human beings. "We are driven to conclude that the Devil too would incarnate in and through man."[4] There is a concentration of evil in a directional pull counter to the will of God. And however intolerable it is when encountered personally, its manifestations are most disastrous when they are social.

There is something sad in the moralistic tirades of fundamentalist preachers terrifying the credulous with pictures of Satan lurking in the shadows, coaxing individuals to violate rules that are often satanic themselves and deserve to be broken, while all the while ignoring the mark of the cloven hoof in economic or political arrangements that suck the life out of whole generations of people. The media have made a sensation out of a few rare cases of possession of pubescent youth, with no comprehension whatever of Satan's grip on our entire civilization. Why should Satan reveal himself more often in individual cases, when he can, from invisibility, preside over an entire global culture that spreads over the whole planet like a cancer: a civilization that systematically erodes traditional religions; that treats people who produce and serve as robots; that denies not only the spiritual but even the poetic, the artistic, and the inner; that propagates belief in the ultimate power of money; and that organizes an economic system exploitative of most of the peoples of the world and anchored in a permanent war economy?

Liberal Christianity has so reacted against the misuse of the Satan image in fundamentalist circles that it has tended to throw out the notion altogether. The absence of any really profound means of imaging radical evil has left us at the mercy of a shallow religious rationalism that is naive, optimistic, and self-deceiving. We need not return to medieval superstition in order to appreciate the power of the Satan image, not as an explanation of evil—for Satan explains nothing—but as a way of keeping its irreducible malignancy before our eyes.

Indeed, a nuclear holocaust would beggar every other evil imaginable. How could Satan benefit from such a catastrophe? As the principle of fragmentation, Satan can never achieve the totalization of evil it desires; there is a contradiction built into the very nature of evil that prevents it from ever gaining

---

4. James Hillman, *Insearch* (New York: Charles Scribner's Sons, 1967), 90.

ascendancy. The whole is too harmonious in its foundations and fabric, and evil must always be conceding too much to the good, since it must mimic the good and pass itself off as desirable in order to win adherents. But a nuclear holocaust—that is as close as we could come to totalizing fragmentation.

"We"? Did I say "we"? When we take away the mask from Satan, do we then find—ourselves? Have we, after all, breathed life into this image and kept it alive by our continually stoking the fires of Armageddon? Does that mean then that there is a retrogressive pull in us that fears the creative possibilities of self-transcendence and that would finally blow everything up to avoid that pain? Is it our own willful refusal of abundant life that has turned Satan from a servant into a monster? Was this our counterattack on God, whereby we seduced God's seducer and won him to our side? Must Satan then after all be redeemed, freed, delivered—not from his own overweening pride, but from ours?

History Belongs to the Intercessors

Intercession is spiritual defiance of what is, in the name of what God has promised. Intercession visualizes an alternative future to the one apparently fated by the momentum of current contradictory forces. It infuses air of a time yet to be into the suffocating atmosphere of the present. Those who have made peace with injustice, who receive their identity from alienated role definitions, and who benefit economically from social inequities are not likely to be such intercessors.

There is a marvelous image of intercession in the book of Revelation. Jesus Christ, the Lion of the tribe of Judah, the Lamb standing though slain—this Lion in sheep's clothing—is opening, one by one, the seals on the Scroll of Destiny (Rev. 5–8). As he opens the first four seals, the sorry spectacle of human violence is laid bare: the endless cycle of conquest, civil war, famine, and death, depicted by the Four Horsemen. When the fifth seal is broken, the martyred witnesses under the altar cry out: "How long, O Lord? Avenge our blood!" And when the sixth seal is opened, the whole creation lurches and totters in agonized anticipation of God's wrath. Now, just before the seventh seal is opened, those who will be saved are marked off for the new "Passover" of the angel of death and destruction. Everything is now ready. We await the final unrolling of the scroll. Toward this climax the whole cycle of the ages has turned.

> Now when the Lamb broke the seventh seal there was silence in heaven for
> about half an hour. I saw the seven angels who stand in the presence of God;

they were given seven trumpets. Another angel came and stood at the altar, holding a golden censer. He was given much incense to offer with the prayers of all God's people on the golden altar in front of the throne, and the smoke or the incense from the angel's hand went up before God with his people's prayers. The angel took the censer, filled it with fire from the altar, and threw it down on the earth: and there came peals of thunder, lightning-flashes, and an earthquake. (Rev. 8:1–5 REB)

Heaven itself falls silent. The heavenly hosts and celestial spheres suspend their ceaseless singing so that the prayers of the saints on earth can be heard. The seven angels of destiny cannot blow the trumpets to signal the next times to be until an eighth angel gathers these prayers—prayers for justice, vindication, and victory—and mingles them with incense upon the altar. Silently they rise to the nostrils of God. Then from the same altar the angel fills the same censer with fiery coals and hurls them upon the earth. The earth is convulsed. The silence is shattered. The heavenly liturgy is complete. Now the seven angels who have the seven trumpets make ready to blow.

This scene reverses the usual unrolling of fate, where heavenly decisions are acted out on earth. Humans have intervened in the heavenly liturgy. The uninterrupted flow of consequences is dammed for a moment. New alternatives become feasible. The unexpected suddenly becomes possible, and the cries of the intercessors have been heard. What happens next happens because people prayed.

The message is clear: history belongs to the intercessors, who believe the future into being. This is not simply a religious statement. It is as true of Communists or capitalists or anarchists as it is of Christians. The future belongs to whoever can envision in the manifold of its potentials a new and desirable possibility, which faith then fixes upon as inevitable.

This is the politics of hope. Hope envisages its future and then acts as if that future is now irresistible, thus helping to create the reality for which it longs. The future is not closed. There are fields of forces whose interactions are somewhat predictable. But how they will interact is not. Even a small number of people, firmly committed to the new inevitability on which they have fixed their imaginations, can decisively affect the shape the future takes. These shapers of the future are the intercessors, who call out of the future the longed-for new present. In the New Testament, the name and texture and aura of that future is God's domination-free order, the reign of God.

As a result of the intercessions of God's people, the seven angels trumpet calamity: hail and fire rain down, mixed with blood, and burn up a third of the earth and trees and grass; the sea becomes blood, and a third of its creatures die; a third of the fresh waters become bitter with wormwood; a third of heaven's light is darkened—and these are but the first of the woes to fall on humanity (Rev. 8:7–13).

John is referring here explicitly to the Domination System currently embodied in the Roman Empire. "The kingdom of the world [*kosmos*]" (11:15 RSV) for him is not geographical or planetary. It refers to the alienated and alienating reality that seduces humanity into idolatry: the worship of political power as divine. The Roman Empire had made itself the highest value and the ultimate concern, arrogating to itself the place of God. Whether it be the Pax Romana or the Pax Britannica or the Pax Americana, empires can maintain cohesion across racial, ethnic, linguistic, and national lines only by creating a bogus solidarity. This they achieve by demanding the worship of the spirituality of empire.

The Romans were a model of lucidity on this point. They did not, at least during the New Testament period, worship the seated emperor, but only his "genius." This Latin term does not refer to the emperor's intellect but to his inspiration, the daemon or god or spirituality that animates the incumbent ruler by virtue of his being incumbent. His genius is the totality of impersonal power located in an office of surpassing might.

The British, for their part, spoke reverentially of their empire as a holy burden and obligation, a vocation to carry Anglo-Saxon light to a darkened world. Americans, however, had rebelled against the British Empire and its spirituality. We could not therefore admit to having an empire; and concurrently, the nature of empire had shifted from political sovereignty to economic hegemony. So when, after World War II, we assumed the burden of empire, we found a scapegoat—Communism—against which we would organize and police the world. Empire could thus appear to have been thrust upon us to save the world. This anti-Communist crusade and its attendant Cold War policies masked the spirit of empire from no one except Americans themselves.

That spirituality—which included as one of its chief tenets the denial that it exists—literally threatened to rain hail and fire mingled with blood to burn up the Soviet third of the earth and trees and grass, turn the seas to blood and freshwater to radioactive wormwood, and darken a third of the heaven—all to preserve the privileged position of the richest nation on the earth. And the Soviet Union, for its part, was fully prepared to return the compliment.

Empires are "unnatural" systems. They cannot exist for a moment without the spiritual undergirding of a persuasive ideology. No wonder John was exiled to Patmos by the powers. A seer whose vision cuts through the atmospherics of imperial legitimation is a far worse threat than armed revolutionaries who accept the ideology of domination and merely desire it for themselves. Churches, which continually complain about their powerlessness to induce change, are in fact in a privileged position to use the most powerful weapon of all: the power to delegitimate. But it is a spiritual power, spiritually discerned and spiritually exercised. It needs intercessors, who believe the future into being.

If the future is thus open, if the heavenly hosts must be silenced so that God can listen to the prayers of the saints and act accordingly, then we are no longer dealing with the unchanging, immutable God of Stoic metaphysics. Before that unchangeable God, whose whole will was fixed from all eternity, intercession is ridiculous. There is no place for intercession with a God whose will is incapable of change. What Christians have too long worshiped is the God of Stoicism, to whose immutable will we can only surrender ourselves, conforming our wills to the unchangeable will of deity.

Not so with biblical prayer. Scripture calls us into the presence of Yahweh of Hosts, who chooses circuitous paths in the desert and whose ways are subject to change without notice. This is a God who works with us and for us, to make and keep human life humane. And what God does depends on the intercessions of those who care enough to try to shape a future more humane than the present. Historian and philosopher Mircea Eliade describes faith operating through prayer as "absolute emancipation from any kind of natural 'law' and hence the highest freedom" that one can imagine: "freedom to intervene even in the ontological constitution of the universe."[5] The fawning etiquette of unctuous prayer is utterly foreign to the Bible. Biblical prayer is impertinent, persistent, shameless, indecorous. It is more like haggling in an oriental bazaar than the polite monologues of the churches.

When Abraham discovers that Yahweh is about to destroy Sodom, where his nephew Lot lives with his wife and two daughters, Abraham blocks God's path: "Suppose there are fifty righteous within the city; will you then sweep away the place and not forgive it for the fifty righteous who are in it? Far be it from you to do such a thing . . . ! Shall not the Judge of all the earth do what is just?" (Gen. 8:24 NRSV). When God agrees to spare Sodom if there are fifty, Abraham presses the issue: Would you spare the city if there were forty? Thirty? Twenty? Ten? God agrees, and although ten are not found there, God saves Lot's family, even though they are but four (Gen. 18). Moral: it pays to haggle with God.

Scripture is full of this motif of spirited give-and-take with God. When Israel, impatient from waiting forty days for Moses to return from Sinai, makes the golden calf, God says to Moses: You'd better get down there. Israel has

5. Mircea Eliade, *The Myth of the Eternal Return* (Princeton: Princeton University Press, 1971), 160–61.

made a golden calf, and I'm fed up with dealing with them. "I have seen this people, how stiff-necked they are. Now let me alone, so that my wrath may burn hot against them and I may consume them; and of you I will make a great nation" (Exod. 32:9–10 NRSV).

Moses refuses to let God destroy Israel and asks: Yahweh, why should your wrath blaze out against this people of yours whom you brought out of the land of Egypt with arm outstretched and with a mighty hand? Why let the Egyptians say, "Ah, it was in treachery that he brought them out, to do them harm and lead them to death in the mountains and wipe them off the face of the earth"? Leave your burning wrath: repent and do not bring this evil on your people.

And we read, "The LORD repented of the evil which he thought to do to his people" (Exod. 32:14 RSV). Moses made Yahweh repent!

Or think of Jacob's wrestling with the angel until it blessed him, or of Jonah's sulking over God's change of heart about Nineveh. Of the latter Ernst Bloch notes "the amazement of the prophet Jonah, who failed to grasp the difference between Cassandra and himself. For Jonah had indeed been sent to inform Nineveh of its destruction after forty days, but when the city did penance and the evil did not occur, he was wrongly but exceedingly displeased (Jon. 4:1)—as if he had told an untruth to the people of Nineveh, whereas it was the change in them that had caused a change in Yahweh (Jeremiah 18, 7f.; 26, 3 and 19)."[6]

Nor is this theme confined to the Hebrew Scriptures. We see it in Jesus's parables of the persistent widow and the friend who came at midnight, both examples of how we are to hammer away in prayer until a breakthrough comes (Luke 18:1–8; 11:5–13). Thus Rudolf Bultmann is speaking not only for Jesus for but the whole Bible when he says, "Prayer is not to bring the petitioner's will into submission to the unchanging will of God, but prayer is to move God to do something which He otherwise would not do."[7]

No doubt our intercessions sometimes change us as we open ourselves to new possibilities we had not guessed. No doubt our prayers to God reflect back on us as a divine command to become the answer to our prayer. But if we are to take the biblical understanding seriously at all, intercession is more than that. It changes the world and it changes what is possible to God. It creates an island of relative freedom in a world gripped by an unholy necessity. A new force field appears that hitherto was only potential. The entire configuration changes as the result of the change of a single part. An aperture opens in the

6. Ernst Bloch, *Man on His Own* (New York: Herder and Herder, 1970), 207.
7. Rudolf Bultmann, *Jesus and the Word* (New York: Charles Scribner's Sons, 1958), 185.

praying person, permitting God to act without violating human freedom. The change in even one person thus changes what God can thereby do in the world.

"Wherever we cast our eye," wrote Karl Barth, "the dynamite is prepared and ready to explode. . . . For impossibility is, as such, nigh at hand, ready at our elbow, possible. Impossibility presses upon us, breaks over us, is indeed already present. Impossibility is more possible than everything which we hold to be possible."[8] Miracle is just a word we use for the things the powers have deluded us into thinking that God is unable to do.

"I believe in a world," exclaimed Nikos Kazantzakis, "which does not exist, but by believing in it, I create it. We call 'non-existent' whatever we have not desired with sufficient strength."[9]

Warfare prayer is indecorous, alarming, and uncouth, and this has put off many people. But this is simply a matter of taste. Warfare prayer is a way of boosting spiritual energy and bringing large numbers into strenuous spiritual struggle. If I found myself in a crisis of health, and I was requesting prayer from others, I would much more prefer having Peter Wagner be my intercessor than some observers of the fine points of etiquette. I affirm belief in miracles in full recognition of the misuse to which it is subject: manipulative magic, superstition, utopian fanaticism, spiritual greed, New Age naïveté. Against such perversions I know no preventive. But the alternative—supine acquiescence to the spirit of the age—is no more desirable. Let us join hands then with faith healers and speakers in tongues. Let us take as allies a few ranters, raving with the vision of a society of justice, health, and love. For intercession to be Christian, it must be prayer for God's reign to come on earth. It must be prayer for the victory of God over disease, greed, oppression, and death in the concrete circumstances of people's lives, now. In our intercessions we fix our wills on the divine possibility latent in the present moment and then find ourselves caught up in the whirlwind of God's struggle to actualize it.

That is why the phrases of the Lord's Prayer are not indicative but imperative—we are ordering God to bring the kingdom near. It will not do to implore. We must command. We have been commanded to command. We are required by God to haggle with God for the sake of the sick, the obsessed, the weak, and to conform our lives to our intercessions. The God of the Bible invents history in interaction with those "who hunger and thirst to see right prevail" (Matt. 5:6 REB). How different this is from the static God of Greek ontology that has lulled so many into adoration without intercession all these years!

8. Karl Barth, *The Epistle to the Romans*, trans. Edwyn C. Hoskins, 6th ed. (London: Oxford University Press, 1933), 380.
9. Nikos Kazantzakis, *Report to Greco*, trans. P. A. Bien (New York: Simon and Schuster, 1965), 371–72.

Praying is rattling God's cage and waking up God and setting God free and giving this famished God water and this starved God food and cutting the ropes off God's hands and the manacles off God's feet and washing the caked sweat from God's eyes and then watching God swell with life and vitality and energy and following God wherever God goes.

Prayer is not a request made to an almighty King who can do anything at any time. It is an act that liberates the origin, goal, and process of the universe from all distortions, poisonings, ravagings, misdirectedness, and sheer hatred of being that frustrate the divine purpose.

When we pray, we are not sending a letter to a celestial White House where it is sorted among piles of others. We are engaged rather in an act of cocreation, in which one little sector of the universe rises up and becomes translucent, incandescent, a vibratory center of power that radiates the power of the universe.

History belongs to the intercessors, who believe the future into being. If this is so, then intercession, far from being an escape from action, is a means of focusing for action and of creating action. By means of our intercessions we veritably cast fire upon the earth and trumpet the future into being. It is no accident then that the seven angels of the Apocalypse make ready to announce the scenes that follow as a direct result of prayer.

Waging Spiritual Warfare with the Powers

Now we must consider more directly the role of the powers in prayer. Most of us were taught that unanswered prayer is a result of either our failure or God's refusal. Either we lacked faith (or were too sinful and impure, or said the wrong thing or asked for the wrong thing) or God said no out of some inscrutable higher purpose.

Perhaps there are times when our faith is weak. But Jesus explicitly states our duty and tells us to exercise whatever faith we do have; and an infinitesimal amount, he says, is enough (Luke 17:5–6). The issue, after all, is not whether we are spiritual giants but whether God really is able to do anything. Faith is not a feeling or a capacity we conjure up but is trusting that God can act decisively in the world. So if we have faith like a grain of mustard seed—that is, if we have any faith at all—we should not blame ourselves when our prayers go unanswered.

Nor should we be too swift to ascribe our lack of success in praying to our sins and inadequacies. Morton Kelsey tells how the first really dramatic healing he was ever involved in took place despite his resentment at having to go to the hospital to minister to people he scarcely knew. God apparently ignored his attitude and healed the person anyway. Many of us were taught at an early age that God hears our prayers in direct proportion to the degree of purity of heart or sinlessness that we bring to our prayers. However, once we accept these terms, no one is "good enough" to pray. The God revealed by Jesus graciously listens to all who pray, perhaps even especially to sinners. It was the corrupt publican, after all, not the morally correct Pharisee, who went home justified (Luke 18:9–14). There may even be a towering conceit in our belief that our inadequacies and sins are so important that they can stand in the way of God answering our prayers.

Nor is it adequate in certain cases to blame God's nonresponse to our prayers on a higher will for us that, for now, requires a no. No doubt what sometimes appears to us as evil is the very explosion necessary to blast us awake to the destructiveness of our habits. Sickness and tragedy are, unfortunately, at times the indispensable messengers that make us recall our life's purpose. We sometimes do pray for the wrong thing or fail to recognize God's answer because we are looking for something else. But there are situations where God's will seems so transparently evident that to assert that God says no is to portray God as a cosmic thug. I still cannot see, after forty-nine years, how the death of a six-year-old boy from leukemia was in any sense an act of God. And don't even try to tell me that the death of approximately forty thousand children a day—over fourteen million a year—is the will of God!

What we have left out of the equation is principalities and powers. Prayer is not just a two-way transaction. It also involves the great socio-spiritual forces that preside over so much of reality. I am speaking of the massive institutions and social structures and systems that dominate our world today, and of the spirituality at their center. If we wish to recover a sense of the importance of these powers in prayer, we can scarcely do better than to consult the book of Daniel. Daniel marks the moment when the role of the powers in blocking answers to prayer was, for the first time, revealed to humanity.

The book of Daniel is the story of Israel's struggle against evil powers in order to stay faithful to Yahweh. Daniel is a Jew who has risen to a high position in the Persian bureaucracy in Babylon. Three years before, Cyrus freed the Jews from captivity and offered to rebuild their temple at royal expense. Yet few Jews responded by returning home. When the story opens, Daniel is in deep mourning and is fasting for his people. In the light of Romans 8:26–27 we might say that the Holy Spirit wanted to prepare him to receive a vision and so released in him a flood of anguish that Daniel wisely chose to face and not repress. So he entered upon a major fast. After twenty-one days an angel came and said, "Daniel, don't be afraid. God has heard your prayers ever since the first day you decided to humble yourself in order to gain understanding. I have come in answer to your prayer" (Dan. 10:12 GNT).

Why then was the angel twenty-one days in arriving, if the prayer was heard on the very first day that Daniel prayed? Because, the angel continues, "the angel prince of the kingdom of Persia opposed me for twenty-one days" (Dan. 10:13a GNT). He could not even have managed to get through to Daniel at all, except that "Michael, one of the chief angels, came to help me, because I had been left there alone" to contend with the angel of Persia (Dan. 10:13b GNT). Now, while Michael occupies the angel of Persia, the messenger-angel has slipped through and is able to deliver the vision of the future for Daniel's exiled people. That mission completed, "Now I have to go back and fight the guardian angel of Persia. After that the guardian angel of Greece will appear. There is no one to help me except Michael, Israel's guardian angel. He is responsible for helping and defending me" (Dan. 10:20b–11:1 GNT).

The angel of Persia is able to block God's messenger from answering Daniel's prayer! For twenty-one days Daniel contends with unseen spiritual powers. Perhaps he also had to slough off internalized elements of Babylonian spirituality; he bore as his own a name compounded from the name of a Babylonian god—Belteshazzar (v. 4:8). But whatever changes in him may have been necessary, the angel was dispatched before he had purified himself. Daniel is heard on the very first day, as the words leave his lips. The real struggle is between the angels of two nations. The angel of Persia does not want the nation he guards to lose such a talented, subjected people. The angel of Persia actively attempts to frustrate God's will, and for twenty-one days succeeds. The principalities and powers are able to hold Yahweh at bay!

Daniel continues praying and fasting; God's angel continues to wrestle with the angel of Persia, yet nothing is apparently happening. God seems not to have answered the prayer. Despite this supposed indifference, there is a fierce war being waged in heaven between contending powers. Finally Michael, Israel's own guardian angel, intervenes, and the angel gets through.

This is an accurate depiction, in mythological terms, of the actual experiences we have in prayer. We have been praying for decades now for the superpowers to reduce their arsenals; for most of that time it seemed an exercise in abject futility.

What does this say then about the omnipotence of God? About God's ability to redeem? God's sovereignty over history? The principalities and powers are able to assert their will against the will of God and, for a time, prevail! The wonder then is not that our prayers are sometimes unanswered but that any are answered at all! We have long accepted that God is limited by our freedom. The new insight in Daniel is that God is limited by choice. In any case, whether

by choice or not, God's ability to intervene, uninvited, is extremely circumscribed—as you may have noticed when you pray. When Daniel was written
(ca. 167 BCE), the Jewish people had been under foreign rulers for over four
hundred years. It was no longer intelligible that the exile from Palestine was
a divine chastisement or the divine will. The predicament we see in Daniel
derives from the fact that God does not effectively rule "this world" (what I
have been calling the Domination System). Satan rules it.

In short, prayer involves not us but God and people and the powers. What
God is able to do in the world is hindered, to a considerable extent, by the
rebelliousness, resistance, and self-interest of the powers exercising their freedom under God.

God is powerful to heal, and all healing, I believe, is of God. But if the powers flush PCBs and dioxin into the water we drink, or release radioactive gas
into the atmosphere, or insist on spraying our fruit with known carcinogens,
God's healing power is sharply reduced. Children (like the boy in my parish
on the edge of one of the largest petrochemical complexes in the world) die
of leukemia. The situation is no different in kind than normal bodily healing.
A clean cut will almost always, wondrously, mend; but if we rub infectious
germs into it, God's capacity to heal is hindered or even rendered void.

God does want people to be free to become everything God created them
to be. I have not the slightest hesitation in declaring such fulfillment to be the
will of God. But when one race enslaves another to labor in its fields or to
dig its mines, or when children's lives are stunted by sexual abuse or physical
brutality, or when whole nations are forced to submit to the exploitation of
other states more powerful, then what is God to do? We may pray for justice
and liberation, as indeed we must, and God hears us on the very first day. But
God's ability to intervene against the freedom of these rebellious creatures is
sometimes tragically restricted in ways we cannot pretend to understand. It
takes considerable spiritual maturity to live in the tension between these two
facts: God has heard our prayer, and the powers are blocking God's response.

If the powers can thwart God so effectively, can we even speak of divine
providence in the world? If our prayers are answered so sporadically, or with
such great delays, can we really trust in God? Can God really be relied on? Is
a limited God really God at all? We have to face these questions because our
capacity to pray depends on some kind of working idea of God's providential
care for us.

The sobering news that the powers can thwart God is more than matched by
the knowledge that our intercessions will ultimately prevail. Whether we have
to wait twenty-one days or twenty-one years or twenty-one centuries changes
nothing for faith. It knows how massive and intractable the Domination System

is. We cannot stop praying for what is right because our prayers are seemingly unanswered. We know they are heard the very first day we pray. Yet we keep praying, for even one more day is too long to wait for justice.

That is why the delay of the kingdom was not fatal to Christian belief. For the church could now see the Domination System for what it was and could never wholly capitulate to it again. And the church had caught glimpses of God's domination-free order and could never give up the longing for its arrival.

Daniel had to wait twenty-one days to receive the vision of his people's future conflicts in Palestine; it would be two centuries before any sizable number returned. Modern-day Jews had to wait nineteen centuries for a Jewish state in Palestine. Gandhi struggled with the angel of the British Empire for twenty-six years; the Aquino revolution, once it mobilized the masses in the Philippines, unseated Marcos in only a matter of days. Whether the water rises drop by drop or through a flash flood, eventually the pressure bursts the dam of oppression and the powers fall. They are but mortal creatures, and they are all the more vicious when they know their time is short (Rev. 12:12). Many innocent people may die, while the powers appear to gain in invincibility with every death, but that is only an illusion. Their very brutality and desperation is evidence that their legitimacy is fast eroding. Their appeal to force is itself an admission that they can no longer command voluntary consent. Whenever sufficient numbers of people withdraw their consent, the powers inevitably fall.

I have a nagging hunch that the gospel's power in our time is about to be manifested in a manner repugnant to the sensibilities of the society at large and to all of us who have accommodated ourselves to it, just as the early Christian message was repugnant to Roman paganism. Our society is possessed, and Christians are possessed as much as anyone. We are possessed by violence, possessed by sex, possessed by money, possessed by drugs. We need to recover forms of collective exorcism as effective as was early Christian baptism's renunciation of "the devil and all his works," that is, the Domination System.

RESPONSE TO WALTER WINK

DAVID POWLISON

Walter Wink makes a notable contribution in describing the scope, depth, and durability of institutional evils. I suspect that most Christians operate with a vague sense that "larger forces are at work" in human affairs. Awareness of the details, however, remains haphazard. A particular person might be attuned to the effects of high school peer pressure or the Hollywood ideal of love, to cultural habits of racism or the impact of watching television, to the pornography industry or the gross inequity between executive compensation and average wages. Wink deepens, widens, and focuses our gaze. He wants us to notice the powerful effects of social arrangements and public policies, our unconscious conformity to popular ideologies and cultural assumptions, the ramifying of evil choices down through history. By becoming aware, we can become free ourselves so that by intercession and action we can actively pursue freedom for others.

These insights are valuable, and these aspirations noble. But I have a problem with the doctrines Wink teaches, the framework within which such insights and aspirations are embedded.

Reading and Misreading Scripture

Have theological assassins misinterpreted Satan for two millennia, persistently maligning humanity's best friend and unfairly portraying God's servant as an evil, demonic, fallen enemy? Or has Wink selected what he likes and scorned what he dislikes in the Bible, pitting one strand of Scripture against another, so the story comes out the way he wants? In effect, he makes a hermeneutical principle out of "every man does what is right in his own eyes." His exegetical method is not exactly the old "allegorical" interpretation of Scripture, but we can certainly call it "imaginative exegesis." He controls the text rather than submitting to what the text actually says.

For example, Wink's interpretation of the Old Testament's use of "Satan" is curiously selective. He takes a proper noun infrequently used in the Old Testament (*ha satan*) and pits it against all other Scripture. He systematically excludes everything else that might bear on a comprehensive and coherent understanding, such as:

> the richly provocative use of *satan* language in places such as the messianic and imprecatory Psalm 109;
>
> the wider "enemy" theme throughout Scripture;
>
> Old Testament portrayals of God's adversary using different terms;
>
> the New Testament's definitive discussion that explicitly draws biblical, theological linkages throughout the Bible (e.g., John 8:44; Rev. 12:9).

This strategy of "illegitimate semantic exclusion" allows Wink to extract an idiosyncratic meaning that is foreign not only to each immediate context but also to the wider context of biblical revelation.

Wink's throwaway accusation about John 8:44 is particularly troubling. No doubt, virulent bigots have twisted and will continue to twist Jesus's words to justify anti-Semitism, but there is nothing "repugnant" in what Jesus actually said and why he said it when he did. He said, "You are of your father the devil, and your will is to do your father's desires. He was a murderer from the beginning, and has nothing to do with the truth, because there is no truth in him. When he lies, he speaks out of his own character, for he is a liar and the father of lies" (RSV).

No "straight line" leads from these words to the Holocaust; only a twisted line makes such connections. The very same twisted line leads from Genesis 2:16–17 to 3:1–5, and from Psalm 91:11–12 to Matthew 4:6. It is the satanic line, the lie that twists truth with murderous intentions—exactly what Jesus said as he interpreted and applied Genesis 3 to people about to pick up stones in order to kill the Lord and Messiah with whom they were speaking face-to-face. Wink accuses Jesus (or perhaps he believes that John was a churchly culprit putting anti-Semitic words in Jesus's mouth?) from a passage that warns us of our actual adversary and of our own propensities.

I believe that the Bible is internally self-consistent and unfolds progressively. Every strand comes into focus in Jesus Christ—the true Prophet, Priest, and

King (and many other fine things) in both Old Testament and New. Jesus was the only person who *did* know where the Old Testament was heading, rather than being the only person in Israel who did not know. Scripture comes "loaded" in Jesus's direction, not the direction of the first-century religious institutions and ideologies that worked in unison with Satan's temptations. Jesus knew well that "yesterday's will of God" is also today's will of God. When tempted, Jesus was not straining every nerve to hear something different. After all, he kept saying, "It is written . . ."

Jesus and his apostles make their hermeneutical method clear: "The new is in the old concealed, the old is in the new revealed" (cf. Luke 24:25–27, 44–49; John 5:37–47; Rom. 9:4–7; 2 Cor. 1:20). Both old and new proceed from the mouth of the same God. Jesus ought to know. Being both God in the flesh and the only man who is only godly, Jesus brings a certain cachet and je ne sais quoi to any conversation about Scripture. These are my a priori assumptions about the Bible.

What Kind of Thing Is Institutional Evil?

As noted at the outset, Wink perceptively describes some significant institutional evils, ideologies, and sedimentations of history.[10] But Scripture uses a different category from Wink to describe these things that oppress, enculturate, socialize, and dominate us. He is actually describing the "world"/*kosmos*, which, like the "flesh"/*sarx*, operates in the image of Satan but is not Satan. Wink's keenest insights come miscategorized. He collapses the cooperating trio of "world, flesh, and devil" into a devilish duo of world and flesh. This has consequences.

For starters, it means that Wink's perception of the scale of evil is human-sized. Here are two metaphors. It's like explaining Nazism by looking at individual atrocities and at the characteristics of German culture, politics, economics, and society, but viewing Adolf Hitler's mesmerizing authority and iron will as simply an emergent aspect of all things Germanic. It's as if

10. I find it curious, however, that Wink's perceptions extend only to the many institutional evils to which liberal politics is attuned: e.g., nuclear weapons, environmental catastrophe, racism, sexism, colonialism, anti-Semitism, economic injustice, the failings of the church. But he makes no mention of the different institutional evils to which conservative politics is attuned: secularism, homicidal Islamicism, the pornography industry, homosexualist ideology, the politics of abortion, regimes that persecute Christians. A Christian gaze seeks to be as impartial as God, identifying institutional evil however it appears, rather than marching to any one political drumbeat. And I was mystified that Wink cited British and American imperialism (surely among the more benign forms of the imperial impulse—Gandhi would have failed anywhere else) and did not indict the cultures of death presided over by Hitler, Stalin, and Mao.

Tolkien's *Lord of the Rings* located evil in the individual activities and collective organizations of orcs, evil men, Ringwraiths, and the fallen wizard Saruman—but no Sauron or One Ring was a power to reckon with. In each case, much evil would remain, but something essential goes missing.

Downsizing Satan into a symbolic resource for institutional evils affects Wink's goals as well as his perception of what's wrong. It is striking—but logical—that political justice is the bottom line and summum bonum ("the highest good") in each of Wink's concrete examples. A Jewish state in Palestine? Gandhi's post-British India and Pakistan? Corazon Aquino's post-Marcos Philippines? Treaties that reduce nuclear arms? Policies that aim to improve the environment? Perhaps one or more of these is unambiguously good (as far as we can see at this moment in history), but history abounds with unintended bad consequences of things that seemed very good at the time. And political good, however good, is never good enough. Political change cannot serve as a summary of the endgame of Christian faith. The Bible's bottom line and summum bonum is the full revelation of the kingdom of God at Jesus's return, seeing God face-to-face, our resurrection from death to eternal life, the destruction of all sin and evil, a new heaven and new earth in which love, joy, and peace will reign forever.

Intellectual Debts

Many of Wink's core doctrines bear a Jungian imprint. Archetypes manifesting the collective unconscious? Satan's fall occurring in the collective psyche of the human race? The nondualistic integration of good and evil—within the Godhead, no less, as well as in self-aware human beings? The resizing of ultimate issues so that life expresses an essentially infrahuman and infrapsychological drama rather than a covenant-relational drama? These ways of thinking exhibit underlying structures from Carl Jung's psychology.

A thoughtful historian of pastoral care commented that the Bible is a text that "resists reduction to the psychological," while noting that "the temptation to allow psychological language to overwhelm or define the religious tradition has often been irresistible" in the liberal Protestant tradition.[11] Wink chides his fellow liberal Protestants for their naive handling of the problem of evil, and seeks to rectify their neglect. But Wink's analysis still misses the cold, pervasive malignity of evil. The Jungian outlook, like other psychological outlooks, overwhelms and redefines Scripture by reducing the cosmic drama

11. E. Brooks Holifield, *A History of Pastoral Care in America: From Salvation to Self-Realization* (Nashville: Abingdon, 1983), 356, 355.

to the scale of the human psyche. Even a collective psyche is not big enough to contain the cosmic drama in which we live or die.

What Is Intercessory Prayer?

I appreciate Wink's vision for prayer as rousing, candid, fiery, complex, direct. Yes and amen, enough already with vague, sanitized, painfully polite, syntactically excruciating prayers. But the pointed candor of the Psalms has a different feel from Wink's edginess. Where is the minor-key sense of weakness, anguish, and need amid besetting threats and personal sinfulness? Where the major-key joy, the refuge even when enemies are about? Where the ambient hope in the Lord's steadfast love and faithfulness? Jesus prayed these prayers and sang these songs. He teaches us to pray passionately and persistently for God's kingdom, but he never makes us sound either heroic or impertinent.

I think Wink is wrong when he asserts that "we are ordering God to bring the kingdom near. It will not do to implore. We must command." Perhaps this way of putting things might serve provocatively—say it once, and then qualify it with a paragraph that works the nuances, the proper "etiquette" if you will. But Wink fails to make straightforward distinctions both between the parties involved and in the grammar. The words "Listen to my voice!" can express two very different standpoints. When God says to us, "Listen to my voice!," he commands—we perish if we fail to do what he says. When we say to God, "Listen to my voice!," we entreat—we perish if he does not do for us what he promises. In the imperative of entreaty, I say to God, "Have mercy, Lord. Your kingdom come!" In the imperative of command, God says to me, "Show mercy to your neighbor. My will be done!" Both are in the imperative mood grammatically, but when creature seeks Creator it is clear which party sits on the throne and which party kneels, which party is strong and which party needy. Submission is as much a part of prayer as boldness. Bold, submissive prayer is not indecisive, mealy-mouthed, or supine. Entreaty expresses the urgency and intelligence of neediness and desire—"implore," "beseech," "importune," and "supplicate" take asking to a whole different level. When Jesus prayed psalmically, he implored, he did not command.

"The Modern Mind"?

If "nothing commends Satan to the modern mind," perhaps the problem lies with modern minds. I have noted what I appreciate in Walter Wink's view and some specific differences. It is worth bearing in mind that he and I express these differences because we build on essentially different foundations. His "liberalism" or "modernism" is not simply a different form that Christian faith takes. The diverse species of historic Christian faith—Roman Catholic, Eastern Orthodox, Lutheran, Reformed, Anglican, evangelical—differ profoundly. But they agree that the Apostle's Creed expresses our common truth; that the Bible is God's Word written; that all Scripture culminates in the coming of Jesus Christ, who saves us by his incarnation, life, death, and resurrection, who is overcoming the triumvirate of dark powers, who reigns by his Holy Spirit amid all the tumults of human life, who will come on the day when both eternal judgment and eternal life are revealed, when God's children of mercy shall rejoice with unutterable joy, and all manner of thing shall be well. Wink's liberalism is a different kind of religion. It offers some fine insights and noble aspirations (as all religions do), but it is not a religion of salvation through the grace and sweat, the tears and blood, the patience and power of the only Son of God who will put all his enemies underfoot. "Amen, come Lord Jesus!"

Response to Walter Wink

Gregory Boyd

I am thankful Walter Wink agreed to participate in the present discussion on spiritual warfare. Over the years, I have benefited greatly from Wink's insightful work, especially his award-winning *Powers* trilogy. While I certainly disagree with fundamental aspects of his thought, as shall be clear below, I deeply appreciate the fact that he has helped mainline theology begin to take the New Testament's teaching on transcendent evil seriously. In what follows I will first discuss two aspects of Wink's essay I agree with and believe are profoundly important. I will then discuss two aspects of his essay I disagree with.

The Importance of Intercessory Prayer

As is true of all his works, Wink's essay highlights the important role humans play in God's redemptive work in history. In his essay he places particular stress on the fact that intercessory prayer influences God, pushes back the powers, and thereby genuinely affects what comes to pass. Because "the future is not closed," he writes, intercession "can decisively affect the shape the future takes." So too, prayer "changes the world and it changes what is possible to God," he contends. While I think Wink occasionally overstates his case, as when he says "God's ability to intervene, uninvited, is *extremely* circumscribed" (my emphasis), I nevertheless concur that, *to some extent*, God genuinely depends on intercessors to bring about his will "on earth as it is in heaven."

This understanding of intercessory prayer confronts the classical understanding of the future as a domain of exhaustively settled facts and of God as an atemporal, immutable, and impassible being.[12] "Before that unchangeable God, whose whole will was fixed from all eternity," Wink writes, "intercession is ridiculous." Moreover, "there is no place for intercession with a God whose will is incapable of change." Unless things genuinely hang in the balance on whether or not God's people pray, intercessory prayer cannot be regarded as any more than a pro forma activity (that is, an activity done as a pure formality). Yet, as I have argued elsewhere, embracing the view that prayer genuinely affects what comes to pass requires that we adopt a more dynamic and relational view of God and a more open view of the future.[13]

The Influence of Demonic Powers

A second aspect of Wink's essay I heartily agree with concerns his understanding of the significant influence demonic powers have over what comes to pass. Wink finds it highly significant that Daniel didn't receive an answer to his prayer for twenty-one days (Dan. 10:13). While those who embrace the classical view of God would be inclined to explain this delay by attributing it to the will of God—for *everything* is ultimately reflective of God's eternal, immutable will in this view—the text rather indicates that the delay was the result of the interference of "the prince of Persia." Hence, according to Wink, this narrative "marks the moment when the role of the powers in blocking answers to prayer was, for the first time, revealed to humanity." It demonstrates that the "the principalities and powers are able to hold Yahweh at bay."

Wink rightly concludes from this that we cannot "blame God's nonresponse to our prayers on a higher will for us that, for now, requires a no." He understandably bristles at the all-too-common suggestion that the reason children starve (for example), despite prayers on their behalf, is because God mysteriously *wills* this. "Don't even try to tell me that the death of approximately forty thousand children a day . . . is the will of God!" Rather, to understand why prayer that is clearly in line with God's will is not "answered," we must

12. For several critiques of the classical view of God, see Clark Pinnock, *Most Moved Mover: A Theology of God's Openness* (Grand Rapids: Baker Academic, 2001); John Sanders, *The God Who Risks: A Theology of Providence*, rev. ed. (Downers Grove, IL: InterVarsity, 2007); Vincent Brümmer, *The Model of Love: A Study in Philosophical Theology* (Cambridge: Cambridge University Press, 1993).

13. On the relationship between a dynamic God, open future, and intercessory prayer, see Robert Ellis, *Answering God: Towards a Theology of Intercession* (Waynesboro, GA: Paternoster, 2005); Vincent Brümmer, *What Are We Doing When We Pray?* (London: SCM, 1984); Gregory Boyd, *Satan and the Problem of Evil: Constructing a Trinitarian Warfare Theodicy* (Downers Grove, IL: InterVarsity, 2001); Boyd, *Is God to Blame? Beyond Pat Answers to the Problem of Suffering* (Downers Grove, IL: InterVarsity, 2003).

keep in mind that "principalities and powers" are able to interfere with God's plan, just as humans can. "Prayer is not just a two-way transaction," he writes. "It also involves the great socio-spiritual forces that preside over so much of reality."

I consider this perspective to be profoundly insightful and important. Indeed, as I shall argue below, I believe it can be utilized not only to explain unanswered prayer but also to play a central role in one's overall theodicy.

Satan as God's Servant

The first disagreement I have with Wink's essay is exegetical in nature. Wink contends that the basic understanding of Satan in Scripture is along the lines of a "fully credentialed member of the heavenly court" who serves God as a "prosecuting attorney" or an "executor of God's wrath." I have elsewhere argued that this view is questionable even in the Old Testament, but Wink believes it to some extent carries over even into the New.[14] For example, Paul told the Corinthians to turn an immoral person in their congregation over to Satan for the "destruction of his flesh" so that "his spirit may be saved in the day of the Lord" (1 Cor. 5:5 NRSV).[15] From this Wink concludes that Satan is "a means of [this man's] deliverance."

Of course, there is a sense in which Satan serves as this man's "means of . . . deliverance," assuming he turned from his immorality as a result of his "flesh" being destroyed. But it is one thing to say that God in his sovereign wisdom is able to put Satan's evil activity *to good use*, and quite another thing to say that Satan *carries out* God's good purposes by engaging in his evil activity. I would argue that all passages in Scripture pertaining to God's relationship to the activity of Satan and other evil agents can and should be interpreted along the lines of the former.

One of the considerations that I believe leads Wink to interpret the biblical depictions of Satan mostly in positive and (at other times) neutral terms has to do with his denial that Satan and the powers exist as agents with their own volition and power, over and against humans. This leads to the second, and much more fundamental, disagreement I have with Wink's view of Satan and the powers.

14. Gregory Boyd, *God At War: The Bible and Spiritual Conflict* (Downers Grove, IL: InterVarsity, 1997), 143–67.

15. The TNIV, which I usually cite, translates *sarx* as "sinful nature," which, in my estimation, is a poor theological interpretation of this word and an even poorer translation of this word. I have thus followed the NRSV.

Demythologizing Satan

In his essay for this volume as well as in all of his writings on this topic, Wink argues that Satan should not be thought of as a personal being that exists independently of humans. He rather demythologizes Satan by understanding him as (at the present time) "the symbol of the spirit of an entire society alienated from God, the great system of mutual support in evil, the spirit of persistent self-deification blown large, the image of unredeemed humanity's collective life." Similarly, Wink believes the New Testament's language about the powers should be interpreted as referring not to personal free agents but to the "spirit" or "interior reality" of people groups (families, tribes, corporations, nations). This does not mean that Wink denies Satan and the powers are *real*, or even in some sense *transcendent*, as is clear from his essay. But it does mean that they have no reality *over and against* humanity, in Wink's view. Indeed, Wink suggests that the concept of Satan as a distinct personal agent is a piece of "medieval superstition."

While this demythologization has helped many contemporaries take seriously the New Testament's talk of Satan and the powers, for which we can be thankful, I cannot myself go along with it. It's not that I am in principle against demythologizing certain biblical concepts when there are good hermeneutical reasons for doing so. In fact, I believe everyone at times does this, whether they are aware of it or not. Few today interpret the Old Testament's references to Yahweh combating "the raging sea," "Leviathan," or "Rahab" literally, for example, though it's very clear that Old Testament authors viewed them as such.

Moreover, I completely accept that we need to demythologize traditional *conceptions of* Satan and the powers if they are to be taken seriously today. The medieval depiction of Satan as a red monster with horns, hoofs, pointed tail, and holding a pitchfork (along the lines of the Greek god Pan) has got to go! In my estimation, Wink's own demythologized conception of Satan is much closer to the truth than this and similar mythic conceptions. Yet I suspect that, in reacting to outdated conceptions of Satan and the powers, Wink has, to some extent, thrown the proverbial baby out with the bathwater.

Conclusion

I will conclude my response by expanding on two of the four reasons I gave in my essay as to why I resist Wink's demythologizing interpretation. First, when understood in their first-century apocalyptic context, I think it is undeniable that Jesus and the authors of the New Testament viewed Satan and other malevolent cosmic powers as transcendent, personal agents who exist independently of humans. While I grant that certain aspects of their thought are culturally conditioned and not binding on us, I have never discovered any reason to consider their views of Satan and the powers to belong to this category.

To the contrary, so far as I can see, Wink's demythologizing hermeneutic is rooted in nothing more than the fact that it is generally unfashionable in Western academic culture to believe in personal, transcendent, invisible beings.[16] This Western perspective is itself not based on any sound assessment of empirical evidence or any sound philosophical argument. To the contrary, as Paul Eddy and I have argued elsewhere, if one sets aside the Western academic prejudice against such notions and adopts a more cross-cultural perspective, one discovers a wealth of evidence that arguably *confirms* the perspective of Jesus and of New Testament authors (as well as most cultures throughout history).[17] In this light, the Western academic assumption that spirit agents do not exist apart from humans can justifiably be judged to be a prejudiced, myopic, chronocentric, and ethnocentric perspective.[18]

Nor is the Western academic perspective rooted in any sound philosophical considerations. To the contrary, while space considerations prevent me from reviewing them now, I would argue that there are a number of philosophical considerations that render belief in independently existing spirit agents plausible, at least. Suffice it for the present to note that the arguments one might give for believing in the existence of a supreme, independently existing, transcendent, invisible personal agent—God—should, at least in principle, allow one to believe in less powerful spirit agents. It strikes me as inconsistent to dismiss the latter as "medieval superstition" while embracing the former. In fact, it's worth noting that all the considerations Wink offers in defense of his demythologized interpretation of Satan and the powers could just as readily be applied *to God*. That is, if we must regard Satan to be merely an "archetypal symbol" of evil, why should we not regard God merely as an "archetypal symbol" of good? Conversely, if Wink accepts that God is more than an "archetypal symbol" of good—and he clearly does—why do he and so many of his theistic academic colleagues find it impossible to accept that Satan is more than this?

16. I specify that it is unfashionable in Western academic culture to believe in invisible agents because, despite the repeated claims from certain academics, numerous studies show that the vast majority of Westerners outside of academic circles continue to believe in Satan, angels, and demons.

17. Paul Eddy and Gregory Boyd, *The Jesus Legend: A Case for the Historical Reliability of the Synoptic Tradition* (Grand Rapids: Baker Academic, 2007), 39–90.

18. See ibid., 71.

Second, I reject Wink's demythologized view of Satan and the powers because of its implications for the problem of evil. As I alluded to above, because Wink does not accept that Satan and the powers have a will and a power over and above the will and power of social systems and people groups, he cannot appeal to them to help explain evil that is not caused by human beings, such as "natural" disasters. Wink is, in fact, explicit on this point. "[As] an explanation of evil," he writes, "Satan explains nothing."

Now, it seems to me Wink is inconsistent on this point inasmuch as he appeals to the activity of the powers to help explain unanswered prayer, which is, after all, simply one aspect of the problem of evil. In any event, the only reason Wink cannot expand this explanation to cover other aspects of the problem of evil that are not directly related to human activity is that he does not acknowledge the powers have any independent existence over and against humans.

By contrast, because they uniformly accepted that Satan and demonic powers exist independent of humans, early church fathers were able to account for all suffering that is not related to human volition by appealing to the volition of these transhuman agents.[19] Only when Augustine and other theologians embraced an understanding of God's omnipotence as omni-controlling did people stop appealing to Satan and the powers as the ultimate explanation for evil not attributable to humans.[20]

In my opinion, it is time to recover the outlook of the pre-Augustinian church.

---

19. See Boyd, *Satan and the Problem*, 39–49, 294–95.

20. I will flesh out the Hellenistic philosophical influences behind this conception of divine power in my forthcoming two-volume work, *The Myth of the Blueprint* (Downers Grove, IL: InterVarsity, forthcoming).

Response to Walter Wink

C. Peter Wagner and Rebecca Greenwood

No one we are acquainted with would quarrel with the statement that Walter Wink is one of the most provocative thinkers of our generation. I (Peter) am privileged to have built a personal relationship with Walter more than twenty years ago, and although we may differ radically from each other on a number of issues, we maintain strong, mutual respect for one another. In fact, at one point he wrote: "I sense here a convergence of aims that may have the disconcerting result of linking charismatics, conservative evangelicals, and social action liberals in a united front of enormous power and divisiveness."[21] For good or for bad, it never turned out as we had envisioned it in those days, but our mutual respect persists.

Wink's chapter falls into two fairly equal sections. The first deals with the ontology of Satan; the second with the nature and power of intercession. Let us look at these in sequence.

The Ontology of Satan

Nothing could be more important in understanding the nature of spiritual warfare than coming to terms with our enemy. The concept of warfare always means a struggle between two powers of one sort or another. Common sense tells us that ordinarily the power we agree with would be "good"; the opponents "evil." The goal would be to overthrow the evil enemy. Our Judeo-Christian

21. Walter Wink, *Engaging the Powers* (Minneapolis: Fortress, 1992), 314.

tradition tells us that the enemy is Satan. One of the first rules of warfare is to know your enemy, so one of our first rules of engagement would be to have as clear an idea as possible of who or what Satan is.

Wink observes that "beliefs about Satan are a matter of debate." He goes on to draw clear lines for the parameters of what must be the heart of any debate about Satan—namely, whether such a being actually exists. Wink says, "In this study I am relatively uninterested in the metaphysical question, is there a Satan?" With all due respect, we are intensely interested in that metaphysical question, to which we would answer with an unequivocal yes, there is a Satan.

One of Wink's stated purposes for his essay is an attempt "to rectify two millennia in which Satan has been so persistently maligned." He then strives to demythologize the Satan of the history of Christian dogma, postulating that "Satan is an archetypal image of the universal human experience of evil." With this in mind, he uses a considerable portion of the essay presenting evidence that Satan, whoever that might be, must be seen, among other things, as a servant of God. In order to make his case, Wink cites several biblical passages both from the Old Testament and the New Testament through which, *assuming that his premise regarding the ontology of Satan is correct*, he can argue that Satan may not be so bad after all. He can conclude, using the words of Sidney Harris's daughter, "If God is really all-powerful, no devil would have a chance against him. So if a devil really exists, it must be because he's secretly in cahoots with God!"

This book is a discussion of spiritual warfare. As we just suggested, literal warfare requires an identifiable enemy. If Satan, traditionally considered the enemy of God, is possibly a servant or secret agent of God, it becomes difficult to conceptualize the form and nature of Wink's enemy, and one is caused to wonder whether there is a real war out there after all.

We do think there is a real war going on, so we will briefly summarize our thoughts. It is notable that, in choosing biblical passages to describe his view of Satan, Wink does not begin with Adam and Eve in the garden of Eden. Satan, in the form of a serpent, entered the garden. True, the name "Satan" is not used here, but the identity is strongly suggested by Revelation 20:2, which tells of the angel laying hold of "the dragon, that serpent of old, who is the Devil and Satan" (NKJV). The crucial question is, why did Satan choose to enter the garden in the first place? We touch on this in our chapter, but we feel it would be important to summarize it at this point of discussion. We believe the traditional answer that Satan entered the garden of Eden in order to make Adam sin is partial and inadequate. Instead, we believe that the underlying reason was that Satan wanted to usurp the dominion over creation that God had offered to Adam as the first representative of the whole human race (see Gen. 1:28).

Satan, under the name of Lucifer, was a created being, one of the most glorious of the archangels. As such, at one point in time, he gathered some other angels and initiated a rebellion to overthrow the government of heaven: "I will ascend above the heights of the clouds; I will be like the most High" (Isa. 14:14 KJV). He lost the ensuing war to Michael and his angels and was cast out of heaven to the earth (see Rev. 12:9). After this happened, while he still possessed his created power, he had lost his authority to use it. In order to regain his authority, Satan entered the garden of Eden. He knew that, because Adam had been created a free moral agent, Adam had authority to take dominion of creation, but he also had authority to give his dominion away. Satan persuaded Adam to obey him rather than God, and he succeeded in taking dominion. That is how he gained titles such as "the god of this age" (2 Cor. 4:4 TNIV), "the prince of the power of the air" (Eph. 2:2 RSV), and "the ruler of this world" (John 14:30 RSV).

Our enemy, then, is not some archetypical image or philosophical concept or compilation of historic human imagination, but a personality, created by God, whose evil purpose has become "to steal, and to kill, and to destroy" (John 10:10 NKJV). However, Jesus came "that he might destroy the works of the devil" (1 John 3:8 NKJV), and Satan's doom is assured. His kingdom will ultimately be replaced by the kingdom of God; meanwhile God has assigned us to the task of being his agents of reconciliation (see 2 Cor. 5:18). This is the real spiritual war we are currently engaged in.

"History Belongs to the Intercessors"

Some of our readers will undoubtedly be interested to know that in our "charismatically inclined evangelical" circles, the name Walter Wink is a favored icon. His phrase, "history belongs to the intercessors," is quoted again and again with the fervency and assurance usually reserved for biblical texts. However, we have been filtering Wink's words through the grid of our understanding of intercession, while Wink's grid turns out to be somewhat different from ours.

To begin with, Wink has a broader concept of who the intercessors might be than we do. He reiterates his premise: "History belongs to the intercessors, who believe the future into being." He then goes on to say, "This is not simply a religious statement. It is as true of Communists or capitalists or anarchists as it is of Christians. The future belongs to whoever [presumably including Buddhists or Druids or Scientologists, etc.] can envision in the manifold of its potentials a new and desirable possibility, which faith then fixes upon as inevitable." These thoughts tend to humanize intercession more than we would like.

In our view, the intercessors whose petitions and proclamations have the potential of moving the hand of God for doing good things here on earth are those who have previously been brought into the family of God either through the old covenant or the new covenant. This is what 2 Chronicles 7:14 would seem to imply: "If my people, who are called by my name, will humble themselves and pray and seek my face, and turn from their wicked ways, then I will hear from heaven, and I will forgive their sin and will heal their land" (NIV). Presumably a healed land would be characterized by righteousness, social justice, peace, material prosperity, morality, unselfishness, love for neighbors, racial equality, and integrity of government. But the intercession to release God to make this happen would come from those "who are called by my name," not just from any good-hearted human individual who could envision a better world regardless of their ultimate allegiance.

Furthermore, we would stress, as Wink admittedly also does at points, that it is God who actually changes history, not intercessors themselves. Look at this Scripture, for example: "The people of the land have used oppressions, committed robbery, and mistreated the poor and needy; and they wrongfully oppress the stranger. So I sought for a man among them who would make a wall, and stand in the gap before Me on behalf of the land, that I should not destroy it; but I found no one. Therefore I have poured out My indignation on them" (Ezek. 22:29–31 NKJV). Here God himself says that if there had been one intercessor, history would have been different. But the intercessor would not have changed history—the intercessor would have released God to change history.

Our differences with Wink here may be quite subtle, but we consider them substantial enough to highlight. For example, we would not have quoted Nikos Kazantzakis to bolster our point of view: "I believe in a world which does not exist, but by believing it, I create it." Kazantzakis is not our kind of an intercessor. Our intercessors do not believe that they create anything. They strive to stand in the gap before the Creator himself, but they do believe that, at times, their prayers (both petitions and proclamations) move God to do things to change history that he would not otherwise have done.

In that sense we agree with Wink that "history belongs to the intercessors"!

2

The Classical Model

DAVID POWLISON

I believe in one God, the Father Almighty, maker of heaven and earth, and of all things visible and invisible." Our forerunners in Christian faith showed good sense when they articulated the core of fidelity to God's Word written and incarnate. Attentive to Scripture's emphases, the framers of the ancient, abiding creeds (Apostles', Nicene, Athanasian) chose to trace the shape of the triune God's person, work, and promises. They made no direct mention of the roiling complex of evil: flesh, world, devil. But every baptismal liturgy contained a dramatic renunciation of the authority of flesh, world, and devil. Proclaiming the light, our fathers marked out the darkness into which light shines.

Our brethren who framed the sixteenth- and seventeenth-century confessions and catechisms (e.g., Augsburg, Thirty-Nine Articles, Heidelberg, Belgic, Westminster) were similarly attentive to Scripture. They chose to elaborate the doctrine of Scripture, the shape of Christ's redeeming work, the complexities of human nature, the scope of the Lord's commandments, the basics of the Christian life, the riches of the Lord's Prayer, and the nature of church and sacraments. They never focused on the evil one. In passing, they marked out the defining characteristics of evil to orient us in our conflict: (1) the adversary seeks to destroy us by our sin; (2) the flesh, world, and devil are mutually consistent and cooperative; (3) Christ works to destroy this triumvirate of evil in setting us free from sin and death.

Scripture points out the person and work of Satan only as he stands in relationship to God's purposes with us, as we live for either good or ill. The emphasis is pastoral. God passes over many questions that might intrigue us.

We might be curious to know more of the biography of Satan. How did he become evil? What is the origin of the collective forces of evil? What is the hierarchy of relationships between the devil and demons? How can it be that Satan and other hostile spirits are utterly malicious, acting to harm and destroy all people, and in particular to subvert God's church—yet they serve God's various purposes and work at his permission?

God seems to think we don't need to know all the details.

We might be curious to know more about how the murderer causes suffering and death. When Jesus healed the hunchbacked "daughter of Abraham whom Satan bound for eighteen years" (Luke 13:16 RSV), he did not explain the interface between her physical disability and the afflicting spirit of weakness. In the deaths of Job's children, how did Satan influence those tribal raiders (who had their own reasons) and the violent weather (which came with inherent dangers)? What was the psychophysiology of Saul's torment at the hands of an evil spirit sent to curse him for his sin?

We don't know.

We might be curious to know more about how the liar exerts moral influence. When Ephesians points out "the spirit that is now at work in the sons of disobedience" (2:2 RSV), how exactly does the liar and enslaver work? What are the psychological and social dynamics—the points of contact and the mechanisms, if you will—by which the deceiver influences the willingly deceived? How did the evil one influence the foolish counsel of Job's wife and friends (who spoke their own minds)? How does the devil connect to the pride that animates empires of institutionalized evil, to the religious activities of false worship, to the pride that incites our daily interpersonal conflicts?

Our enemy works within the fog of war, and God does not explain all that goes on in the fog.

God tells us what we need to know. His purposes are always practical, never theoretical, so that we can live faithfully, courageously, and fruitfully (Deut. 29:29). He teaches us just enough, so that we can oppose the flesh, world, and devil that oppose Christ's glory and our welfare.

We learn, for example (because we need to know), that the evil one does not operate as an independent cosmic agent of evil. He is not God's opposite number ontologically. Good and evil are not equally ultimate. Satan lives on our side of the distinction between Creator and creatures. As a creature, he depends on God for existence. The Bible's first mention of the evil one carefully underscores creatureliness: "the serpent . . . more crafty than any other beast of the field . . . the LORD God made" (Gen. 3:1 ESV). He hates God, but his continued existence and his malice operate within the larger purposes and permission of the Lord God. The people who marveled at Jesus—"He commands even the unclean spirits and they obey him" (Mark 1:27 ESV)—knew that the Lord is the one who commands all created things.

We learn (and need to know) that "Satan" is not merely a personification of impersonal forces (like "Mother Nature"). Evil comes in person, a perverse covenant lord aiming to command our disloyalty to the true King. The devil is a purposeful, intelligent, malevolent personal agent. As an immoral being, he is potent, culpable, and doomed. To react against Jesus is to live in the image of this devil, obeying his desires and loving darkness (John 3:19; 8:44). Behind the webs of deception spun by individuals and ideologies, a liar works. Behind the violence and violation done by evildoers, whether individual or institutional, a murderer works.

We learn (and need to know) that the devil is not merely a metaphor for human darkness, reducible to psychological or sociocultural forces ("your inner demons"; "the powers that be"). Rationalism debunks the personhood of the evil one, considering all that is evil to have human origins. This fails to fully recognize the uncanniness of the power of evil. Allergy to Christ expresses an inexplicable irrationality. Individual *sarx* and corporate *kosmos* intimately connect and cooperate with *diabolos*, expressing diabolical instincts for falsity, for empire building, for destroying love. But none of the partners in the dance of darkness reduces to either of the others.

We learn (and need to know) that the animistic, occult, superstitious view of demonic agencies is false. Animism exaggerates the personhood and autonomy of the forces of darkness. It locates the human drama within a haunted universe. It diminishes the significance of personal and sociocultural evils. One of the consistent purposes of the Old Testament is to demythologize the superstitious worldview. Common animistic beliefs and practices—for example, the influence of ancestral spirits or of territorial demons, demon-inhabitants as the agency behind human sins, techniques to do combat with evil spirits—are systematically undermined by Scripture's revelation of evil.

We learn, and need to know above all, that Jesus Christ is working the cosmic overthrow of evil in all its forms.

Jesus will destroy the curse of death and every shadow of death—sickness, disability, demonization, and poverty, as well as all the pain caused by being lied to and sinned against. Jesus began rolling back the curse during his earthly ministry: "He went about doing good and healing all who were oppressed by the devil" (Acts 10:38 ESV). He gave foretastes of eternal life. Then he bore the curse for us, drinking the cup of death and hell, being raised to indestructible life, that we might drink the cup of life forever. On the day when death dies and life lives, seeing his face, we shall live.

Jesus will destroy sin, the intricate powers that deceive and enslave—the reason we are cursed with death. By his incarnation, life, death, resurrection, gift of the Spirit, and founding of the church, he has begun to set us free of the moral infection of evil. "Whoever makes a practice of sinning is of the devil," but Jesus came "to destroy the works of the devil" (1 John 3:8 ESV). We have foretastes of freedom when we love God, his other children, and our human enemies. We still sin, but in the place where sin is no more and love is all, seeing his face, we shall be like him.

What Is Spiritual Warfare?

The phrase "spiritual warfare" never appears in the Bible. It is a pastoral, theological term for describing the moral conflict of the Christian life. It is a metaphor for our lifelong struggle with our lies and other liars, our lusts and other tempters, our sins and other evildoers, the present darkness that continually unsettles us. Our sufferings, whatever their form or cause, provide occasions either to stumble or to stand. Our warfare is over which it will be.

The pages that follow explore Ephesians 6, the classic passage on spiritual warfare. In the light of Ephesians, we will then consider other important questions. What does spiritual warfare look like? What about people who are involved in the occult? What about people enslaved to sin? What about the demon deliverances that Jesus and the apostles perform? What about the experiences reported by "spiritual warfare ministries" and in animistic cultures?

The Lord's teaching in his Scriptures is both source and test for our views and practices. The church has always looked to Ephesians 6:10–20 as the centerpiece for understanding how to engage complex evil. My comments will be brief and summative.

It is of first importance to recognize that Ephesians 6:10–20 is not introducing a new topic. This paragraph pulls together everything that Paul has already been saying and puts a sharp point on it: "OK, here's the bottom line. Here's what you need to do right now."

Failure to recognize this turns "spiritual warfare" into a wild card that can mean things antithetical to the Lord's intentions. For five and a half chapters Paul has spoken of how Jesus Christ—the Lord in person and in power—has come bringing life, light, and love to an accursed humanity. He is overthrowing the kingdom of moral evil, the infection that poisons us all. We have forgiveness through his blood. Christ is changing children of disobedience into children of light, creating one people for himself from all nations. The spirit that was at work in us produced unfruitful works of darkness. The Spirit now at work in us produces the fruit of light.

So now what? We are to walk worthy of his calling as the dozens of positives scattered through Ephesians 1:15–19; 2:8–10; and 3:14–6:24 describe. The triune God is reversing instinctive human nature. We are to walk in the active, constructive goodness that characterizes Christ Jesus himself. This is what we are by God's new creation. We are not to return to what once held us, what surrounds us, what still beckons us. Will we walk in faith and love, strengthened by God, or will we revert to the rathole of sin?

We formerly lived wholeheartedly in the deadly darkness, as the dozens of negatives scattered through Ephesians 1:7; 2:1–13; and 4:14–6:16 describe. An extensive cooperation and sympathy of purpose exists between the instincts of individual sinfulness, the characteristics of corporate sinfulness, and the purposes of the devil's inworking power. The overwhelming majority of evils, individual and collective, are not atrocities or paranormal oddities. They are everyday trespasses and sins; the common passions and fears; the unbelief, anger, lusts, and lies of our foolishness.

We easily regress. The struggles we go through today, personal history, family history, church history, and world history collectively testify to our failures. How often do we get irritated or anxious? How often do we obsess about our responsibilities or escape into our pleasures? How broken was our family? How many church scandals and splits have we witnessed? Have we read history? Do we follow the news? But by grace, we progress. The fruit of light (amid today's struggle, and in each layer of history) quietly testifies to Christ's presence, kindness, and power. Ephesians is about this warfare in which the fruit of light silences the noisy darkness, to the praise of his glorious grace. *Kyrie eleison*, have mercy, O God of strength.

Paul has repeatedly asked our Father to strengthen us. Now, in Ephesians 6:10, he tells us to take action. Find strength in the Lord. Stand up. Step out. Walk in the light, not reverting to darkness. The new thing about this passage is not the topic; it is the sharp point Paul puts on the topic. The pieces of weaponry (6:11–17) are an extended metaphor, a proclamation of Christ, fleshing out how faith and love operate.

It is of first importance that we rightly envision the "panoplian of God" (usually translated "whole armor of God"). Teaching on this passage often puts the emphasis in the wrong places. For starters, *panoplian* does not mean

protective armor. It is most accurately the "complete weaponry" needed to
wage war, or "all the tools" needed to do a job. Paul chose this metaphor to
create a vivid mental picture. We want to get the right picture.

When we examine each individual piece of weaponry, it is clear that Paul did
not dream up his metaphor by noticing the outfit worn by Roman soldiers (as
the metaphor is usually explained). He had been pondering Isaiah and Psalms
in the light of Christ. When Paul lists individual implements, the soldier we
are to imagine is not Roman but divine and messianic. We are to imagine the
Lord God in person.

"Girding on the belt of truth"? Paul took this from Isaiah 11:5, which describes a man characterized by truth and faithfulness. Isaiah 11:1–12 portrays
the Messiah arising from the lineage of David. He is filled with the Holy Spirit
beyond measure. He invades the earth, bringing justice and mercy for the meek
and destruction to the godless. His warfare is an offensive. He is not playing
defense. Peoples from the whole earth seek him. Isaiah's theme is the theme
of Ephesians. We recognize Jesus Christ.

"The breastplate of righteousness"? Paul takes both this and the "helmet of
salvation" from Isaiah 59:17. Who arms himself in these ways? Isaiah 59:1–21
makes clear that the Lord God comes armed. He alone can make right all that
is so wrong. The whole earth, including God's people, is dark, sinful, and
condemned. No one on the scene can fix it. So the Lord comes in wrath and
mercy, pouring out his Spirit and his words on those who turn from transgres-
sion. Again, this is Jesus Christ. Only when wrenched out of its missional
context does the military hardware seem to be defensive armor.

"Shoes for your feet" that express "the readiness given by the gospel of
peace"? This also comes from Isaiah:

> How beautiful upon the mountains
>   are the feet of him who brings good news,
> who publishes peace, who brings good news of happiness,
>   who publishes salvation,
>   who says to Zion, "Your God reigns." (52:7 ESV)

Isaiah 52:6–10 makes clear that this is the Lord: "It is I who speak; here
am I" (ESV). Every eye sees the Lord returning to Zion, bringing comfort
and redemption. A few sentences later, we learn how he does this: the Lamb
of God bears the iniquity of us all. How wide is the scope of his salvation?
"The ends of the earth shall see the salvation of our God" (Isa. 52:10 ESV).
Again, that's Ephesians. Jesus Christ brings good news of peace because he
is the good news.

"Taking up the shield of faith"? This is the only image that does not arise from Isaiah, and the only image intended to communicate an essentially protective and defensive role. In every life circumstance our shield repels "the flaming darts of the evil one" (Eph. 6:16 ESV). In many Psalms, the Lord is called our shield, strength, and refuge. Faith takes refuge in him from enemies. Psalm 18:1–3 (ESV), for example, piles up every safe-place metaphor David can think of. This is what faith looks like in operation:

> I love you, O LORD, my strength.
> The LORD is my rock and my fortress and my deliverer,
>   my God, my rock, in whom I take refuge,
>   my shield, and the horn of my salvation, my stronghold.
> I call upon the LORD, who is worthy to be praised,
>   and I am saved from my enemies.

Notice the themes: strength, shield, salvation, prayer, enemies. These are the words of Ephesians 6 made flesh. The psalm catches faith in the act of looking with confidence to the one who strengthens and shields. Who first and fully lives this psalm? The Messiah is going out to war, and he is both shielded (Ps. 18:30–31, 35) and strengthened to pursue his enemies (Ps. 18:29, 32–42). Even the "defensive" weapon of Ephesians 6 is portrayed as being used for a divine offensive. Ephesians expands our understanding of the varied enemies we face and pours in the glory of Christ, who has now come. But the pattern of faith operates exactly as in Psalm 18 (and other psalms of protection). Notice, the Lord *is* our shield. Faith per se has no protective power; faith seeks and finds our protector.

"The sword of the Spirit, which is the Word of God"? Paul is beginning to phase out his weaponry metaphor, and here he alludes to, rather than quotes, Isaiah. Isaiah 11:4 and 49:2 provide the most obvious references to a weapon of divine words. This sword expresses the wisdom of the Spirit, destroys evil, and brings in the peaceable kingdom. Isaiah 49:1–13 (like Isaiah 11, discussed above) proclaims the light of life to the whole earth. It identifies a man whom the Lord calls by name from his mother's womb, who will be glorified, in whom the Lord will be glorified. His life will apparently come to nothing when he is despised and rejected by his own people. But in the end, he will be their Redeemer and a light to the nations. Again, we recognize the biography of Jesus Christ.

In Ephesians 6:18, Paul drops the metaphor of weaponry entirely in wrapping up this call to faith and love. As in 6:10, he speaks directly. Pray at all times in the Spirit, with all prayer in all perseverance for all the saints. In 6:10, he says, "Be strengthened in the Lord" (NET). Now he calls them to also pray that others will be strengthened. Our need leads us to consider the needs of our brothers and sisters. This is just how Jesus prays. In John 17 he intercedes for us, that our Father will keep us from the evil one and sanctify us to himself. In John 17 and the Lord's Prayer, Jesus shows us how to pray: deliver us from evil, that we might become one in your love.

That's the divine weaponry for the great war between sin and love, lies and truth, Satan and God. Jesus says, "Follow me." As the parallel passage in Romans 13:8–13 puts it, "Put on the weapons of light" (NET) and throw away all that is not loving. "Put on the Lord Jesus Christ" and leave no room for corrupt desires. Faith and love destroy darkness.

With so much light and good pouring forth from Christ, why then is life so hard and the process so messy? Paul underscores the devil (Eph. 6:11–13, 16) so we won't be surprised. We live in evil days. Paul alerts us to the irrational, relentless nature of evil. In the clash of two kingdoms, we aren't thrown off by the confusing fog of war and the fact that we take hits. When children of light lapse into what we once were, hurting and fighting each other, it helps to know that our deepest enemies are not flesh and blood. It "lowers the temperature" amid human conflicts, the church's many failures, and the stubbornness of our own sin. We take heart and seek Christ's merciful strength that we might persevere with all humility, with patience, bearing with one another in love, eager to live out the unity of the Spirit. The powers of darkness are canny, pervasive, intentional; but the powers are under Christ's feet (1:21–22); and every deed of light builds up the church into a visible demonstration of God's glory, wisdom, and grace (3:10). Ephesians 6 gives us marching orders, not foolproof techniques.

Spiritual warfare is usually portrayed as defensive, trying to hold our ground against waves of attackers. This gets the major emphasis exactly backward. Spiritual warfare arises because God is carrying out his invasion, piercing the darkness with light. We who were formerly darkness have been made part of the light that he brings—and every photon of faith and love illumines and destroys darkness. Ephesians envisions a war in which the fighting is hot but the initiative and conquering power are on our side. The enemy is on the defensive. Fiery darts are return fire and counterattack. Dangerous, with deadly intent? Yes. When darts hit home, the children of light go dark, relapsing into trespasses and sins, living like the sons of disobedience that we once were. But light will prevail. When we stand at the end of the day, having done all, we will have swept the field of battle and overthrown the dictatorship of evil.

In applying Ephesians, people often rush past the fact that the Lord himself continues to wear and use his own weapons. Christ came with the tools to do what needed doing. He equips us in order to work through us. Christ on his mission *is* the weaponry, and we join in. This is how light contradicts and undoes the slave-kingdom of darkness.

Paul has already been doing everything he tells us to do. Throughout Ephesians we witness true spiritual warfare in operation. The entire letter is a self-disclosure of Paul's message, purpose, mission, and lifestyle. Paul demonstrates the assault on darkness wearing the weaponry of light.

Paul wears the belt, speaking truth in love with constructive, timely, and grace-giving words. He wears the breastplate of righteousness, a living demonstration of a man redeemed by grace through faith, who lives fruitfully as God's workmanship in Christ. His feet walk in the readiness of the gospel of peace, reconciling people with God and once-estranged peoples with each other, making one body in which the triune God dwells (2:11–22). Paul takes up the shield of faith (on our behalf, no less), audibly seeking the God of power and strength. He wears the helmet of salvation: his message, his ministry, his incandescent awareness of Jesus our Savior. Of course, Paul takes up the Word of God in the power of the Spirit. Ephesians *is* the Word of God, after all. And throughout Ephesians Paul continually cites and applies other Scriptures in ways that are both faithful and fresh. Dropping the weaponry metaphor but continuing the warfare, Paul prays for others. His intercessions so seamlessly weave into all he says that it's hard to tell where prayer ends and teaching picks up. His prayers are wondrously normal. Our deepest need meets Christ's present help.

Paul's core intercession is very simple: "God, personally strengthen us to know you." No fireworks, no fuss and feathers, no binding and loosing, no authoritative pronouncements, no naming and claiming. His prayers are new Psalms, familiar patterns overflowing with fulfillment in Christ. For example, Psalm 103 says, "Bless the LORD, O my soul, and don't forget any of the good things he does" (author paraphrase). David then lists the core blessings: forgiveness, life, renewal, steadfast love, mercy, participation in a people, God's fatherly care, his kingdom. These patterns of human need and divine generosity do not change. Ephesians 1 is almost identical to Psalm 103, yet strikingly different: "Blessed be the God and Father of our Lord Jesus Christ, who has blessed us in Christ with every spiritual blessing" (ESV). Paul then lists the *same* core blessings, now ten thousand times brighter, bigger, more immediate.

How does Paul invade the kingdom of darkness? He stands up and walks straight in, clothed in light. We fight the same way. Put on the complete weaponry of God's goodness and power. Christ did it. Paul did it. You do it. Be strengthened in Christ and pray for others to be strengthened in Christ. For the first readers of Ephesians, their faith got right down to business by immediately praying for Paul (6:19–20). Who do you know who needs the same things you need?

To win spiritual warfare is simply to live as light in a dark world. It is to treat others with humility, patience, and thoughtful consideration. It is to live as a conscious and contributing member of "we the people" whom God has brought together by mercy. It is to have things to say that are worth saying: true, constructive, timely, and filled with grace. It is to live purposefully amid a thousand distracting voices. It is to seek God's grace and strength. At its core, to win this war is to know God and consciously serve him. You serve in Christ, becoming formed into his image. It is the hardest thing in the world because blinding darkness clings so closely. It is the best thing in the world. This is what Ephesians proclaims, models, and enables, putting the powers of darkness underfoot, revealing the glory of God's grace.

To lose spiritual warfare is to live the darkness, to revert to what comes naturally to every fallen heart. It is to walk "under the influence," in the image of the powers of evil. It is to live as a world of one: willful, inconsiderate, bitter, fearful. It is to speak thoughtlessly, impulsively, falsely, and destructively. It is to live carelessly, unwisely, drifting with the zeitgeist of your time and place. At its essential core, to lose this war is to forget God and consciously serve yourself. You serve the devil and are conformed to his image. This is what Ephesians opposes and sets out to destroy.

Five Important Questions

In light of what Ephesians teaches, the rest of this chapter will address five questions.

What is the look and feel of spiritual warfare?

How do we understand and help those involved in the occult?

How do we understand and help those living in addictive bondage to sin?

How do we understand the exorcisms in Matthew, Mark, Luke, and Acts?

What about the experiences that are common in "spiritual warfare ministries" and in animistic cultures?

Scripture clears our minds and focuses our efforts in each of these areas.

What Is the Look and Feel of Spiritual Warfare?

It looks like the Christian life.

In 2003 our sixteen-year-old daughter was diagnosed with a rare, painful, and progressive illness. Its effects were potentially disfiguring, disabling, even deadly. The cause was a mystery. It had no cure. Some symptoms could be treated or would spontaneously abate. But one never knew when the next episode might strike, with ever-worsening symptoms. Doctors did say that in 30 percent of cases, for unknown reasons, the illness disappeared as mysteriously as it had appeared. If there were no recurrence and decline over the next three years, they would consider her cured. These were the particular circumstances in which we needed to take up the shield of faith.

High-pressure situations bring many temptations. Facing a dire diagnosis, there are many ways to lose the spiritual battle, reverting to the darkness of flesh, world, and devil. Will we go blind to God, becoming absorbed in the immediate threat? Will we worry, feeling an undercurrent of anxiety or even stark fear? Will we obsess about medical intervention? Will we go into denial? Will we numb our apprehensions by escaping into work, TV, or drink? Will we get irritable with each other, exacerbating the tension by bickering? Will we become stoic, short-circuiting honest human need with a quick "God is in control" that is more Islamic than psalmic? Will we pray repetitively, even superstitiously? There are many ways to revert to the darkened understanding that expresses alienation from the life of God (Eph. 4:17–18). The flaming darts of the evil one aim to recapture us for the godless darkness.

We could revert, or we could face our troubles the way Ephesians and the Psalms encourage us to face trouble. In our case, Psalm 28 gathered up our experience and took us in hand. It is one of many psalms that describes human need finding God's strength and shielding care. It puts feet on Ephesians 6. Psalm 28:1–2 gives voice to a sense of utter need, of vulnerability in the face of threat.

> I call to you, O Lord, my rock. Do not turn a deaf ear to me. If you remain silent, I will be like those who go down to the pit. Hear my cry for mercy as I cry to you for help, as I lift up my hands toward your most holy sanctuary. (author's paraphrase)

This is no routine "say your prayers." It's not just an item added to your prayer list. It's not just a change in your self-talk, as if faith's sphere of operations happens inside your mind: "Just remember that God is in control. Just remember your identity in Christ." Faith's sphere of operations is in relating to another: "I need you, merciful God, our King. When you consider my need, remember who you are. Remember your promises of compassion and help." Need cries out to one able and willing to help. The act of turning in actual need to the Lord was an act of sanity and light.

David then grapples with the specific evils (Ps. 28:3–5) animating his plea for mercy. In his case (intensified for Jesus), he faced the enmity of godless men who did the evils that their hearts incubated, as well as the deeper hostility of the adversary of God's Messiah. Flesh-and-blood hostilities are one of the perennial evils every one of us faces. But this was not our current situation. Ephesians (and the rest of Scripture) extends the scope and depth of our awareness of evil. We don't only wrestle with flesh and blood but with every enemy that Jesus will put underfoot (1 Cor. 15:25).

The power of "the enemy" (Matt. 13:39; Luke 10:19) works to blind and confuse us, attempting to reassert mastery over us by deforming us into his image.

Our daughter's illness was a precursor of "the last enemy" (1 Cor. 15:26 ESV), a shadow of death darkening the steps of a sixteen-year-old girl.

The "passions of our flesh . . . the desires of the body and the mind" (Eph. 2:2–3 ESV) manifest our own hearts' sympathy for the devil. Will we insist on healing, or demand a comfortable life, or place our deepest hopes in doctors? We become obsessive, angry, escapist, or fearful when driven by the tyranny of our desires.

There are subtle human enemies as well. Ephesians 4:14 warns of false messages blowing through the world around us. Anyone facing illness simultaneously faces widely enculturated and well-institutionalized assumptions. The air we breathe insinuates an ideology and value system: good health, medical care, and medical cure are the summum bonum (rather than a *bonum*—the highest good rather than just a good). Will we be misled and never realize what is shaping our attitudes and choices?

Psalm 28:3–5 portrays one of many possible variants on "all circumstances." We needed to find God's strength and shielding in our circumstances. In our plea for mercy, we named our exact troubles to the Lord.

This psalm moves quickly across the emotional register, arriving at joyful peace (28:6–7) more quickly than we did. David gives us a template, not a timetable. He shows the direction in which to walk. It is striking how the general exhortations of Ephesians 6 (and 5:18–20!) recapitulate these exact themes:

> The LORD is my strength and my shield;
>> in him my heart trusts, and I am helped;
> my heart exults,
>> and with my song I give thanks to him. (Ps. 28:7 ESV)

Honest gratitude and joy are intrinsic to spiritual warfare. God's Spirit creates exultation and thankfulness throughout Ephesians, as in many Psalms. Spiritual warfare is not grim or apprehensive, not paranoid or superstitious, not magical or talismanic. The Lord proved to be our strength and shield in the crisis. And, mercifully, our daughter's symptoms abated. Months passed, and then years. We did not forget the threat, though it became distant with time. We trusted, and we were helped.

A bolt out of the blue hit exactly three years out. Our daughter was in Uganda for a semester abroad. The university doctor was instructing the students on the importance of the antimalarial medicine they were taking. He mentioned in passing that this medicine could trigger the rare syndrome that she had faced. She changed medicines. My heart trusts and I am helped.

What if our daughter's condition had degraded rather than improved? What if she were not fine now, but her body had become inflamed and broken with pain? That would be a hard road, bringing many temptations. But the path of life that Ephesians and the Psalms mark out for us would still be the path of life.

Psalm 28:8–9 concludes the same way that Ephesians 6:18–20 concludes. David reaches beyond himself and reaches out for others who need what he has been given. He intercedes for God's people in their need for strength, refuge, and the saving care of the Lord our Shepherd. You face the same kinds of enemies, temptations, and struggles that David did, that Jesus did, that we did. If we need our Lord to strengthen and shield us, so do you. And I pray that this very story might be a gift that leads you to know more deeply the ways of our Christ through the wisdom of Psalm 28 and Ephesians.

How Do We Understand and Help Those Involved in the Occult?

It is often argued that people with a history of occult involvement need some sort of demon deliverance. This is invariably paired with firsthand experiences of how deeply people become enmeshed in darkness, how difficult it is to break free, how confused or vile they become, and the almost palpable aura of evil that such people emit. But in interpreting and responding to such experiences, would-be helpers often ignore the Bible's striking examples of those who traffic with the dark side. The pattern of ministry and description of the change process is strikingly uniform. It is consistently and vividly "normal." Deliverance from the sin of pursuing the occult never includes any sort of deliverance from inhabiting spirits.[1] We will consider three examples.

First, Manasseh did it all when it came to "the despicable practices of the nations" (2 Kings 21:2 ESV). His biography reads like an encyclopedia article on occult involvement: worshiping multiple idols; burning his sons in human sacrifice; using fortune-telling, omens, and sorcery; and consulting mediums

---

1. Acts 16:16–18 is seemingly an exception to this comment. See note 4 below.

and necromancers. Manasseh also murdered others besides his sons; he "filled Jerusalem with innocent blood" (2 Kings 24:4 ESV). It sounds like dry understatement when the list of his vile and violent transgressions concludes, "He did much evil in the sight of the LORD, provoking him to anger" (2 Kings 21:6 ESV).

So what happened to Manasseh? The prophets pointedly spoke the Lord's words to Manasseh (2 Kings 21:10; 2 Chron. 33:18). He paid no attention. God brought painful consequences on him. He was captured with hooks, bound in chains, and led into exile. Then Manasseh changed. In the midst of his distress, he humbled himself before God, pleading for mercy. God was moved by his plea and mercifully restored him. Manasseh lived out his days as a man of faith (2 Kings 21:10; 2 Chron. 33:18).

Notice the pattern: (1) deep immersion in vile practices; (2) pointed ministry of the Word; (3) negative consequences for intransigence; (4) deeply repentant faith; (5) restoration and a fruitful life. The degree of spiritual perversity in his sin did not change either the mode of ministry or the dynamics of change. Later we will look at how Scripture portrays the casting out of demons. Here it is worth noting that when the problem is moral bondage to Satan, demon deliverance is never the practice.

Second, Philip was proclaiming Christ in Samaria, where a man named Simon practiced magic arts with great power (Acts 8:9–24). When Simon heard the gospel, he believed and was baptized. He saw signs and works of power done through Philip, including casting out unclean spirits and other healings (8:6–7, 13). He saw the Holy Spirit given through Peter's and John's hands, and he offered money to get that power for himself. Many Christians would immediately suspect a demonic stronghold at work in Simon's soul, "a bat in the cave" from his preconversion life. As a ministry approach, they would seek to cast it out.

If exorcism were the way to deal with the sins of an occult practitioner, it would seem that this is the moment. Demon-deliverance healings are taking place right in the context. But Peter goes in a completely different direction. He speaks pointedly to Simon, holding the man himself responsible for both behavior and motives, calling him to repentance. Here are Peter's words (Acts 8:20–23 ESV, emphasis added).

> May *your* silver perish with *you*, because *you thought you* could obtain the gift of God with money! *You* have neither part nor lot in this matter, for *your heart is not right* before God. *Repent*, therefore, of *this wickedness of yours*, and *pray* to the Lord that, if possible, the *intent of your heart* may be forgiven *you*. For I see that *you are in the gall of bitterness and in the bond of iniquity*.

This is the most extended personal reproof in the entire Bible. It is sinful to engage in occult practices and to covet. Sin is dealt with by repentance, not exorcism.

Third, it is worth noting that when the good news of Jesus Christ broke out to the nations, most first-century Christian converts came from a background in idolatry, polytheism, occult practices, and demon worship. The exceptions to the rule are pointed out: monotheistic Jews and their gentile followers, and a few rationalistic philosophers (Acts 17). But the majority worshiped the dark side. The New Testament epistles were written to them. That's where we learn how the church is to do ministry: speaking truth that is pointedly convicting and full of mercies, praying honestly and dependently, living what we say we believe, worshiping together, doing genuine good to meet human need, admitting and repenting of our failures, and so forth. The fact that a person came from an occult background did not change the game plan. Paul, Peter, James, and John developed the game plan for such people. In our contemporary Western world, overt idolaters, occult practitioners, and Satan worshipers stand out as unusual. But "normal" ministry methods are designed for such sins, as well as every other form of sin.

How Do We Understand and Help Those Living in Addictive Bondage to Sin?

How does ministry proceed to help people held in extreme bondage to sin and blinded by falsehood? Here too many people think demon deliverance is called for once a certain line has been crossed and "normal" sin has progressed into "bondage." Such a view finds no support in the Bible. We have already seen that Peter described Simon's "bondage to iniquity" and approached him with a straightforward call to repent to God and pray for forgiveness. Similarly, when Jesus defined Paul's ministry as turning people "from the power of Satan to God," he called him to the intensely normal things that characterize ministry of the Word (Acts 26:18, 20).

The Bible uses strong language to describe the blinding and enslaving power of Satan's moral lordship. We noted earlier the enslavement to darkness expressed, for example, in Ephesians 2:1–3 and 4:17–19. In another letter Paul speaks this way: "If our gospel is veiled, it is veiled to those who are perishing. In their case the god of this world has blinded the minds of unbelievers, to keep them from seeing the light of the gospel of the glory of Christ" (2 Cor. 4:3–4 ESV).

How does anyone come to see? The answer is not to cast out an evil spirit. The gospel is unveiled by the God whose power created the world and raised

Jesus. If anyone awakens, it is because God shines the light of Christ into hearts (2 Cor. 4:6). Sinners are blinded by the devil, and they culpably choose blindness. Everyone is a slave; but no one is a puppet. God enlightens; people turn and believe.

The Bible's most forceful portrayal of moral bondage occurs in 2 Timothy 2:25–26. Paul piles up words for slavery to Satan: morally ignorant, out of their minds, trapped by the devil, captured alive by him, obeying the devil's will. In the context, Paul describes how to do ministry to such people. Their slavery is more than matched by their deliverance: repentance leading to knowledge of the truth, coming to their senses, escaping the devil's trap, and being freed from his captivity, so they no longer serve his will. What changes such people? "God may perhaps grant them repentance" (2 Tim. 2:25 ESV). There is no possibility of self-liberation, but there is no bondage too difficult. Nothing we do can impart life or cast off chains, but we play a significant role. Given the magnitude of the problem, our part in the solution sounds astonishingly modest.

> Flee youthful passions and pursue righteousness, faith, love, and peace, along with those who call on the Lord from a pure heart. Have nothing to do with foolish, ignorant controversies; you know that they breed quarrels. And the Lord's servant must not be quarrelsome but kind to everyone, able to teach, patiently enduring evil, correcting his opponents with gentleness. (2 Tim. 2:22–25 ESV)

Ministry to enslaved people begins with fleeing our own slavish propensities, bringing us into the community of those who call on the Lord and pursue Christ's character (note the parallels to the Ephesians' weaponry). We learn to do Christ's work of deliverance in Christ's way: breathing forth the fragrance of kindness, speaking relevant truth, being patient when others wrong us, correcting gently, relying on the Lord. Jesus sets slaves free, using us. God tells us what to do to liberate the enslaved. He doesn't need our attempts at a show of power.

How Do We Understand the Exorcisms in Matthew, Mark, Luke, and Acts?

Matthew, Mark, Luke, and Acts proclaim numerous works of power whereby Jesus and the apostles perform healings by casting out evil spirits. This brings joy to those who had suffered and amazement to those who witness the display of merciful power. In various works of mercy, Jesus shows his divine power: he feeds the hungry, stills a storm, heals the sick, casts out demons, raises the dead, even procures tax money for Peter—all at a word of command or a touch of his hands.[2]

The Bible never connects these deliverances to Satan's *moral* lordship and our battle with sin. They are part of mercy ministry to sufferers, not our fight against the triumvirate of dark masters. In the Gospels and Acts, supposed "demons" of sin (e.g., pride, anger, lust, addiction) are never identified, spoken to, bound, or cast out. Sins are not even mentioned as bringing on the afflictions and disabilities caused by demons.[3] As with the man born blind, the point was not "who sinned?" but that the merciful works of God might be displayed in Jesus (John 9:3). It's a sign of the Messiah when good things happen in a world where suffering and anguish always get the last say.

Demon deliverance is a subset of the category of healing.[4] In the Bible, some afflictions have a demonic cause; others have other causes. This is clear not only in individual incidents but also in the summary of Jesus's work. For example:

> He went throughout all Galilee . . . healing every disease and every affliction among the people. So his fame spread throughout all Syria, and they brought him all the sick, those afflicted with various diseases and pains, those oppressed by demons, epileptics, and paralytics, and he healed them. (Matt. 4:23–24 ESV; cf. Luke 7:21)

Demonization is an item on the list of sufferings to be cured. In the Bible's descriptions of demon deliverance, people afflicted by demons are blind or deaf, crippled or convulsive—or in the most extreme cases, driven to madness

2. It is beyond the scope of this article on spiritual warfare to explore other questions about how Jesus's mercy ministry (and now ours) alleviates suffering. For example, Jesus's mode of doing good is by dramatic, performative words and actions. For us, the mode of doing good changes into dependent prayer and loving action. This has wide-ranging implications for how we approach healing of afflictions, whatever their cause. For a discussion of the significance of the mode of doing ministry, see David Powlison, *Power Encounters* (Grand Rapids: Baker, 1995), 77–92.

3. All sufferings ultimately connect to the curse on sin, but the Gospels head in a different direction: mercy to sufferers is the constant theme (with warnings of curses for the unrepentant). In the Old Testament, Saul was punished for his sins by a tormenting evil spirit sent from God (1 Sam. 16:14–23). The evil spirit neither caused Saul's sins nor held him into bondage. It inflicted pain because of Saul's sins; David's music (singing psalms?) drove off the spirit and alleviated the pain.

4. The one exception occurs in Acts 16:16–18, where a slave girl had a spirit that enabled divination and fortune telling. Paul ignored her for many days. Finally, out of annoyance (!), he told the spirit to get lost. The spirit had caused the minor suffering of being a bother—to Paul. The exception proves the rule. The girl is portrayed as a slave, both to human masters who exploit her and to the paranormal gifts of a dark spirit. As with every exorcism, the story never even hints at the girl's possible sins (pursuit of occult power? unbelief?). She had heard the word of Christ repeatedly, and there is no evidence that the message met with faith.

by unlocalized pain and torment (Mark 5:1–20; cf. 1 Sam. 16:14–23). Their sufferings have a demonic agency; Jesus heals them. Even in places where a demonic voice cries out through a person and speaks in recognition of Jesus (e.g., Mark 5:7–12; Luke 4:34), the Bible never makes the point that the victim was sinfully participating. Every incident is simply portrayed as a merciful healing, demonstrating that Jesus is the Messiah and giving us reasons to believe.

No moral stigma is assigned to being painfully afflicted. In fact, the most plausible interpretation of Paul's thorn in the flesh, "a messenger of Satan to harass me" (2 Cor. 12:7 ESV), is a demonically caused physical torment. Not only is Paul's tormentor not connected to any moral stigma or habitual sin, but also the painful weakness actually serves to guard Paul from the sin of conceit, keeping him dependent on God's mercy and power (2 Cor. 12:7–9).

This leaves us with the question: How did Jesus himself fight spiritual warfare? When Satan attempted to gain moral authority over Jesus, seeking to shape Jesus's choices, Jesus fought in the Ephesians 6 way. He spent forty days with the Word of God and prayer in his heart and on his lips (mention of fasting is shorthand for intensive prayer and fasting). Of course. This is the invading Lord of Isaiah and Psalms, doing the very things Paul will tell us to do in putting on Christ.[5]

The temporary alleviation of the suffering of others played a particular role in Jesus's overall mission. Jesus's mercy ministry does sheer good, rolling back the curse. These healings, feedings, stilling of a storm, and resurrections are true goods—but they are temporary. They point to something better by far. Every person healed, fed, saved from drowning, or raised later suffered and died in some other way. Jesus was on a mission to win the ultimate cosmic warfare. The Gospel of John never mentions a demonized sick person, but it proclaims the supreme "exorcism." When Jesus says, "Now will the ruler of this world be cast out" (John 12:31–33 ESV), he points to the cosmic exorcism of all that is wrong—sin, death, and Satan overcome forever—by the death, resurrection, and return of the Lamb of God. Even so, come Lord Jesus.

What about the Experiences That Are Common in "Spiritual Warfare Ministries" and in Animistic Cultures?

I hesitate to write anecdotally. Both Christian understanding and Christian practice regarding the forces of darkness are best served by establishing biblical grounds. But personal experiences are often cited as authoritative by those

---

5. When Ephesians 6:11; James 4:7; and 1 Peter 5:9 tell us to "oppose the devil," they portray faith and love standing up to the devil's schemes. There is no whiff of demon deliverance in Ephesians, James, or 1 Peter.

who argue for casting out demons as a way of overcoming sin. If those who disagree with those theories and methods never tell stories, the conversation can sound like bookish theory arguing with nitty-gritty, eyewitness testimony. In addition to the consistency and clarity of biblical witness, telling a couple of stories is worthwhile.

My first example concerns a European friend of mine who went to rural West Africa in the 1980s as a long-term missionary. He taught in a theological college and did church planting and pastoral ministry. When he arrived, the implicit rationalism of his Western worldview was severely threatened by the disturbing forces he encountered: animism, witchcraft, amulets, manifestations of bizarre voices and various other physical effects, trance states, hallucinations, and a visceral sense of being in the presence of uncanny evil. He encountered these phenomena both in professing Christians and in non-Christians. He began to adopt the common demon-deliverance practices and experienced apparent success.

But as the years went by, he increasingly doubted both the legitimacy and efficacy of what he was doing. For one thing, a deliverance event, however dramatic in the moment, proved to be no predictor of any good thing in a person's life over the long term. It did not result in blessing, stability, spiritual growth, or freedom from symptoms. In contrast, people whose lives changed—who turned from their sins, who came under Christ, whose lives became fruitful—were people who did "normal" things. "Normal" did not mean rote, perfunctory, or mechanical. It meant the reality of Scripture, confession, repentance, faith, prayer, worship, fellowship, accountability, obedience. People in whom normal things did not take root continued to live in sin, fear, and animistic chaos. Normal things were the difference in delivering people from Satan's power. Deliverance ministry made a lot of noise but made little difference. It even reinforced the core assumptions of animism.

As my friend continued to reflect on Scripture and his experience, he concluded that the demon-deliverance worldview and practice did not add up biblically and failed practically. So what was going on with the darkly bizarre symptoms that he was encountering? The evil one and his agents were intimately involved. But most of the varied phenomena—the sense of uncanny moral evil, the lies, fear, confusion, and hostility—point toward normal spiritual warfare in a world of suffering. As we touched on in the discussion of Psalm 28, people suffer terribly under many things: the hardships of life, the brutality of others, anguish of conscience, the cruelty of the slave master, the threat of death. It is always right to earnestly cry out to God, "Deliver us from evil. Be merciful, O Lord." But the animistic worldview suggested that the brokenness of life calls for a power encounter with an inhabiting spirit. My friend began to change his approach.

He started to dig carefully, to proceed more patiently, to do more pointed ministry of Word and prayer. He sought to find out what else was going on in the lives of people. He found dark secrets and relational problems—and the miseries of life that both tempt to sin and result from sin. He found secret adulteries. He found financial corruption. He found Christians who, in their anguish over a sick child or extreme poverty, began visiting witch doctors and wearing amulets. Most frequently, he found bitterness and hatred, relationships that had been broken and never reconciled. False accusations were also a common relational problem. In the context of suffering and unexpected death, the traditional culture looked for someone to blame. The finger of accusation often pointed to "witches" or "witch children" as the cause.[6] In all these cases, bizarre manifestations appeared. The liar, accuser, and murderer is at work in all this—but not quite in the way it was being interpreted. The environing animistic worldview was yet another lie—a "teaching of demons" about demons (1 Tim. 4:1). My friend was uncovering complex spiritual and moral problems. We don't need to sort out where "flesh" ends and "world" begins, where "world" ends and "devil" begins. We don't need to determine where the devil's role in moral blinding and in inflicting destruction begin and end. We can't see through the fog of war. But Christ's truth and power address all dimensions simultaneously. We intercede with our Lord to comprehensively deliver us from evil.

My friend normalized the abnormal and humanized the bizarre, seeking to get behind confusing appearances, seeking to minister. He dealt with bizarre evil the way the Bible tells us to deal with evil of any sort: clear scriptural truth; bold, faith-expressing prayers that plead the mercies and power of Christ; heartfelt worship; meaningful fellowship. People brought their sins, fears, and confusion to the light. They found Christ's mercy and aid, and acted in newness of life. The bizarre symptoms disappeared. They found deliverance from evil, and biblical reality increasingly supplanted the fear-filled animistic worldview.

My friend had come to mission work with a Christian faith somewhat tilted toward Western rationalism. The initial shock of cross-cultural experience had somewhat tilted his faith toward the traditional animistic worldview. Further ministry experience and biblical reflection increasingly shaped a humble, bold, truth-speaking, prayerful, loving approach to people: spiritual warfare against the powers that enslave people in the confusion of sin and fear.

6. Even secular studies of witchcraft observe that relationship breakdowns lie behind the bizarre phenomena and that the problem is solved by confession and forgiveness.

My second example concerns a colleague and friend at the Christian Counseling and Educational Foundation. He is a wise counselor, with a marked ability to keep his bearings amid bizarre, complicated problems. He loves very troubled people. One Sunday after church, he heard a commotion in the fellowship hall and went to find out what was going on. A slender, twentysomething woman had lost control of herself. An excited group of people had gathered close around her. She was writhing on the floor, biting people, switching between several different personalities and voices, screaming hysterically, growling blasphemies in a deep, animalistic voice, trying to escape. Some of those gathered were attempting to physically restrain her, but she exhibited herculean strength, and they couldn't control her writhing. Others were praying loudly and authoritatively over her, attempting to cast out demons. One man in particular, a veteran of "warfare ministry," was taking charge in a confident, domineering manner. He interpreted her cowering as "the demons are afraid"; her growling, blasphemous voice and switches between multiple personalities meant demons had taken over and were using her as their mouthpiece; her supernatural strength was animated by these evil spirits, which he was binding and commanding to depart.

My friend is a respected elder and was able to get the group to back off. He sat down about eight feet away from the woman and talked quietly and reassuringly with her. She began to calm down enough to respond. That led to hours of conversation over the weeks that followed. She was an extremely fearful person. In normal life, she projected a sense of overwhelming fragility and vulnerability. It came out that she had never been able to come to terms with being sexually abused as a young teen (something that many exorcism ministries interpret as opening a door to demon-inhabitants). She'd been unable to tell her parents. She'd been unable to tell anyone. A sense of pain, horror, and fear never left her. She couldn't shake vivid memories of horrible things that the rapist said to her. She could find no words for her experience of unspeakable evil—only helpless agony. In daily life, she often felt on the verge of shattering into a thousand tiny pieces. When other people "got too close," violating her physical or psychological space, she would violently react, flipping into multiple-personality episodes. She was filled with an all-consuming sense of shame and personal dirtiness, afraid of exposure before the eyes of others. Her universe was fear-colored. Whenever fear started to rise inside, she had no resources, no idea of how to turn to Christ for help. She had no refuge and strength, no very present help in her very real troubles.

Why had she first lost control that morning after church? Why did she manifest multiple personalities? Why did she act and sound like an animal? It is a puzzle. Giving her a descriptive label—"MPD" or "DID"[7]—can comfort those who like to use medical-sounding words for complicated human things, but it explains little if anything. Naming her problems as demonic inhabitants is speculation: people in the Bible whose afflictions were demonically induced didn't do and say the kinds of things she did and said.

She was able to describe what happened that morning. People crowding her, loudly and authoritatively invading her physical and psychological space, had utterly terrified her. Hearing her problems named as demons had further terrified her. Her own hysterical reactions had added to her terror. Unassuming human kindness and simple good sense slowly reassured her. My friend was able to draw her out. Could he explain every kink and wrinkle in this young woman's life? No. Could he explain the unspeakable evil of what had happened to her? No. But where we find the reign of fear, lies, pain, violence, oppression, shame, stifling darkness, confusion—we know that these are characteristics of Satan's kingdom, not Christ's. My friend worked with what the Bible teaches us to know, normalizing the abnormal and humanizing the bizarre.

What helped this young woman? My friend prayed silently for her (God hears and answers honest intercession, not according to the volume). He talked gently with her (not bypassing her by loudly challenging supposed demonic agencies). He prayed clearly with her and for her (not praying loudly against supposed demons). He lived, modeled, and communicated how Christ meets a very fearful young woman (not how the animistic worldview feeds fears). His prayers and counsel gathered up her sufferings and fears within the promises of our Lord's mercies and shielding strength. They talked about listening to God's voice—the Lord bless you and keep you; the Lord make his face shine on you and be gracious to you; the Lord turn his face toward you and give you peace. They exposed the false authority of the rapist's contrary voice. He was a liar, and the murderer of a girl's innocence, in the image of *the* liar and murderer. How might she put her hopes in Christ rather than in the hopeless hope that her past would somehow go away? They talked about small obediences—what Ephesians 4:29 words might look like as she entered into conversations with people at church, the small practicalities of building genuine, mutual friendships. They talked about being known fully by God, and loved. My friend's conversations embodied the things he spoke about.

Did this young woman's problems all go away? Of course not. Do your problems or mine all go away? She was coming out of a deep pit, and that's almost always a long process. But she subsequently spoke of that time after church as a true turning point. The bizarre experience forced her to consider

7. Multiple Personality Disorder; Dissociative Identity Disorder.

crucial spiritual realities with more urgency: Who is in control? Who is her rock and fortress? Whom does she trust? Trusting herself was no longer a viable option.

She became able to talk about her fears of people with depth and directness. Her world became organized. As inner panic lost its dominion, outer hysteria was no longer her only option. She learned to name evil—the real evils of sin, the real devil who lies and kills, not the spooks of the animistic worldview—and to call on the name of the Lord. As she began to learn faith, she began to learn love. In other words, my friend practiced spiritual warfare with her. He taught her how to fight, how to find strength in the God of strength, shelter in the God who shields. She learned to pray. She learned to believe, standing against the world of fear. She learned to love, standing against the world of hate. She learned to live within the body of Christ, the light of the world. In a world that often feels precarious—because it is precarious—she learned to stand.

These stories don't prove my view of spiritual warfare any more than other stories prove other points of view. But I hope that I've given readers a coherently biblical vision to ponder and rich encouragement to live and minister wisely and lovingly. Our warfare with evil plunges into deep, dark waters. Experiences that seem uncanny, bizarre, and frightening do express the power of this present darkness—everyday grumbling and self-centeredness also express dark power. Both the bizarre and the everyday easily conceal the "normal" abyss of deadly sin and suffering. The bizarre overexcites us; the everyday lulls us. In the abyss of evil, the evil one holds men and women in the bondage that is bondage indeed. Spiritual warfare in the pastoral wisdom of Jesus Christ goes to the depth that is depth indeed.

RESPONSE TO DAVID POWLISON

WALTER WINK AND MICHAEL HARDIN

It was a pleasure to read this essay with its sober assessment of spiritual warfare and exegesis of Ephesians 6. Several themes offer points of convergence with our perspective, most notably Powlison's emphasis on the christocentric focus of spiritual warfare. His emphasis on the pastoral is admirable. We have one primary objection, which concerns Powlison's insistence that the devil is a "perverse covenant lord." In our response to Greg Boyd we observe that the personification of the satan is part of an antiquated mythological worldview and has been supplanted by the recognition that the satan is the spiritual dark side of humanity. To recognize this does not detract from evil, nor does it make evil less evil. In fact to correlate the satanic and the Adamic (as does the writer of the second creation narrative in Gen. 2–4) places the problem of evil right where it belongs: on human shoulders. We no longer need to do a theological Flip Wilson ("The devil made me do it").

Like so many who wrestle with the problem of evil, what is missed is the problem of human violence, its origins and effects. Evil manifests itself as destruction in human relationships (deception and death). As Jesus says in the Fourth Gospel, Satan is a liar and a murderer from the beginning (John 8:44). We would like to focus this response by adding to Powlison's exegesis of Ephesians 6 by noting what is omitted in the armor of God and why this omission is critical for understanding spiritual warfare.

The author of Ephesians[8] is not the first to take up the notion of God's armor. There are two places in the Jewish canonical tradition that do so, Isaiah and the Wisdom of Solomon.

Isaiah 59:15b–18 (NRSV)

> The LORD saw it, and it displeased him
>   that there was no justice.
> He saw that there was no one,
>   and was appalled that there was no one to intervene;
> so his own arm brought him victory,
>   and his righteousness upheld him.
> He put on righteousness like a breastplate,
>   and a helmet of salvation on his head;
> he put on garments of vengeance for clothing,
>   and wrapped himself in fury as in a mantle.
> According to their deeds, so will he repay;
>   wrath to his adversaries, requital to his enemies;
>   to the coastlands he will render requital.

The Wisdom of Solomon 5:17–20 (NRSV):

> The Lord will take his zeal as his whole armor,
> and will arm all creation to repel his enemies;
> he will put on righteousness as a breastplate,
> and wear impartial justice as a helmet;
> he will take holiness as an invincible shield,
> and sharpen stern wrath for a sword,
> and creation will join with him to fight against his frenzied foes.

When Paul takes up the armor of God in Ephesians 6, what is notable is what is not there: violent retribution and zeal. This will become significant in our response to Wagner and Greenwood, but its omission in the discussion of Ephesians 6 is symptomatic of Christianity held captive to the myth of redemptive violence. All interpreters argue that deception and violence are key elements of the satanic. Most interpreters see the deception of Genesis 3 and the violent killing of Abel in Genesis 4 as the referent to those "attributes" associated with the satan in John 8:44. Yet few connect the two. Violence is deceptive.

This omission of vengeance and zeal is not happenstance but purposive. By omitting the words *orgē* and *zēlos*, the writer eliminates an offensive posture.

---

8. Like many, we are not persuaded that Paul wrote Ephesians, although we do believe that a serious student of Paul has admirably captured Pauline theology in this letter.

Contrary to Powlison, the armor is defensive, not offensive, in character. Un-like Phineas, the prototypical figure of Jewish zeal, the Christian is not called to purify the community through the imposition of holiness codes.[9] Sadly, some conservative Christians have taken certain offensive postures to cast out the demonic, which results in social acrimony, hostility, and marginalization from America. This is to turn the pacifistic armor of God into the violent weaponry of the satanic.

On the contrary, the apostle Paul contends in 2 Corinthians 10:3–5 (NRSV):

> Indeed, we live as human beings, but we do not wage war according to human standards; for the weapons of our warfare are not merely human, but they have divine power to destroy strongholds. We destroy arguments and every proud obstacle raised up against the knowledge of God, and we take every thought captive to obey Christ.

The weapons of the Christian life here are not for the casting out of de-mons but are epistemological in character. They are intended to change the way people think, to alter their perspective. The purpose of spiritual warfare is to create obedience to Jesus and his way, which is not oriented to zeal or wrath, like Phineas, but is a war waged with love of the enemy Other, forgive-ness for the sinner, and esteem for the marginalized. If the armor of God is given in Ephesians 6, the strategy and tactics are given in the Sermon on the Mount (Matt. 5–7).

Why might Paul have omitted wrath and zeal as part of God's armor if it was part of scriptural tradition? What wrought this change of perspective for Paul? His encounter with the risen Christ and the recognition of the problem of zeal. This is seen clearly in the letter to the Galatian churches. In both Philippians 3:6 and Galatians 1:13–14 Paul identifies his preconversion issue as that of zealous violence. His conversion was not a change in religion, from Jew to Christian, as much as it was a change in perspective on the problem of violence within religion itself.[10]

The myth of redemptive violence depends on the ability of the community (mob, crowd) to frame their persecution of the Other as divinely sanctioned. Paul's preconversion belief was that God had ordained his persecution of the Christian movement, in line with that of Phineas and the great Maccabean

9. On Phineas and zeal, see Num. 25:1–13; Ps. 106:28–31; Sir. 45:23–25; 1 Macc. 2:54; 4 Macc. 18:10; Philo, *On the Life of Moses* 55 (301); Josephus, *Antiquities* 4.6.12; Midrash Rabbah on Num. 25:13; Targum Pseudo-Jonathan on Num. 25.

10. See J. Louis Martyn, *Galatians* (New York: Doubleday, 1997), esp. 161; Robert Hamerton-Kelly, *Sacred Violence: Paul's Hermeneutic of the Cross* (Minneapolis: Fortress, 1992), 71; Martin Hengel, *The Pre-Christian Paul* (Philadelphia: Trinity Press, 1991), 68.

leaders. But when he encountered the innocent victim he realized that his zealous demonization of Jesus and the Christians not only was wrong but also was itself satanically inspired. If Jesus were innocent and God had vindicated his innocence by raising Jesus from the dead even though the law had denounced him ("Cursed is everyone who hangs on a tree," Deut. 21:23 cited in Gal. 3:13 NRSV), the problem was with a law that could condemn innocents. This is why Paul eliminates the words "by God" when he cites the Deuteronomic text. God does not nor has ever "cursed" Jesus. That is something we humans do. Violence, retribution, and punishment are not part of the divine economy according to Paul.[11]

Paul's change in perspective occurred in his revaluation of the meaning of the crucifixion of Jesus. The spiritual warfare Paul had engaged in as a zealous Pharisee (most likely as a Shammaite) was invested in attacking and destroying the enemy Other. Paul read his Jewish texts as though it was God's will for him to scapegoat Jesus and Christians. This hermeneutic is as much a problem today as it was in Paul's time. When texts like Ephesians 6:10–17 are read through a Constantinian-Augustinian lens, they lend themselves to pogroms, wars, inquisitions, witch hunts, holocausts, and so-called just wars. This is to read the text opposite from the very position that it seeks to deconstruct. It is to read the text from the perspective of divinely sanctioned sacred violence or, we might say, from the pagan perspective of the mythmaking community.

Mimetic theory explains the rationale for such a militant (anti)reading. From the perspective of the mimetic theory, when a group is in crisis (experiencing social chaos or loss of identity) it reverts to the single-victim mechanism, blaming the Other for its woes. The perceived reason for the lack of "blessing" or divine approval for the community is then traced back to the victim to whom can be attributed many and varied taboo violations.[12] This is precisely what occurred to Jesus in the Passion Narratives. Paul continued this line of thinking and behavior until he encountered the crucified and risen Christ and had his entire theological model turned on its head. One can be certain that Paul believed he was carrying out God's will to do spiritual and physical warfare against the early Christians.

Yes, it is crucial to recognize the stratagems of the satanic (transliteration: *tas methodeias tou diabolou* [Eph. 6:11]), but these wiles or methods have been and will always be oriented to zealous violence and the desire to purify the community through extermination or marginalization of those who do not

11. This is explored in detail for both Jesus and Paul in Michael Hardin, *The Jesus Driven Life* (Lancaster, PA: JDL Press, 2010), esp. chaps. 2 and 7.

12. René Girard, *Things Hidden from the Foundation of the World* (Stanford: Stanford University Press, 1987); Girard, *The Scapegoat* (Baltimore: Johns Hopkins University Press, 1986).

hold to the perceived divine order. Spiritual warfare is less about casting out supposed demons than it is about assisting those, who through enthrallment to sacred violence, justify their exclusionary and violent tactics to see that overcoming the principalities and powers is already accomplished in the cross of Christ (Col. 2:13–15). A crucial component of the satanic, sacred violence enshrined in the law is overcome in the death of Jesus, the innocent and vindicated scapegoat. This last remark is now an indication that a hermeneutic shift has taken place: the recognition that the Jewish canonical tradition(s) are not God's Word in toto. It means, following Paul and Jesus, the renunciation of all demonization of the Other, of a critically selective rendering of God's works and ways in the history of Israel, and a complete reorienting of oneself to inclusive principles and behaviors, seeking only what is best for the other, as God in Christ has done for us (2 Cor. 5:16–21).

In short a Muslim (or anyone else) committed to peace and nonviolence is more of a brother or sister than a Christian who justifies or commits violence and exclusion. Our battle is not against "flesh and blood" but against the justification of violence and the making of victims. Karl Barth, quoting Johan Blumhardt, has reminded us that Jesus is Victor! The battle is won; Christians are only engaged in mop-up operations. This is still the world of our heavenly Father; God has not abdicated the throne; Jesus reigns (Phil. 2:5–11). By living lives that exemplify forgiveness, not accusation; love, not hate; generosity, not acquisitiveness; peace, not the justification of violence, we shall be children of our heavenly Father (Matt. 5:48), and only then shall we be soldiers of the Almighty.

RESPONSE TO DAVID POWLISON

GREGORY BOYD

I want to thank David Powlison for contributing a well-written and tightly argued essay for this volume. I found myself in agreement with most of what he had to say. Over against Wink, I concur with Powlison that Satan is "not merely a personification of impersonal forces." While we can only rely on analogies to understand the nature of these invisible agents, based on the things Jesus and New Testament authors say about them, they clearly possess *something like* personal characteristics such as volition and intelligence. They are, in other words, *something like* personal agents who exist independent of us.

So too, over against Wagner and Greenwood, I agree with Powlison that there are no compelling grounds for thinking a distinct sort of spiritual warfare is required to free people who have been, or who continue to be, involved in occult activity. Jesus and his earliest disciples treat people who were steeped in occult practices no differently than they treat others. In sharp contrast to many deliverance ministries today, we never find Jesus or his disciples doing "background checks," as it were, on people's personal or familial involvement with the occult. Indeed, they never exhibit the least bit of interest in discovering *how* a person came under demonic oppression. The only thing that mattered to them, and the only thing that should matter to us, is manifesting the power of God against demonic strongholds and setting people free.

On a related note, I deeply appreciate Powlison's concept of the "fog of war," by which he calls attention to our need to always bear in mind our massive ignorance of the hows and whys of spiritual warfare. Far too much energy is needlessly expended in far too many deliverance ministries trying to answer these sorts of questions. The way I have elsewhere fleshed out the impenetrable ambiguity of the cosmic conflict that envelops us is somewhat different from Powlison, due to our different understandings of divine providence and free will (more on this in a moment).[13] Yet I fully concur with him on the basic point that we must humbly accept that we can know next to nothing about the particulars of how or why things unfold the way they do. Fortunately, as I mentioned above, we don't need to know any of this to effectively engage in the warfare Christ has called us to.

Finally, though I will shortly argue that he takes it too far, I heartily agree with Powlison's emphasis on lifestyle warfare. To "win spiritual warfare is simply to live as light in a dark world," he contends. "It is to treat others with humility, patience, and thoughtful consideration," he continues. Indeed, "at its core," Powlison says, "to win this war is to know God and consciously serve him." I heartily agree with this focus. Jesus manifested God's reign and waged war against the powers (we can't do one without the other) primarily by living a selfless servant lifestyle of love that revolted against every aspect of society that was not in line with God's will, thus (when understood in Jesus's apocalyptic context) revolting against the powers that fueled those aspects of society. In substantial agreement with Powlison, therefore, I affirm that our central calling is to imitate Jesus's countercultural lifestyle and to thus engage in *this form* of warfare of Jesus.[14]

Despite these agreements, however, there are two aspects of Powlison's essay that I have reservations about.

Warfare and Providence

First, though he never addresses this issue head-on, I have reservations about the manner in which Powlison seems to relate spiritual warfare to divine providence. At one point Powlison states that, while "Satan and other hostile spirits are utterly malicious" and seek "to harm and destroy all people," they nevertheless "serve God's various purposes and work at his permission." Now, if by this Powlison means merely that God permits spirit agents to engage in

13. In *Is God to Blame? Beyond Pat Answers to the Problem of Suffering* (Downers Grove, IL: InterVarsity, 2003), I argue that the impenetrable mystery of why things happen the way they do attaches to the unfathomable complexity of a creation populated with a myriad of human and angelic free agents, not to the mystery of God's character and will; for this, I hold, is clearly revealed in Christ.

14. For an overview of ten aspects of Jesus's life that were "revolutionary"—they revolted against ungodly aspects of his culture, and therefore against the powers that fuel them—see Gregory Boyd, *The Myth of a Christian Religion: Losing Your Religion for the Beauty of a Revolution* (Grand Rapids: Zondervan, 2010).

evil by virtue of giving them free will and that God in his infinite wisdom is always able to bring good out of their evil, I have no problem. But given everything else Powlison says in his essay, including his emphasis that "the Lord . . . commands all created things," I suspect Powlison was instead suggesting that every *particular* thing evil agents do is *specifically* permitted by God and fulfills a *specific* divine purpose. In this case I have significant problems with Powlison's position.

Embracing this position requires us to accept that every particular evil thing that Satan, the powers, and demons have ever done, as well as every particular evil thing that humans have ever done, *conforms to God's specific will*. We must accept, for example, that behind every horrific episode of a child being kidnapped, tortured, and raped, there is a divine yes! With all due respect to "the fog of war," I cannot for a moment imagine Jesus saying yes to such unthinkable, diabolic activities. And since Jesus is the "radiance of God's glory" and the one and only "exact representation of his being" (Heb. 1:3 NIV), I cannot imagine God saying yes to such activities.[15]

An Overly Domesticated Warfare

While I appreciate Powlison's emphasis on lifestyle warfare, as I mentioned above, my second reservation is that he almost seems to *reduce* spiritual warfare to the moral struggles involved in living a Christlike life. For Powlison, "spiritual warfare" language, such as we find in Ephesians 6, is simply a way of "describing the moral conflict of the Christian life." Indeed, reflecting his (questionable) conviction that the focus of the New Testament's talk of Satan and spiritual warfare is always "pastoral," Powlison contends that the only reason Paul "underscores the devil" in Ephesians 6 is "so we won't be surprised" when we find that "life is so hard and the process so messy." Along the same lines, after describing how Paul waged spiritual warfare by engaging in Christlike actions and by "normal" prayer, Powlison notes that this warfare involved "no fireworks, no fuss and feathers, no binding and loosing, no authoritative pronouncements."

While I fully empathize with Powlison's concern to avoid unbiblical and sensationalist practices that unfortunately characterize far too many deliverance ministries, I worry that Powlison has gone to the other extreme, suggesting

15. For a biblical defense of free will and response to passages typically cited to support the view that God controls every specific event, see Boyd, *Is God to Blame?*, and Boyd, *Satan and the Problem of Evil: Constructing a Trinitarian Warfare Theodicy* (Downers Grove, IL: InterVarsity, 2001).

that spiritual warfare *never* involves unusual practices such as "binding and loosing" and making "authoritative pronouncements."

The primary challenge to Powlison's view, as I see it, is that Jesus's ministry was full of demon-confronting and infirmity-confronting activities such as "binding and loosing" and making "authoritative pronouncements." Indeed, aside from teaching, the two activities Jesus engaged in most frequently were casting out demons and healing people from afflictions.[16] Not only this, but Jesus passed this ministry and this authority on to his disciples, and according to the book of Acts, they used it in a manner that closely followed his example.[17] While I grant that Jesus's primary form of warfare was his servant lifestyle, it seems evident that spiritual warfare was for him and his disciples much more than merely a way of "describing the moral conflict of the Christian life." Often, it seems, their warfare also involved "fireworks."

The question, therefore, is why we should think that spiritual warfare today would not follow the pattern of Jesus and his earliest disciples. Consider the example Powlison provided of his friend who ministered to the young lady who "freaked out." According to Powlison, she withered on the floor, bit people, spoke with different voices, exhibited "Herculean strength," screamed hysterically, and growled "blasphemies in a deep, animalistic voice." In short, she behaved quite a bit like demonized people in the New Testament behaved. Some people responded to this apparent demonic manifestation by trying to speak "loudly and authoritatively over her, attempting to cast out demons." Disapproving of this response, Powlison's friend intervened and broke up their "fireworks." He simply "talked quietly and reassuringly" until the young lady calmed down.

We are of course thankful this young lady got into counseling and subsequently experienced some improvement in her struggle with various psychological issues. Indeed, setting aside for the moment the issue of how we should respond *in the moment* when a person exhibits behavior that appears demonic, I always strongly encourage people who exhibit this sort of behavior to receive follow-up counseling after a deliverance. But this doesn't alter the fact that whenever Jesus and the disciples confronted people behaving the way this young lady did, they responded much more like the people Powlison and his friend disapproved of than like the calm and quiet "no-fireworks" approach of Powlison's friend. And Powlison unfortunately provides no explanation for this discrepancy.

16. See Gregory Boyd, *God at War: The Bible and Spiritual Conflict* (Downers Grove, IL: InterVarsity, 1997), chap. 7.

17. E.g., Matt. 10:1; Mark 6:7; John 14:12; cf. Acts 3:6; 5:16; 8:6–7; 19:12. It's worth noting that healings and exorcisms continued to play a central role in the ministry of the postapostolic church.

The closest Powlison comes to providing an explanation is found in a cryptic footnote in which he asserts that, while "Jesus's mode of doing good is by dramatic, performative words and actions," our "mode of doing good changes into dependent prayer and loving action." He then points out that this has "wide-ranging implications for how we approach healing of afflictions." Unfortunately, these opaque statements simply beg the question. They reassert Powlison's conviction *that* our mode of "doing good" should look calmer than Jesus's, but they don't explain *why* he holds this view. When we consider that the earliest disciples closely followed the precedent of Jesus and continued to "do good" by means of "dramatic, performative words and actions," it seems to me an explanation is in order. Perhaps Powlison has provided this in other writings, but I could not find one in his essay for this volume.

Along similar lines, Powlison at one point recommends that we "humanize the bizarre," such as his friend did in response to the young lady. My concern is that this recommendation is tantamount to advising we "*Westernize* the bizarre." While Powlison rightly rejects the Western naturalistic worldview, it is undeniable that the calm and quiet "no-fireworks" response of his friend to the apparently demonized young lady conforms much better to the "normal" of Western society than it does to the precedent set by Jesus and his disciples.

In fact, I would argue that Powlison's assessment of what constitutes "bizarre" behavior in the first place, as well as what constitutes "fireworks" and "fuss and feathers," is completely predicated on the modern Western worldview. In the culture of Jesus and his disciples, as well as in most cultures outside modern Western culture, it is not all that unusual to have people manifest demons by behaving the way this young lady did and the way demonized people in the Gospels and Acts behaved. Nor is it all that unusual to have people respond to these manifestations in the confrontational way Jesus and his disciples did.[18] The question for Powlison thus becomes: Why should modern Western disciples of Jesus allow the "normal" of their culture to take precedence over the example set by Jesus and his disciples?

To conclude, I want to again register my agreement with Powlison that our primary warfare is rooted in our call to revolt against the powers by the countercultural, Jesus-imitating way that we live. But I believe Powlison has unwittingly overreacted to the excesses of many contemporary deliverance ministries and has consequently overly domesticated, and overly Westernized,

18. For an overview and list of sources, see Paul Eddy and Gregory Boyd, *The Jesus Legend: A Case for the Historical Reliability of the Synoptic Jesus Tradition* (Grand Rapids: Baker Academic, 2007), 67–73 and notes.

another important dimension of spiritual warfare. As we fight the powers by loving and serving others the way Jesus did, we must expect at times to confront demonized people in ways that involve "fireworks . . . fuss and feathers . . . binding and loosing" as well as "authoritative pronouncements"—in short, in ways that look like the warfare ministry of Jesus and his disciples.

RESPONSE TO DAVID POWLISON

C. PETER WAGNER AND REBECCA GREENWOOD

We read what David Powlison calls a classical view of spiritual warfare with a mixture of appreciation and consternation. The appreciation relates to his desire that every Christian win the individual struggle against the world, the flesh, and the devil. We of course agree with this as part of the ongoing challenge of living lives exemplified by holiness. The struggle does indeed involve personal spiritual warfare.

However, consternation enters the picture when the focus of an entire essay on spiritual warfare is on such a minute part of the whole picture. It is like writing about the Olympic Games and focusing on fencing. Or writing about business and focusing on expense accounts. Or writing about dentistry and focusing on filling cavities. All are important but somewhat minor parts of the whole.

Ministering with Jesus's love and compassion to people in need and helping them to repent of sin, receive forgiveness, and commit their lives to serve the Lord and his kingdom releases great power to bring healing and freedom. Powlison understands and applies this well, but we feel that there is much additional God-assigned ministry relating to overt confrontation with and deliverance from demons that he does not highlight in his essay.

Let's take a look at the case of Simon the sorcerer, which Powlison refers to. He uses this case to make his point that "sin is dealt with by repentance, not exorcism." However, there may be an alternative way of understanding the story in Acts 8. The extraordinary evangelistic experience of Philip in Samaria took place in an environment of straightforward demonic deliverance. Accompanying miracles and healings, "unclean spirits, crying with a loud voice, came out of many who were possessed" (Acts 8:7 NKJV). Then Simon comes on the scene, and he also believed and was baptized. It is common knowledge among those who have observed and practiced deliverance that in many cases of severe demonization, the tormenting demons leave at baptism. Thus it would not be beyond reason to assume that Simon would have been delivered when he was born again. If that were the case, Simon's later sin of wanting to purchase the power of the Holy Spirit might not have been caused by a demon. Keep in mind that born-again Christians remain susceptible to the world, the flesh, and the devil. In this case, Simon most likely would have yielded to the world and the flesh, and that would explain why repentance and not exorcism would be called for at the time and in that particular case.

However, there is no principle asserting that strong reproof and aggressive counseling trumps direct confrontation with and literal ejection of evil spirits in dealing with people who are oppressed. Powlison may not want to put it in such blunt terms, but we believe that most readers of his essay would feel that he seems to be leaning in that direction. We just might think for a moment of Jesus's dealing with another demonized person, this time the one who broke his chains and shackles and terrorized the whole region of the Gadarenes. In this case, the legion of demons had to be cast out and the man was instantly made whole (Luke 8:28–40).

Jesus's pattern, when he sent out his disciples to preach the gospel of the kingdom, was almost invariably to direct them to cast out demons and heal the sick. We believe that this applies to Christian workers today. We don't train our people to *counsel* out demons but to *cast* them out, using the weapons of spiritual warfare that God has provided in the power of the Holy Spirit.

The Classical View

The title of Powlison's essay is "The Classical Model." On the one hand, if by this he means that the majority of Christian leaders and believers through the centuries, including theologians, have tended to ignore or trivialize spiritual warfare, it would be an accurate title. If, on the other hand, he means to imply that issues of spiritual warfare such as those discussed in this book have appeared on the Christian landscape only in recent times, it would be inaccurate.

If we look back to the first three centuries or so of the Christian movement, we find that spiritual warfare was high on the agendas of churches. An extraordinary scholarly tool for understanding this in some detail is Ramsay MacMullen's *Christianizing the Roman Empire (AD 100–400)*.[19] MacMullen,

19. Ramsay MacMullen, *Christianizing the Roman Empire (A.D. 100–400)* (New Haven: Yale University Press, 1984).

Dunham Professor of History and Classics at Yale University, analyzes the factors contributing to the historical phenomenon where the Roman population went from zero Christians to an entire Christian empire in a relatively short period of time.

MacMullen's well-documented conclusions will be surprising to many readers. In the book, he highlights a number of factors contributing to the amazing spread of Christianity, but he regards the primary factor to be *the casting out of demons*! Toward the end of the book, MacMullen says, "This . . . sums up and sharply delineates a great deal that has been discussed in the preceding pages: emphasis on miraculous demonstration, head-on challenge of non-Christians to a test of power, head-on confrontation with supernatural beings inferior to God, and contemptuous dismissal of merely rational . . . paths toward true knowledge of the divine."[20]

This is precisely the kind of spiritual warfare that we advocate in our essay. By the way, if MacMullen's conclusions are historically correct and if overt confrontation with demons was part of the lifestyle of the church through its first three hundred years or so, could not a case be made that this is, in fact, the classic view of spiritual warfare?

Even though deliverance ministries gradually slackened after Constantine established a state church and persecution ceased, a cursory reading of church history reminds us that spiritual warfare continued strongly. For example, Martin of Tours was the pioneer missionary who first took the gospel to France. In a certain village he discovered that the territorial spirit that dominated the area was located in a large pine tree that had been dedicated to the demon. When he started cutting the tree down, the people rose up and tried to stop him. They finally agreed to let him cut down the tree if he would stand in the exact spot it was going to fall. Trusting God, Martin did just that. The tree made a loud cracking noise and fell toward Martin. But historian Sulpicius Severus says, "Then, indeed, after the manner of a spinning top (one might have thought it driven back), it swept round to the opposite side, to such a degree that it almost crushed the rustics who had taken their places there in what was deemed a safe spot."[21]

What happened? Severus goes on: "The well-known result was that on that day salvation came to that region. For there was hardly one of that immense multitude of heathens who did not express a desire for the imposition of hands, and, abandoning his impious errors, made a profession of faith in the Lord Jesus."[22]

20. Ibid., 112.
21. Sulpicius Severus, *Life of St. Martin*, in *Classics of Christian Missions*, ed. Francis M. DuBose (Nashville: Broadman, 1979), 121–22.
22. Ibid.

Other stories could be told. St. Benedict, founder of the Western monastic movement, had many recorded face-to-face battles with Satan and demons at Monte Cassino, including smashing in pieces the idol of Apollo. Boniface, one of the first missionaries to the Germans, cut down a famous oak tree that was believed to be used by Thor as his base of evil in the region. Both of these were historic power encounters that opened the way for the spread of Christianity. Spiritual warfare has been with us since Paul wrote: "We do not wrestle against flesh and blood, but against principalities, against powers" (Eph. 6:12 NKJV).

The Animistic View

We found it a challenge not to take offense at Powlison's caricature of our position on spiritual warfare as "the animistic, occult, superstitious view of demonic agencies," which he regards as false. He goes on to denounce "the influence of ancestral spirits," "the influence of territorial demons," "demon-inhabitants as the agency behind human sins," "techniques to do combat with evil spirits"—all of which we teach and practice within certain rules of engagement. He dismisses these as "animistic beliefs and practices."

After seeing this, a reader might well suspect that the two of us must be animists. Well, strange as it may seem, we might well be! Here is how one of our most respected missionary anthropologists, William A. Smalley, defines animism: "Animism is the belief in personalized supernatural power. As such it contrasts with impersonal power (*jimana* and related phenomena). Its manifestations range from one God as the only spirit being, through orthodox forms of the great monotheistic religions (including angels, demons, souls of the dead, and other forms of spirits), to innumerable ghosts, ancestor spirits, spirits in natural objects, and other phenomena characteristic of many 'primitive' religions."[23] In general terms, and with certain disclaimers, this might describe us.

This may not be the definition of animism that Powlison has in mind. Whatever it might be, however, he claims that it is the root of believing in the influence of territorial spirits, in which we sincerely believe. But he also claims that the Old Testament "demythologizes the superstitious worldview." This does not fit well, for example, with Daniel 10, where Daniel says, "The prince of the kingdom of Persia withstood me twenty-one days" (Dan. 10:13 ESV),

23. William A. Smalley, "Animism," *Concise Dictionary of the Christian World Mission*, ed. Stephen Neill, Gerald H. Anderson, and John Goodwin (Cambridge, UK: Lutterworth Press, 1971), 24.

and later Michael says, "I must return to fight with the prince of Persia; and when I have gone forth, indeed the prince of Greece will come" (Dan. 10:20 NKJV). It seems here that these territorial spirits are being personalized, not demythologized.

All of this raises interesting issues of epistemology that we should discuss at another time, since space does not permit it here. But we must deal with questions relating to whether the Bible is our only dependable source of information about the spirit world. Those of us who believe in biblical authority would not accept other information that *contradicts* the Bible, but this does not necessarily imply that we are not open to information that *supplements* the Bible. The phenomenon of extrabiblical revelation must be accepted in principle, since our very definition of the Bible as having sixty-six books does not come from the Bible itself but through extrabiblical revelation. We say this to point out that some non-Christians who are deeply embedded with the demonic forces of darkness in the world today might possess valid information about the spirit world, which can be used to help spread the kingdom of God. To know what is valid and what is not requires discernment of spirits, but this is supplied as a gift from the Holy Spirit, as we see in 1 Corinthians 12:10. We love Greg Boyd's phrase: "democratized epistemology"!

3

The Ground-Level
Deliverance Model

GREGORY BOYD

D ue largely to the influence of Augustine, a dominant strand of the theological tradition of the West over the last fifteen hundred years has held that everything that comes to pass, good or evil, ultimately reflects God's sovereign will. "The will of the omnipotent is always undefeated," Augustine avers.[1] This perspective, I argue, conflicts with a fundamental motif that runs throughout Scripture in which God battles cosmic powers and humans to establish his will "on earth as it is in heaven."[2] Hence, while it's certain God will eventually triumph over his cosmic and earthly foes, much of what comes to pass in history does not reflect God's benevolent will but rather reflects the wills of agents working at cross-purposes with God. The world we live in

1. Augustine, *Enchiridion*, in *Enchiridion and Confessions*, ed. Albert C. Outler, Library of Christian Classics (Philadelphia: Westminster, 1955), 7:400.

2. This is the central thesis of Gregory Boyd, *God at War: The Bible and Spiritual Conflict* (Downers Grove, IL: InterVarsity, 1997). Following the practice of Walter Wink in his renowned *Powers* trilogy, I will refer to the various categories of angelic agents mentioned in the New Testament as "the powers." See esp. Walter Wink, *Naming the Powers: The Language of Power in the New Testament* (Philadelphia: Fortress, 1984). However, in my view demons constitute a distinct category of spirit agents, so I will continue to refer to them separately.

looks like a war zone because the world *is* a war zone, and followers of Jesus have an important role to play in how this conflict unfolds.

In this essay I will first demonstrate that the motif of cosmic conflict runs throughout the biblical narrative. I will then respond to the frequent claim that modern Western people can no longer believe in the reality of angels, powers, or demons and instead argue that we have good biblical, theological, and even empirical reasons for accepting the biblical depiction of these agents. I will then conclude with several reflections on how followers of Jesus are called to participate in the ongoing cosmic conflict that engulfs our planet.

The Bible and Spiritual Warfare

Some scholars argue that the cosmic-conflict worldview expressed throughout the New Testament had little or no precedent in ancient Judaism.[3] In this view, a robust belief in a devil, rebel powers, demons, and spiritual warfare didn't arise until the second century BCE. While there is certainly some truth to this claim, it should be balanced with the observation that, throughout the Old Testament, the authors assume that God must battle the powers to accomplish his will.

Yahweh and Hostile Cosmic Waters

As was common among ancient Near Eastern (ANE) cultures, Old Testament authors frequently depict cosmic powers that oppose God as personified hostile waters that surround and perpetually threaten the earth.[4] While Israel's ANE neighbors credited Baal, Marduk, or some other deity with protecting the earth from these anticreational forces, Hebrew authors uniformly give the credit to Yahweh. For example, in a biblical creation account that has parallels in Canaanite literature, the Psalmist proclaims that it was Yahweh (not Baal) who "rebuked" the chaotic waters and caused them to flee (Ps. 104:7; cf. Ps. 29:3; 77:16). So too, it was none other than Yahweh who assigned a place for these rebel waters to go and who set boundaries they could not trespass (Ps. 104:8–9; cf. Prov. 8:29). And it was Yahweh, not any other god, who imposed order on these waters so that they would give life rather than destroy it (Ps. 104:10–11, 16). As the psalmist says elsewhere in a poem that echoes a Ca-

3. See, e.g., Richard Horsley, " 'By the Finger of God': Jesus and Imperial Violence," in *Violence in the New Testament*, ed. Shelly Matthews and E. Leigh Gibson (New York: T&T Clark, 2005), 51–80.

4. For a fuller discussion on the ANE concept of hostile waters and sea monsters (to be discussed below) as Yahweh's foes, see Boyd, *God at War*, 73–100.

naanite celebration of Baal's conflict with the sea monster *Yamm*, Yahweh's victory over the hostile waters enables him to sit "enthroned over the flood . . . as King forever" (Ps. 29:10 NIV).[5]

In another important passage that has strong echoes in other ANE creation accounts, we find Yahweh chiding Job by asking:

> Who shut up the sea behind doors
>   when it burst forth from the womb,
> when I made the clouds its garment
>   and wrapped it in thick darkness,
> when I fixed limits for it
>   and set its doors and bars in place,
> when I said, "This far you may come and no farther;
>   here is where your proud waves halt"? (Job 38:8–11 NIV)

As Jon Levenson notes, this passage depicts the sea "as a somewhat sinister force that, left to its own, would submerge the world and forestall the ordered reality we call creation. What prevents this frightening possibility is the mastery of YHWH, whose blast and thunder . . . force the sea into its proper place."[6]

Similarly, Robert Fyall discerns in this passage "a powerful metaphor for that great and elemental struggle of God with the forces of chaos which will end only when the sea is no more" (cf. Rev. 21:1).[7] In fact, Fyall argues that the reference to the sea being "shut up" (*sûk*) is likely intended to echo Job 1:10, which depicts "the satan" (*ha satan*) being held at bay by a protective "hedge" around Job.[8] This suggests that the images of the satan and of the personified hostile sea (and, I would add, of Leviathan and Behemoth) are simply different ways of referring to Yahweh's formidable cosmic foe.

In sharp contrast to the way chief gods are presented in ANE mythologies, biblical authors portray Yahweh as the Creator of all that exists and thus as one who never had to fight for his supremacy. At the same time, biblical authors do not, on this account, deny that the hostile sea is a truly formidable foe. To the contrary, it's precisely because they believed the raging cosmic waters were so

5. On the parallel of Yahweh and Baal in this passage, see John Day, *God's Conflict with the Dragon and the Sea: Echoes of a Canaanite Myth in the Old Testament* (Cambridge: Cambridge University Press, 1985), 53.

6. Jon Levenson, *Creation and the Persistence of Evil: The Jewish Drama of Divine Omnipotence* (San Francisco: Harper & Row, 1988), 15; see also 122.

7. Robert Fyall, *Now My Eyes Have Seen You: Images of Creation and Evil in the Book of Job* (Downers Grove, IL: InterVarsity, 2002), 93.

8. Ibid.

powerful that they viewed Yahweh's victory over them as praiseworthy.[9] The psalmist captures the sentiment well when he proclaims:

> The seas have lifted up, LORD,
>   the seas have lifted up their voice;
>   the seas have lifted up their pounding waves.
> Mightier than the thunder of the great waters,
>   mightier than the breakers of the sea—
>   the LORD on high is mighty. (Ps. 93:3–4 NIV)

While today we might be tempted to interpret references to these personified waters as mere poetry, this is certainly not how ancient Hebrews or any other ANE people group would have interpreted them. These raging waters represent anticreational forces that threaten creation and that the Creator must therefore continually keep at bay.

Yahweh and Anticreational Cosmic Monsters

Closely related to the mythic imagery of personified anticreational waters are various cosmic monsters that ANE people believed menaced the earth. Perhaps the most renowned monster in the ancient Near East was Leviathan.[10] Job 41, which contains the fullest description of Leviathan, claims that there is "nothing on earth" that is equal to this creature, which is why Leviathan has no fear (v. 33 NIV). Even the gods are terrified of this cosmic beast and "retreat before its thrashing" (v. 25 NIV). When Leviathan snorts, lightning, fire, and smoke come out of its nose (vv. 18–21). Elsewhere we find Leviathan described, in typical ANE fashion, as a multiheaded slithering sea serpent (Ps. 74:13–14) and as a dragon that threatens to reverse creation by swallowing the moon (during an eclipse) when aroused by soothsayers (Job 3:8).

Something similar could be said for a number of other monsters spoken of in the Old Testament, including Rahab, Behemoth, *Yamm* (a Canaanite deity associated with the chaotic sea), *Mot* (a Canaanite deity associated with death), and *Resheph* (a Canaanite deity associated with archery).[11] All have

9. So argues Levenson, *Persistence of Evil*, 27, and Adrio König, *New and Greater Things: Reevaluating the Biblical Message of Creation* (Pretoria: University of South Africa Press, 1988), 46.

10. For works on the meaning and ANE background of "Leviathan," see Boyd, *God at War*, 323n4.

11. See, e.g., Job. 9:13; 26:12–13 (Rahab); 40:15–24 (Behemoth). For discussions of the presence of *Yamm*, *Mot*, and *Resheph*, as well as of possible allusions to other Canaanite deities, see Fyall, *My Eyes*, 83–156 and passim; J. C. L. Gibson, ed., *Canaanite Myths and Legends* (Edinburgh: T&T Clark, 1978); Frank Moore Cross, *Canaanite Myth and Hebrew Epic* (Cambridge, MA: Harvard University Press, 1973); Nicholas J. Tromp, *Primitive Conceptions of Death and the*

clear ANE parallels and all represent menacing cosmic forces that Yahweh must contend with to preserve order on the earth. As with Yahweh's battles against hostile waters, Old Testament authors are confident that Yahweh is capable of defeating these cosmic foes. Indeed, sometimes they emphasize God's sovereignty over these cosmic forces by engaging in hyperbolic mockery, as when they depict Yahweh as sporting with Leviathan or as carving him up and giving him as food for animals (Ps. 104:26; 74:14; cf. Ezek. 29:4–5). Yet the general portrait of this and other anticreational monsters is that they are formidable foes that Yahweh must genuinely battle to preserve the earth and accomplish his will.

Yahweh and Rebel Gods

Alongside hostile waters and cosmic monsters we find Yahweh confronting rebel gods throughout the Old Testament.[12] While today some define monotheism as the belief that only one God exists, biblical authors never thought this way. While they acknowledge Yahweh as the only Creator, and while they consistently emphasize Yahweh's superiority over other gods, they never deny the existence of other deities.[13] Hence we repeatedly hear that Yahweh is "greater than all other gods" (2 Chron. 2:5; cf. Ps. 135:5), is to be "exalted far above all gods" (Ps. 95:3; cf. 97:9; 136:2), and is "to be feared above all gods" (1 Chron. 16:25; cf. Ps. 96:4).

While a myriad of deities constitute God's "heavenly council" and "heavenly army," other gods are depicted as resisting Yahweh's good purposes.[14] For example, while all gods are commanded to worship Yahweh (Ps. 97:7), it seems

---

Nether World in the Old Testament (Rome: Pontifical Biblical Institute, 1969); and William J. Fulco, *The Canaanite God Resep* (New Haven: AOS, 1976).

12. For a fuller discussion on rebel gods, see Boyd, *God at War*, 114–42. See also the probing and comprehensive work of Ronn Johnson, "The Old Testament Background for Paul's Use of 'Principalities and Powers'" (PhD diss., Dallas Theological Seminary, 2004).

13. Isaiah and Jeremiah at times appear to deny the existence of gods alongside of Yahweh (e.g., Isa. 43:10; Jer. 2:11; 5:7), yet both affirm their existence elsewhere (e.g., Isa. 6:2–8; Jer. 23:18, 22). Their apparent denials should likely be understood as hyperbolic expressions of mockery, similar to the way Isaiah mocks nations and armies as being "nothing" (Isa. 40:17, 23; 41:12). So argues, Ulrich Mauser, "One God Alone: A Pillar of Biblical Theology," *Princeton Seminary Bulletin* 12, no. 3 (1991): 255–65; and Richard Kent Eaton, "The Nature of the Non-human Opposition of the Church in the New Testament" (PhD diss., Fuller Theological Seminary, 1985), 34–38.

14. For a comprehensive discussion on the background, nature, and significance of the Old Testament concept of "divine council" and rebel gods, see Johnson, "Old Testament Background," 24–111. See also E. Theodore Mullen Jr., *The Assembly of the Gods: The Divine Council in Canaanite and Early Hebrew Literature* (Chico, CA: Scholars Press, 1980); Cross, *Canaanite Myth*, 186–90.

that many, if not most, of the gods who were commissioned to oversee nations rebel against God and operate out of their own self-interest. Because of their rebellion, D. S. Russell notes, these gods are no longer regarded as legitimate "sons of God" but have instead become "demons" (Deut. 32:17 TNIV; cf. Ps. 106:37).[15] Rather than leading their people to the worship of Yahweh, rebel gods make themselves idolatrous objects of worship, which is why Israelites were strictly forbidden from following them (Deut. 29:26; cf. 6:13–17; 32:17). According to Zephaniah, all the nations will someday come back under the lordship of Yahweh, but this will only happen once Yahweh has vanquished "all the gods of the earth" (Zeph. 2:11 NIV).

The only passage that fleshes out in any detail how a god of a nation might work at cross-purposes with Yahweh is Daniel 10. In this intriguing apocalyptic chapter we learn that Daniel had been mourning, fasting, and praying for three weeks when an angel suddenly appears (vv. 2–6). This angel informs Daniel that he (the angel) had been immediately dispatched in response to Daniel's prayer. But, he adds, "the prince of the Persian kingdom resisted me twenty-one days" (vv. 12–13). Only when "Michael, one of the chief princes," showed up to fight on his behalf was he able to get free and deliver his message (v. 13). After a short conversation he informs Daniel he has to "return to fight against the prince of Persia" because the "prince of Greece" was coming, and there was no one else to help him except Michael (vv. 20–21 NIV).

While there is obviously much that remains mysterious about this passage, it's evident that the god of the Persian nation was trying to intercept Yahweh's response to Daniel's prayer and that he had succeeded for twenty-one days. The passage thus demonstrates that, though rebel gods never threaten Yahweh's supremacy, they can, within limits, "hold Yahweh at bay," as Walter Wink notes.[16]

Cosmic and Earthly Conflicts

Daniel 10 also highlights another important aspect of the Old Testament's cosmic-conflict motif. The warfare between the prince of Persia and the prince of Greece, on the one hand, and Michael and Yahweh's messenger angel, on the other, was intertwined with the hostility between Persia and the Israelites they were oppressing. While modern Western believers tend to separate the

15. D. S. Russell, *The Method and Message of Jewish Apocalyptic* (Philadelphia: Westminster, 1964), 244. For a discussion on issues surrounding the proper translation of Deuteronomy 32:7–9, which arguably plays a central role in an Old Testament understanding of the "gods of the nations," see Johnson, "Old Testament Background," 99–100; Mullen, *Assembly of Gods*, 202.

16. Walter Wink, *Engaging the Powers: Discernment and Resistance in a World of Domination* (Minneapolis: Fortress), 310.

"spiritual realm" from the "the natural realm," ANE people, including ancient Jews, had a more holistic perspective. Throughout the Bible "earthly" and "heavenly" battles were viewed as two dimensions of one and the same battle.

To illustrate, reflecting the common ancient belief that stars are angelic beings who are part of the divine council, Deborah proclaimed that when the Israelites went to battle against Sisera, "the stars fought . . . from the heavens" and "from their courses" (Judg. 5:20 NIV). So too, when the prophet Joel envisioned a time of reckoning for those nations that had abused Israel, he called not only on Israelites to prepare for battle but also on Yahweh to "bring down your warriors" (Joel 3:11 NIV). Similarly, when David marched into battle against earthly enemies, an army of gods that were aligned with Yahweh marched into battle against spiritual opponents (2 Sam. 5:24; 1 Chron. 12:22). And while it looked like Elijah and his servant stood alone against the invading army of Aram, the truth was that they were surrounded by a host of heavenly warriors prepared to fight on their behalf (2 Kings 6:15–17; cf. Ps. 34:7). As Wink correctly notes, the prevailing assumption in the biblical narrative is that "what occurs on earth has its corollary in the heavens."[17]

While much more could be said about the motif of cosmic conflict in the Old Testament, what we've reviewed suffices to show that the intense cosmic-conflict worldview of the New Testament is hardly "unprecedented" in the Old Testament. As we've seen, Old Testament authors were keenly aware that Yahweh's sovereignty was something he and his people had to fight for if his will was to be established "on earth as it is in heaven" (Matt. 6:10 NIV).

The Battle against Satan

As pervasive as the theme of Yahweh battling cosmic foes is in the Old Testament, it became, for a variety of reasons, much more pervasive and intense in the two centuries leading up to Christ. Among other things, apocalyptic writers all attribute significantly more influence to gods, angels, and demons than does the Old Testament.[18] Jesus and his earliest followers not only share this apocalyptic worldview but, in certain respects, they also intensify it. Most importantly for our purposes, the authority and influence ascribed to Satan by Jesus and the authors of the New Testament is unprecedented.

17. Wink, *Naming the Powers*, 131. Throughout his *Powers* trilogy Wink rightly emphasizes that "for ancients heaven and earth were a seamless robe, a single interacting and continuous reality" (ibid., 16).

18. With the exception of Daniel, though most scholars agree this is because Daniel (or at least parts of Daniel) is itself a second-century-BCE apocalyptic work.

According to John, for example, Jesus believed that Satan was "the prince of this world" (John 12:31; 14:30; 16:11 NIV). The word translated "prince" (*archon*) customarily referred to "the highest official in a city or a region in the Greco-Roman world."[19] While Jesus and his followers of course believed that God was the *ultimate* Lord over all creation, they clearly viewed Satan as the *functional* lord of earth at the present time. Along the same lines, Satan is depicted as possessing "all the kingdoms of the world"—to the point that *he* is able to give the authority to rule these kingdoms to anyone he pleases (Luke 4:5–6). Indeed, in the book of Revelation, the various kingdoms of the world are depicted as constituting *a single kingdom* under Satan's rule (Rev. 11:15), represented as the mighty Babylon. Similarly, Satan and his cohorts are depicted as deceiving and enslaving "all the nations" and "all the inhabitants of the earth, except those who bear the seal of the Lamb" (Rev. 13:3, 7–8, 12, 14 NIV; cf. 20:8). And in his first epistle, John goes so far as to claim that the *entire world* is "under the power of the evil one" (1 John 5:19 NRSV). Paul doesn't shy away from labeling Satan "the god of this world" (2 Cor. 4:4 NRSV) and "the ruler of the power of the air" (Eph. 2:2 NRSV). It is because of this pervasive and oppressive diabolic influence that Paul, in typical apocalyptic fashion, depicts this entire present world system as fundamentally evil (Gal. 1:4; Eph. 5:6).

Jesus's Victory over Satan

According to the New Testament, the central reason the Son of God came into the world was to drive out the "prince of this world" (John 12:31 NIV), to "destroy the works of the devil" (1 John 3:8 NRSV), and to "destroy the one who has the power of death, that is, the devil" in order to "free those who all their lives were held in slavery by the fear of death" (Heb. 2:14–15 NRSV). Jesus lived, died, and rose again to establish a new reign that would ultimately "put all his enemies under his feet" (1 Cor. 15:25 NRSV). Though "a strong man" was "fully armed," one who was "stronger than he" had finally arrived who could attack him and overpower him (Luke 11:21–22 NRSV). While the cosmic "thief comes only to steal and kill and destroy," Jesus came to vanquish this thief so that all "may have life and have it abundantly" (John 10:10 NRSV). Jesus "disarmed the rulers and authorities and made a public example of them, triumphing over them" (Col. 2:15 NRSV). In a word, Jesus came to bring a victorious end to the cosmic war that had been raging from time immemorial and to set Satan's captives and all of creation free.

19. Clinton Arnold, *Powers of Darkness: Principalities and Powers in Paul's Letters* (Downers Grove, IL: InterVarsity, 1992), 81.

The centrality of cosmic conflict in the ministry of Jesus is reflected in the first messianic prophecy given in Scripture—indeed, the first prophecy *period*—which focuses on his victory over the serpent (Gen. 3:15).[20] Related to this, Jesus's victory over the serpent and all other cosmic opponents pervades the New Testament. This much is evident simply because Psalm 110:1, which celebrates the victory of God's anointed one over his foes, is the most frequently alluded to passage in the New Testament, and it always applies to Jesus. The significance of this is captured well by Oscar Cullman when he writes: "Nothing shows more clearly how the concept of the present Lordship of Christ and also of his consequent victory over the angel powers stands at the very center of early Christian thought than the frequent citation of Ps. 110:1, not only in isolated books, but in the entire New Testament."[21]

The centrality of Jesus's conflict with, and victory over, Satan and the powers is also evident in the fact that salvation in the New Testament is portrayed not primarily as a matter of individuals being forgiven their sin (as is often the case in American evangelicalism) but of humans and the whole cosmos being delivered from the power of Satan and brought into the kingdom of God's Son.[22]

Healing and Deliverance Warfare

Jesus's battle against Satan, the powers, and demons didn't take place only on the cross, nor was his victory only accomplished with his resurrection. Understood in its original apocalyptic context, every aspect of Jesus's life can be understood as part of his battle against, and a victory over, the powers of darkness. Every one of Jesus's healings and deliverances, for example, should be viewed as an act of war that advances God's kingdom and diminishes Satan's kingdom. Peter captures the motif well when he summarizes Jesus's ministry by announcing to Cornelius that Jesus "went about doing good and healing *all who were oppressed by the devil*" (Acts 10:38 NRSV, emphasis added). Gustaf Wingren expounds on the point when he writes: "When Jesus heals the sick and drives out evil spirits, Satan's dominion is departing and

20. On the messianic interpretation of Gen. 3:15, see Ralph A. Martin, "The Earliest Messianic Interpretation of Genesis 3:15," *Journal of Biblical Literature* 84 (1965): 425–27. This interpretation seems to lie behind several New Testament texts (e.g., Rom. 16:19–20; 2 Cor. 11:3; Rev. 12).

21. Oscar Cullmann, *Christ and Time*, rev. ed., trans. Floyd V. Wilson (London: SCM, 1962), 193. For a thorough exposition on the importance of Psalm 110 in the New Testament, see David M. Hay, *Glory at the Right Hand: Psalm 110 in Early Christianity* (Nashville: Abingdon, 1973).

22. For a fuller discussion, see Gregory Boyd, "The Christus Victor View," in *The Nature of the Atonement: Four Views*, ed. James Beilby and Paul Eddy (Downers Grove, IL: InterVarsity, 2006), 23–49, esp. 32–35.

God's kingdom is coming (Matt. 12:22–29). All Christ's activity is therefore a conflict with the Devil. . . . God's Son took flesh and became man that he might overthrow the power of the Devil, and bring his works to naught (Heb. 2.14f.; 1 John 3.8)."[23]

Jesus's Lifestyle Warfare

Jesus's countercultural lifestyle also must be understood as a sustained revolt against the powers once we frame his lifestyle in its original apocalyptic context. There is a growing consensus among scholars that Paul's references to "angels," "rulers," "principalities," "authorities," "dominions," "thrones," "spiritual forces," and "elemental spirits of the universe" refer to various categories of cosmic powers that were believed to exercise a destructive influence over systemic aspects of society, over particular social groups and institutions, and over systemic aspects of creation.[24] Paul taught that the *real* struggle for disciples was never against other humans ("flesh and blood") but against "the rulers, against the authorities, against the cosmic powers of this present darkness, against the spiritual forces of evil in the heavenly places" (Eph. 6:12 NRSV; cf. 2 Cor. 10:3–5). Framed within this apocalyptic framework, we can see that Jesus's unique countercultural lifestyle was not merely a revolt against aspects of his culture but was also against the fallen powers that lay behind and fuel every aspect of society and creation that is inconsistent with the reign of God he came to inaugurate.[25]

For example, when Jesus set aside the riches of his divine prerogatives and sided with the poor and oppressed (2 Cor. 8:9; cf. Phil. 2:5–11), he was revolting

23. Gustaf Wingren, *The Living Word: A Theological Study of Preaching and the Church*, trans. T. V. Pague (Philadelphia: Muhlenberg, 1960), 53. I have elsewhere argued that even Jesus's "nature miracles" (e.g., calming the raging sea, cursing the barren tree) are manifestations of the kingdom of God over and against the kingdom of Satan. See Boyd, *God at War*, 205–14; see also Gregory Boyd, "Evolution as Cosmic Warfare: A Biblical Perspective on Satan and 'Natural' Evil," in *Creation Made Free: Open Theology Engaging Science*, ed. Thomas J. Oord (Eugene, OR: Pickwick, 2009), 125–45, esp. 132–34.

24. See Rom. 8:38; 13:1; 1 Cor 2:6, 8; 15:24; Gal. 4:3, 8–9; Eph. 1:21; 2:2; 3:10; 6:12; Col. 1:16; 2:8, 10, 15; 1 Pet. 3:22. For an overview of the discussion, see Peter T. O'Brien, "Principalities and Powers: Opponents of the Church," *Evangelical Review of Theology* 16 (October 1992): 353–84. No one has explored and developed this thesis more thoroughly and insightfully than Walter Wink in his previously mentioned *Powers* trilogy. Other works arguing in this general direction are Heinrich Schlier, *Principalities and Powers in the New Testament* (Freiburg: Herder, 1961); G. B. Caird, *Principalities and Powers: A Study in Pauline Theology* (Oxford: Clarendon, 1956); Vernard Eller, *Christian Anarchy: Jesus' Primacy over the Powers* (Grand Rapids: Eerdmans, 1987); Hendrikus Berkhof, *Christ and the Powers* (Scottdale, PA: Herald, 1977); and Albert H. van den Heuvel, *These Rebellious Powers* (New York: Friendship, 1965).

25. For a fuller development and application of this theme, see Gregory Boyd, "The Kingdom as a Political-Spiritual Revolution," in *Criswell Theological Review* 6, no.1 (Fall 2008): 23–41.

against cosmic powers that fuel sociopolitical systems that privilege the few by oppressing the masses. So too, when Jesus praised the faith of a Roman centurion (Matt. 8:5–10) and held up Samaritans as heroes (in contrast to Jewish leaders) in some of his illustrations (Luke 10:29–37), he was revolting against the powers that fuel sociopolitical hierarchical systems that privilege some over others on the basis of their ethnicity. Similarly, the respectful way Jesus treated women revolted against oppressive powers that fuel sociopolitical and religious systems that empower men and dehumanize women. Moreover, the dignifying way Jesus identified with beggars and others on the fringe of society revolted against the cosmic forces that fuel sociopolitical systems that ascribe worth to people on the basis of class, wealth, and power. And the manner in which Jesus uniformly resisted all attempts to lure him into the heated nationalism of his day revolted against powers that support idolatrous nationalistic ideologies and allegiances.

Finally, given that all dehumanizing aspects of society are rooted in violence, we must understand Jesus's refusal to use power available to him to defend himself and crush his enemies as his most fundamental revolt against the powers—in this case, the cosmic forces that fuel all violence. In fact, it was this refusal of violence and this act of self-sacrificial love that ultimately "disarmed the powers and authorities" (Col. 2:14–15 NIV). On a physical level, it looked as if Jesus's conflict was with earthly authorities, but his *real* struggle—and, we shall later see, *our* real struggle—was against fallen powers that continually resist God's purpose and exercise a destructive influence in society and creation.

In sum, everything about Jesus and the early church presupposed a cosmic-conflict worldview in which God had to battle powers to establish his will "on earth as it is in heaven" and that God's people have a significant role to play in bringing this about. As we shall discuss later in this essay, we are first and foremost soldiers who are called to live and minister in ways that reflect the unique character and values of God's reign by waging war on the powers that continue to oppress his creation.

The Reality of Satan and the Powers

The Modern Denial

Having surveyed the centrality of spiritual warfare throughout the biblical narrative, we turn now to the question of whether or not this perspective is any longer believable. For the last century a large number of Western theologians and other academicians have claimed that it is not. Rudolf Bultmann expressed the skeptical, "modern" perspective when he famously wrote: "It is impossible to use electric light and the wireless and to avail ourselves of modern medical and surgical discoveries, and at the same time to believe in the New Testament world of spirits and miracles."[26]

Many contemporary scholars have followed suit. "In this day and age," David O'Connor writes, "an ontology of angels, fallen or unfallen, is hardly credible."[27] Similarly, the great Catholic theologian Hans Küng dismissed the belief in Satan and demons as a piece of "outdated medieval thought," which, when accepted, "throws away all credibility for theology and church."[28] Some have gone so far as to argue that if we accept the "primitive" belief in demons and angels, then we must out of consistency accept every aspect of the Bible's archaic scientific worldview, including "a flat earth" and "a six thousand year old creation."[29]

What can be said in response to this claim? To begin, there is no denying that there is a mythological element to the various conceptions of spirit agents in Scripture. Twenty-first-century people obviously cannot be asked to conceive of an evil cosmic agent along the lines of a many-headed sea monster (Ps. 74:14) or angels riding in chariots of fire (2 Kings 6:17). Yet it's one thing to grant that the way someone *conceived* of a cosmic agent was mythic and quite a different thing to claim the *very idea* of cosmic spirits is mythic. Indeed, *all* of our conceptions of spirit agents—including God—are mythic inasmuch as these agents are nonphysical, while all our mental conceptions are inescapably rooted in our embodied experience of the physical world.[30] The important question, therefore, is not whether biblical depictions of angels, demons, and the powers are mythic, but whether these mythic portrayals *point to ontological entities.*[31]

In what follows I will offer four critical responses to the claim that modern people can no longer accept the reality of spirits and then offer an empirical observation that I believe supports belief in their reality.

26. Rudolf Bultmann, *New Testament and Mythology, and Other Basic Writings*, ed. and trans. Schubert M. Ogden (Philadelphia: Fortress, 1984), 4.

27. David O'Conner, *God and Inscrutable Evil: In Defense of Theism and Atheism* (Lanham, MD: Rowman & Littlefield, 1998), 114.

28. Hans Küng, *On Being a Christian* (Garden City, NY; Doubleday, 1976), 369.

29. Howard Munro, "Are Demons Real?," *St. Mark's Review* 145 (Autumn 1991): 38.

30. On the manner in which all our mental conceptions are rooted in our concrete physical experience of the world and the significance this has for philosophical reasoning, see George Lakoff and Mark Johnson, *Philosophy in the Flesh: The Embodied Mind and Its Challenge to Western Thought* (New York: Basic Books, 1999).

31. Karl Rahner argues along these lines in "Devil," in *Sacramentum Mundi*, ed. Karl Rahner et al. (New York: Herder & Herder, 1968–70), 2:73–74.

Four Objections to the Alleged Impossibility of Believing in Spirits

First, the argument that if we accept the reality of spirits we must accept every aspect of the Bible's premodern worldview is a classic non sequitur. While we obviously have compelling grounds for believing that the cosmology of biblical authors was scientifically incorrect, we have no similar grounds for concluding that their belief in spirits was mistaken. Not only this, but this all-or-nothing way of thinking fails to acknowledge the central role the powers, angels, and demons play throughout the biblical narrative in contrast to the utterly insignificant place occupied by the premodern cosmology of biblical authors. One could extract the prescientific cosmology from the Bible, and nothing pertaining to its central story line and message would be lost. If one were to extract all references to spirit agents, however, the entire narrative would become unraveled.[32]

Second, Bultmann's frequently echoed claim is demonstrably false. It is refuted by the simple fact that the vast majority of modern Western people have had no difficulty whatsoever believing in spirits and miracles while continuing to believe in science and use modern technology.[33] And the reason we've had no difficulty is because *there is none*. The objection to believing in spirits and miracles is rooted not in science or technology but in a naturalistic metaphysic. Only if one assumes at the outset that natural law as described by science provides an *exhaustive* account of reality does one find no place for things like spirits and miracles. The vast majority of people throughout history, and the vast majority of people yet today, have not shared this metaphysical assumption.

Third, and closely related to this, inasmuch as the assumption of naturalism that lies behind the Western academic claim regarding the impossibility of believing in spirits or miracles is not rooted in any compelling arguments or evidence and has not been shared by the vast majority of people throughout history, it is liable to the charge of being *chronocentric* (it presupposes the superiority of what these academicians interpret to be the "modern" age), *ethnocentric* (it presuppose the superiority of the cultural perspective of these academicians), and elitist (it presumes that the masses lack the intellectual acuity to perceive the "impossibility" these academics claim to see). For these same reasons, it is also vulnerable to the charge of being uncritical—a point that is particularly ironic given that naturalistic Western academicians tend to

---

32. So argues Paul Minear regarding the New Testament in "Satan Returns from Holiday," *Religion in Life* 12 (1943): 191.

33. According to the 2008 Pew U.S. Religious Landscape Survey, 79 percent of Americans believe miracles occur and 68 percent believe "angels and demons are active in the world." Report available at http://religions.pewforum.org/, accessed September 29, 2010.

view themselves as quintessential critical thinkers.[34] To be sure, these academics are highly critical of premodern and contemporary views that don't share their assumed naturalism, but they seem to have difficulty turning this same critical eye to discern the arbitrariness of their own assumptions.

Peter Berger astutely addresses this curious double standard with reference to the demythologizing program of Bultmannian New Testament scholars when he writes:

> The *past* . . . is relativized [by these scholars] in terms of this or that socio-historical analysis. The *present*, however, remains strangely immune from relativization. In other words, the New Testament writers are seen as afflicted with a false consciousness rooted in their time, but the contemporary analyst takes the consciousness of *his* time as an unmixed intellectual blessing. The electricity- and radio-users are placed intellectually above the Apostle Paul.[35]

In short, in the name of "critical scholarship," Berger argues, this Bultmannian view assumes that the "modern consciousness is . . . the embodiment of superior cognitive powers."[36] With justification, Berger finds the arrogance and duplicity of the whole enterprise to be almost comical.[37]

This leads to my fourth and final critique of the modern denial of spirits. While the naturalistic worldview that has no place for the belief in spirits or miracles was never widely shared outside of a small cauldron of Western academics, it has over the last several decades become increasingly antiquated even within these circles. In keeping with the "postmodern turn" of Western culture as a whole, an increasing number of anthropologists and ethnographers are acknowledging the extent to which many past ethnographic studies were distorted because they were laden with presuppositions of cultural and intellectual imperialism.[38] Increasingly, scholars in these fields are

34. See Alvin Plantinga's comment regarding the supposed "implausibility" of his personal belief in good and evil nonhuman beings in *Alvin Plantinga*, ed. James E. Tomberlin and Peter Van Inwagen (Dordrecht: D. Reidel, 1985), 43. See also the discussion in Wilberforce Omusula Mundia, "The Existence of the Devil" (PhD diss., Boston University School of Theology, 1992), 197–205.

35. Peter Berger, *A Rumor of Angels: Modern Society and the Rediscovery of the Supernatural* (New York: Doubleday, 1969), 51.

36. Ibid., 52.

37. Ibid., 51.

38. On the impact of the postmodern turn for anthropology and ethnography, see George E. Marcus and Dick Cushman, "Ethnographies as Texts," *Annual Review of Anthropology* 11 (1982): 25–69; Paul Stoller, "Eye, Mind, and Word in Anthropology," *L'Homme* 24 (1984): 91–114; John R. Bowlin and Peter G. Stromberg, "Representation and Reality in the Study of Culture," *American Anthropologist* 99 (1997): 123–34; Robert Feleppa, "Emics, Etics, and Social Objectivity," *Current Anthropology* 27 (1986): 243–55. Most of what follows concerning the postmodern approach to anthropology and ethnography as well as the subsequent cross-cultural

maintaining that an accurate understanding of other cultures can only be arrived at if we acknowledge at the start that the culture being studied is on the same level as our own. Along the same lines, some are calling for a "new democratized epistemology," wherein the worldviews of other cultures are taken seriously as rival interpretations of a shared reality.[39] In this light, one could plausibly argue that the metaphysical naturalism that grounded the Bultmannian denial of spirits is transitioning from being *chronocentric* to being *antiquated*.

The self-critical relativization of Western naturalism that Peter Berger called for need not lead to wholesale cultural relativism, as some fear. In reality, it only entails that Western scholars drop the dogmatic assumption that their cultural perspective provides an exhaustive account of reality. It thus entails that Western scholars should strive to remain open to the real possibility that other cultural perspectives and experiences that clash with the academic "Western worldview" might have something important to teach them. John Bowlin and Peter Stromberg put the matter starkly: "It should regularly occur that good ethnography encourages us to conclude that beliefs and warrants held by members of another society track the truth better than our own. An ethnography sufficiently humble about matters of belief must concede this possibility and should regard this kind of critical revision of our own beliefs as a welcomed consequence of careful inquiry."[40]

I would argue that one way in which most societies "track the truth" better than the subculture of the Western academy is in their belief that spirits are real. An increasing number of ethnographers and anthropologists agree, which leads to an empirical observation that arguably supports the belief in spirits.

A Cross-Cultural Argument for the Reality of Spirits and "Demon Possession"

We should begin by noting that reports of something like "demon possession" and "exorcism" can be found in most cultures and religions throughout history.[41] What is most interesting about these reports is how much they have

---

argument for the reality of spirits and "demon possession" is derived from research contained in Paul Eddy and Gregory Boyd, *Apology for the Devil*, unpublished manuscript, 2004.

39. Dan Rose, *Living the Ethnographic Life* (Newbury Park, CA: Sage, 1990), 46.

40. Bowlin and Stromberg, "Representation and Reality," 130.

41. I use the terms "demon possession" and "exorcism" when speaking of cross-cultural experiences because they are most commonly used in the secondary literature. I will place them in quotes, however, since I'm aware these are Western categories that are in some instances being imposed on non-Western phenomena. I will for the same reason place the word "supernatural" in quotes.

in common with each other and with the New Testament, despite the vast differences in cultures and belief systems in which they are found.[42]

For example, it is commonly reported that people familiar with a "possessed" person have a sense that he or she has been taken over by a foreign personality. It is not uncommon to read that the "possessed" spoke in a voice other than his or her own. During "exorcism" the "possessed" are often reported to convulse, become violent, and occasionally exhibit uncharacteristic, if not "supernatural," strength. Not infrequently one finds reports that "possessed" people twitch uncontrollably and contort their bodies in unnatural, if not physically impossible, ways. Occasionally it is reported that the "possessed" know things they couldn't "naturally" know and speak in languages they did not learn. And sometimes one finds in these reports other "supernatural" phenomena taking place as well, such as the "possessed" person levitating and objects moving or even flying about on their own, especially during "exorcism."

Explaining the transcultural and "supernatural" features of "demon possession" and "exorcism" in strictly naturalistic terms is no easy feat, though multitudes of naturalistic theories have been offered. While there is undoubtedly merit to some of these theories, they fail to explain all that needs to be explained. Certainly for people such as myself who have witnessed firsthand "supernatural" phenomenon associated with "demon possession," purely naturalistic theories fail to convince.[43] What is most intriguing, however, is that increasing numbers of anthropologists, ethnographers, sociologists, and psychologists are reporting their own experiences with these sorts of phenomena while acknowledging the inadequacy of natural explanations.[44]

42. For discussions, see Erika Bourguignon, "Spirit Possession Belief and Social Structure," in *The Realm of the Extra-Human: Ideas and Actions*, ed. A. Bharatic (Paris: Mouton, 1976), 17–26; A. R. Tippett, "Spirit Possession as it Relates to Culture and Religion," in *Demon Possession,* ed. John Warwick Montgomery (Minneapolis: Bethany, 1976). The remarkable cross-cultural commonality has been frequently observed. See, e.g., Eric D. Wittkower, "Trance and Possession States," *International Journal of Social Psychiatry* 16 (1970): 156; P. Stevens Jr., "Spirit Possession: Non-Pharmacological Bases for Understanding a Cultural Universal" (paper presented to the Jesus Seminar, Rutgers University, New Brunswick, NJ, October 1992), 21; Paula H. Salmons and David J. Clark, "Cacodemonomania," *Psychiatry* 50 (1987): 53.

43. On a personal note, in one of the dozen or so episodes of "demon possession" I've been involved in, a demonized person's right eye rotated counterclockwise three times while the left eye stared at me without movement.

44. Up until recently (and in some circles yet today), there has been significant peer pressure felt by academic field-workers to suppress their experiences of the "supernatural" in academic environments. See Stoller, "Eye, Mind, and Word," 93; Stoller, "Beatitudes, Beasts, and Anthropological Burdens," *Medical Anthropology Newsletter* 13 (August 1982): 2; Lola Romanucci-Ross, "On Analyses of Event Structures as Philosophical Derivations of the Investigating Cultures," in *Essays in Humanistic Anthropology*, ed. Bruce Grindal and Dennis Warren (Washington, DC: University Press of America, 1979), 57–60.

For example, representing the new self-critical ethnographic approach advocated by Bowlin and Stromberg, the anthropologist Felicitas Goodman challenges naturalistically inclined academics to treat reports of "demon possession" with "respect" and not dismiss them with inadequate naturalistic explanations. In her extensive cross-cultural field studies of this phenomenon, Goodman reports firsthand experiences with things that simply defy the naturalistic Western paradigm.[45] Similarly, in his research on the Orisha religion of Trinidad, James Houk witnessed a possession event that decisively shook his faith in purely naturalistic categories of explanation. He writes of his struggle to "incorporate this incredible experience into my personal belief system." Yet, he confesses, "no matter how I tried . . . I could not reconcile the scholarly or 'scientific' explanations of ritual dissociation with what I was witnessing. Certain aspects of spirit possession are, perhaps, simply ineffable and must be personally experienced before they can be grasped."[46]

Others have had similar experiences. Jeanne Favret-Saada's field research on witchcraft in the Bocage region of western France led to her having several experiences for which she could find no adequate naturalistic explanations.[47] Richard Nelson's investigation of the shamanistic hunters of Wainwright, Alaska, led him to reverse his earlier naturalistic assessment and concede the possibility that these hunters were somehow getting assistance from spiritual agents.[48]

Even more impressive is the report of Larry Peters regarding his study of Tamang shamans in Nepal. As a Western-trained academician, Peters held to a social theory that stipulated that "spirit possession occurs only in societies where people believe in it." Hence, he reasoned, "spirit possession could not exist for me because I don't hold the same animistic beliefs as my informants." This "way of thinking was completely turned around," however, when he experienced things that simply had no place in his Western academic paradigm.[49] He thus "stepped across cultural boundaries and was freed from [his] previous intellectual inflexibility."[50] More dramatic still was the conversion Michael Harner underwent as a field-worker with the Shuar (Jivaro) of Ecuador and

45. Felicitas Goodman, *How About Demons?: Possession and Exorcism in the Modern World* (Bloomington and Indianapolis: Indiana University Press, 1988): 126.

46. James Titus Houk, *Spirits, Blood, and Drums: The Orisha Religion in Trinidad* (Philadelphia: Temple University Press, 1995), 4.

47. Jeanne Favret-Saada, *Deadly Words: Witchcraft in the Bocage*, trans. Catherine Cullen (Cambridge: Cambridge University Press, 1980), 22.

48. Richard K. Nelson, *Make Prayers to the Raven: A Koyukon View of the Northern Forest* (Chicago: University of Chicago Press, 1983), esp. 225–37.

49. Larry Peters, *Ecstasy and Healing in Nepal* (Malibu, CA: Undena, 1981), 47.

50. Ibid., 53. For a description of his experiences, see 37–54.

the Conibo of the Peruvian Upper Amazon.[51] On the basis of all he witnessed and personally experienced, Harner not only relativized his prior naturalistic worldview, but he also became a practitioner and advocate of shamanism.[52]

Yet perhaps the most impressive account to date of a Western anthropologist breaking free from dogmatic naturalism and discovering the spirit world is that of Edith Turner. Edith was the wife and associate of the renowned anthropologist Victor Turner. For years they lived among and studied an African tribe known as the Ndembu. Like most traditional people groups, the life of the Ndembu largely revolved around their understanding and experience of the spirit world. Yet, because of their Western academic training, the Turners never considered the possibility that the Ndembu perspective on the spirit world was actually accurate (and thus that their naturalistic Western worldview was limited). After her husband died, Edith returned to live among this tribe but decided to step out of her role as a Western academician and to instead "go native." It was only after she became a full participant in the spiritual practices and rituals of this tribe that she first discovered "the reality of spirits."[53]

As Turner tells her bizarre story, a member of the Ndembu tribe had purportedly been "invaded" by a magical tooth (called the "ihamba") of a dead hunter. The tooth had been passed on for generations among the Ndembu and purportedly had the power to bring good fortune to the tribe. But the tooth, kept and cared for by a tribal priest named Singleton, had disappeared, and things among the Ndembu had consequently been going badly (e.g., rampant sickness, poor hunting, frequent accidents). It was discerned that the tooth had invaded the body of a woman (Meru) to feed on her blood.[54] As a result, the woman had become ill and was acting peculiar. An "ihambu ritual" was thus needed to extract the ihamba out of the afflicted woman.

After relating in meticulous detail aspects of the ritual leading up to the "exorcism," Turner narrates the following from her journal:

> Singleton pressed Meru's back, guiding and leading out the tooth—Meru's face in a grin of tranced passion, her back quivering rapidly. Suddenly Meru raised her arm, stretched it in liberation, and I *saw* with my own eyes a giant thing emerging out of the flesh of her back. This thing was a large gray blob about six

51. See Michael J. Harner, *The Jivaro: People of the Sacred Waterfalls* (Garden City, NY: Doubleday/Natural History Press, 1972).

52. Harner has written a guide book for Westerners titled *The Way of the Shaman: A Guide to Power and Healing* (San Francisco: Harper & Row, 1980).

53. Edith Turner, "The Reality of Spirits," *ReVision* 15 no. 1 (1992): 28–32.

54. The curious way in which the ihamba was both a protector *and a threat* to the Ndembu tribe conflicts with the traditional Christian assumption that spirits are either unambiguously good or unambiguously evil, but it reflects a perspective that is common among traditional people.

inches across, a deep gray opaque thing emerging as a sphere. I was amazed—delighted. I still laugh with glee at the realization of having seen it, the ihamba, and so big! We were all just one in triumph. The gray thing was actually out there, visible, and you could see Singleton's hands working and scrabbling on the back—and then the thing was there no more. Singleton had it in his pouch, pressing it in with his other hand as well. . . . He transferred whatever it was into the can and capped the castor oil leaf and bark lid over it. It was done.

Following this, Turner reports that Singleton "squatted down and dredged a long time in the bloody mixture [in the can]." Finally, he "drew out an old tooth, a molar, natural size, ordinary and concrete, with a dark root and one side sheared off as if by an ax. It was the ihamba."[55] Reflecting on this surreal experience, Turner concluded: "I saw with my own eyes a large gray blob of something like plasma emerge from the sick woman's back. Then I knew the Africans were right. There *is* spirit stuff, There [sic] *is* spirit affliction: it isn't a matter of metaphor or symbol, or even psychology."[56]

While we Western Christians may find it challenging to make theological sense of the cross-cultural experiences of Turner and others we've reviewed, I would argue that, whatever else we make of them, they provide empirical support for the New Testament view that spirits and "demon possession" are real. The claim that modern Westerners can no longer believe in such things was never warranted or accurate, but in light of the postmodern turn and the demise of dogmatic naturalism, its fallaciousness is now more apparent than ever.

The Powers and Social-Systemic Realities

Before turning to the final section of this essay, a word needs to be said in response to a perspective on the powers that has become quite popular in some circles. Championed especially by Walter Wink, this perspective doesn't dismiss the powers as mere expressions of a premodern worldview, but neither does it accept that the powers are cosmic agents that possess anything like a consciousness or will over and against human beings. Going beyond merely *associating* the powers with "the spirit" of people groups, institutions, and systemic aspects of society, it identifies them as such. The New Testament's language about the powers is thus interpreted as referring to "the inner aspect of material or tangible manifestations of power," or "the inner or spiritual

55. Edith Turner, *Experiencing Ritual: A New Interpretation of African Healing* (Philadelphia: University of Pennsylvania, 1992), 149–50.
56. Turner, "The Reality of Spirits," 28.

essence, or gestalt, of an institution or state or system."[57] Hence while the "powers do not . . . have a separate spiritual existence," they nevertheless are not "simply a 'personification' of institutional qualities." Rather, they exist "as a real aspect of the institution even when it is not perceived as such."[58] This perspective allows Wink and others to take the language of the powers seriously and even integrate it with the nonreductionistic perspective of certain branches of contemporary science (e.g., emergent property theory), while at the same freeing them to dismiss belief in conscious and volitional spirit agents as mythic.[59]

Responding to the Revisionist Interpretation

What can be said in response to this view? To begin, as I intimated earlier, I am fully persuaded by Wink and scholars who preceded him that the apocalyptic conception of powers in the New Testament is indeed closely associated with social groups, institutions, systematic aspects of society, and structural aspects of creation. At the same time, I cannot follow these scholars in *identifying*, without remainder, the powers with the aspects of society and creation with which they are associated. I offer four arguments in support of my conviction that we should continue to understand the powers to be agents, each of whom possesses something like a mind and a will over against humans.

First, if we interpret his language in its original apocalyptic milieu, it's very hard to deny that Paul thought of the powers as conscious, volitional agents, though modern scholars such as Heinrich Schlier, G. B. Caird, and Wink easily interpret Paul's reference to "the ruler of the power of the air" (Eph. 2:2 NRSV) as a reference to something like "spiritual atmosphere." But as Clinton Arnold has shown, "Air was regarded as the dwelling place of evil spirits in antiquity."[60] By depicting Satan as the "ruler of the power of the air," therefore, Paul was envisioning Satan as an evil agent who lords over

57. Wink, *Naming the Powers*, 104.

58. Ibid., 105. While there is a great deal of novelty in Wink's works, the groundwork for his understanding of the powers as the "interiority" or "spirit" of corporate wholes, etc., was laid by Heinrich Schlier, G. B. Caird, Louis Berkhof, and others.

59. For several examples of this perspective on integrating angels or the powers (or something approximating it) with holistic aspects of contemporary science, see Wolfhart Pannenberg, "The Doctrine of Creation and Modern Science," *Zygon* 23, no. 1 (March, 1988): 3–21; Joseph Bracken, SJ, *Society and Spirit: A Trinitarian Cosmology* (Cranbury, NJ: Associated University Presses, 1991); Matthew Fox and Rupert Sheldrake, *The Physics of Angels* (San Francisco: HarperSanFrancisco, 1996).

60. Clinton Arnold, *Ephesians, Power and Magic: The Concept of Power in Ephesians in Light of Its Historical Setting* (Cambridge: Cambridge University Press, 1989), 60.

lesser evil spirits—which, I submit, goes well beyond an oblique reference to "spiritual atmosphere."

Not only this, but Paul immediately adds that this reign of the power of the air is "the spirit that is now at work among those who are disobedient" (Eph. 2:2 NRSV). In keeping with the apocalyptic conception of the time, this passage depicts the evil one as an agent who intentionally, and intelligently, tempts and deceives people into sinful and rebellious behavior.[61] In fact, the New Testament ascribes a large number of activities and attributes to Satan that can only be said of a conscious, volitional agent. For example, Satan accuses, lies, murders, steals, destroys, afflicts, plans, searches for people to devour, and so on.[62] It seems to me that this sort of language is rendered quite meaningless once we define the powers, including Satan, along the lines suggested by Wink, Schlier, Caird, and others.

Second, Paul says that Christ created all things "in heaven and on earth . . . , things visible and invisible, whether thrones or dominions or rulers or powers" (Col. 1:16 NRSV). Through the victory on the cross, Paul adds, God shall reconcile to himself all these things, "whether on earth or in heaven" (Col. 1:20 NRSV; cf. Phil. 2:9–11; Eph. 1:10). As it concerns the nature of the powers, what's significant about this language is that it distinguishes between powers "in heaven" and powers "on earth." And this, I maintain, argues against all attempts to identify, without remainder, powers in heaven with powers on earth. To be sure, I fully embrace Wink's perspective that all distinct social groups and organizations have a "spirit" that is an emergent property of these groups and organizations and that therefore transcends the individuals that constitute them. But I see no good grounds for identifying without remainder this emergent property with the transcendent powers referred to throughout Scripture.

Third, I am aware that one could argue that the personal manner in which Paul and his contemporaries envisioned the powers reflects a mythic aspect of their culture that must be demythologized if their language is to remain credible and significant for modern people, just as we must (for example) demythologize the ancient Israelite conception of evil as a multiheaded dragon. But while I grant that there are mythic elements involved in every ancient (and

---

61. Consider, for example, the crafty intelligence exhibited by Satan in the temptation narratives (e.g., Luke 4:1–13). See also Acts 5:3; 1 Cor. 5:4–5; 7:5; 2 Cor. 2:11; 6:15; 11:14; Rev. 12:9.

62. Satan accuses (Rev. 12:10), lies and murders (John 8:44; cf. Heb. 2:14), steals and destroys (John 10:10), afflicts (2 Cor. 12:7), plans (2 Cor. 2:11), and searches for people to devour (1 Pet. 5:8, cf. Luke 22:31). Paul also ascribes the ability to scheme to other powers (1 Cor. 2:8), while the Gospels, and arguably Paul as well, assume demons are personal agents (e.g., Mark 5:9–10; 1 Cor. 10:19–21).

modern) conception of spirits, I see absolutely no reason to conclude that the Bible's uniform way of conceiving of spirits as conscious, volitional agents belongs in this category. Indeed, if it's true that we must extract the concept of personal agency from our conception of transcendent powers for the language of the powers to remain credible and significant for us today, must we not do the same for our language about God, the ultimate transcendent spirit power? Few Christian theists are willing to go this far. Yet, if we are willing to accept language about a personal God, on what grounds can we possibly claim it is no longer credible and significant to speak of lesser spirit agents in personal terms? I, for one, have never understood the logic (if it can even be so labeled) that affirms faith in a personal God but finds belief in a personal devil, powers, or demons to be incredible.

This brings me to my fourth, and I believe most important, response to the postmodern revisionist conception of the powers. While nothing substantial is altered when we no longer conceive of cosmic forces as (say) raging waters or many-headed sea monsters, something substantial *is* lost if we no longer conceive of the powers as conscious, volitional agents who exist over and against us. For one thing, as I suggested above, all the personal activity ascribed to the powers becomes altogether meaningless once we deny they are personal agents. And this is not merely an exegetical grievance on my part; it has, I believe, serious practical ramifications. We cannot abandon the concept of the powers as personal agents without thereby seriously compromising the New Testament's understanding that we live in a cosmic war with real, spiritual agents who are continuously strategizing against us. Among other things, as I'll flesh out shortly, once we lose our conviction that we have real enemies "in the heavenlies" that we are to struggle against, we invariably, and unwittingly, begin to view other humans as our enemies.

Not only this, but once we deny that Satan and the powers exist over and against humans, we can no longer appeal to their malevolent, free decisions as part of our overall explanation for the problem of evil. It is no coincidence that, for all of his insightful discussions of "the powers" in his renowned *Powers* trilogy, Wink never appeals to them as a means of explaining any dimension of evil in the world. This loss is extremely significant, in my estimation, for it is difficult, if not impossible, to adequately explain "natural" evil unless there are suprahuman free agents who have the capacity to misuse their free will and authority over nature in malevolent ways.[63]

---

63. See Gregory Boyd, *Satan and the Problem of Evil: Constructing a Trinitarian Warfare Theodicy* (Downers Grove, IL: InterVarsity, 2001), 242–318. I appeal to fallen powers to account for the massive carnage involved in evolution in "Evolution as Cosmic Conflict."

For all these reasons, as much as I appreciate the wealth of insight and overall theology of his work on the powers, I have to part ways with Wink and others who deny the autonomy and personal agency of the powers.

Engaging in Spiritual Warfare

Having surveyed the centrality of the cosmic-conflict motif in Scripture and discussed the reality of the fallen powers involved in this conflict, I would like to conclude my essay by exhorting readers to become participants in spiritual warfare in several biblically grounded ways while addressing several issues that surround the concept of spiritual warfare. I will group my reflections around three challenges.

Wake Up

A soldier in battle conducts himself very differently from a civilian on vacation. The vacationer naturally wants to indulge his or her interests and desires, while avoiding inconveniences as much as possible. But soldiers understand they are called to sacrifice their interests and desires and suffer major inconveniences, if not their lives, to advance the cause for which they fight. The question every follower of Jesus must honestly ask is this: Do I live my life with the mind-set and values of a vacationer or a soldier?

The New Testament clearly calls us to live like a soldier. As good soldiers, we are to always seek to please our "enlisting officer" and not become involved in civilian affairs (2 Tim. 2:4). We are to always be on guard against our enemy who perpetually seeks to lure us into sin and lull us into compromise (e.g., 2 Cor. 2:11; 11:3; 2 Thess. 2:9–10; 1 Pet. 5:8–9). We are to crucify ourselves daily (Luke 9:23), set aside all concerns for worldly comfort and security, and at every moment seek first the kingdom of God (Matt. 6:24–34). We are to live with the singular mission of advancing God's kingdom by the unique way we live, the self-sacrificial way we love, the humble way we serve, and the power we demonstrate against oppressive forces. In sharp contrast to this, almost everything about the consumeristic, materialistic, and hedonistic culture in the West encourages us to live as if we were on vacation. From childhood on we are bombarded with messages that in various ways tell us "the good life" is centered on pursuing "the American dream": indulge yourself as much as possible; acquire as much wealth as possible; live with as much comfort, convenience, and pleasure as possible.

Inasmuch as it's hard for the proverbial fish to notice the water it swims in, this cultural indoctrination presents the biggest challenge facing Western

Christians who are serious about orienting their lives around the worldview and values of the New Testament. The extent to which Western Christians have succumbed to the vacation culture that engulfs us is evidenced by the numerous studies that reveal that the lifestyle and core values of most profess- ing Christians in American are almost indistinguishable from those of their secular neighbors.[64] For this reason, I'm convinced the first and most funda- mental challenge for Western followers of Jesus is to simply *wake up* to the reality of the spiritual warfare that engulfs us and to stop living and thinking as though we were on vacation. While it's understandable that secular people would want to live life as self-indulged and carefree as possible, for a solider this is equivalent to going AWOL. We are rather to understand that our time for rest and relaxation is coming, and once it is here it will be forever. In the meantime, we are called to wear the armor and retain the mind-set of a good solider.

Live a Revolting Lifestyle

While popular American Christianity places a premium on *believing in* Jesus "as your personal Lord and Savior," the New Testament places the call to *imitate* Jesus at the center of the faith. Our profession of faith is devoid of meaning except insofar as it translates into a Jesus-looking way of living (James 2:26). "Whoever claims to live in him," John says, "must live as Jesus did" (1 John 2:6 NIV; cf. John 13:15; Eph. 5:1–2; 1 Pet. 2:20–21). As we noted earlier, when we understand Jesus's life in its first-century context, it becomes clear that every aspect of his countercultural lifestyle manifested the beauty of God's reign while revolting against the powers that fuel and sustain everything ungodly within society and creation. To imitate Jesus, therefore, necessarily involves joining his lifestyle revolt against the powers, and this, I submit, is the primary way Jesus followers are called to participate in God's ongoing battle against the forces of evil. To live like Jesus lived *is* to revolt against the powers the way Jesus revolted.[65]

To be specific, just as Jesus waged war against the powers that fuel greed and sustain poverty by setting aside his riches and entering into solidarity with the poor, we who have committed our lives to Christ are called to manifest the beauty of God's reign and revolt against the powers by swimming upstream

64. See, e.g., "Faith Has Limited Effect on Most People's Behavior" at http://www.barna.org /barna-update/article/5-barna-update/188-faith-has-a-limited-effect-on-most-peoples-behavior/; accessed September 29, 2010.

65. This is the central thesis of Gregory Boyd, *The Myth of a Christian Nation* (Grand Rapids: Zondervan, 2009).

in our culture of greed, by refusing to cling to whatever privileges the fallen system affords us, and by living lives in solidarity with the poor. And just as Jesus revolted against the powers that fuel socioeconomic and political oppression, we who follow Jesus are called to manifest the beauty of God's reign and revolt against the powers by cultivating a lifestyle that refuses to benefit from, or in any way participate in, socioeconomic and political oppression, and by doing everything we can (consistent with the nonviolent call of the kingdom) to push back on this fallen system on behalf of others.

Along the same lines, just as Jesus manifested God's beautiful reign and revolted against the powers that reinforce systemic racism by intentionally violating social norms that keep people divided along racial lines, we who are committed to imitating Jesus are called to manifest the beauty of God's reign and live in revolt against the powers by intentionally defying racist norms and cultivating multiethnic relationships that manifest the "one new humanity" Jesus came to create (Eph. 2:13–14 NIV). And just as Jesus revolted against the powers that inspire systems that oppress and dehumanize women, we who follow Jesus are called to manifest the beauty of God's egalitarian reign and revolt against the powers by cultivating mutually respectful, egalitarian relationships between men and women.

Similarly, just as Jesus revolted against the powers that fuel dehumanizing religion by intentionally violating religious norms that put religious observances before the welfare of people, we who profess faith in Christ are called to manifest the beauty of God's reign and revolt against the powers by refusing to participate in oppressive, judgmental, and dehumanizing forms of religion. And just as Jesus manifested God's universal reign and revolted against the powers that fuel idolatrous patriotism by refusing to buy into the religiously motivated patriotism of his Jewish contemporaries, we who follow Jesus are called to revolt against the powers that fuel idolatrous patriotism by refusing to have any master but Christ or swear allegiance to any kingdom but God's (Matt. 6:24; Phil. 1:27; cf. Heb. 11:13; 1 Pet. 1:17; 2:11).

Finally, and most fundamentally, just as Jesus revolted against the powers that fuel violence by loving his enemies and refusing to use his power to retaliate against them—preferring to be killed rather than to kill—we who are submitted to Jesus are called to manifest the beauty of God's nonviolent reign and revolt against the powers that fuel violence by choosing to love, serve, bless, and pray for our enemies while continually putting off all violence in our mind, heart, word, and deed (e.g., Matt. 5:21–22, 39–45; Eph. 4:30–32). We are to remember that our struggle is *never* "against flesh and blood"—that is to say, against humans (Eph. 6:12)—but against the powers that perpetually try to deceive us into thinking that our enemies are "flesh and blood." Hence, a primary way we wage war against the powers is by unconditionally refusing to ever act violently or nonlovingly toward anyone, even if we consider the person our enemy.

In short, to imitate Jesus is to manifest the beauty of God's reign by living a countercultural life that revolts against everything on earth and in "the spiritual realm" that stands against this reign. This is the primary way we wage war against the powers and thereby bring about God's will "on earth as it is in heaven."

Stand against Demonic Oppression and Infirmities

Finally, Jesus waged war and revolted against forces of evil not only by the way he lived but also by using his divine authority to free people from demons and from physical afflictions. As the New Testament and postapostolic church uniformly understood, God imparted this same authority to drive out demons and heal infirmities to his people, for he wants us to imitate Jesus's warfare in this area as well.[66] There is absolutely no reason to think that people today no longer suffer from demonic oppression or from demonically influenced afflictions. Nor is there any reason to think that Christians today are no longer called and empowered to follow the example of Jesus and the early church to manifest God's reign by freeing people from their oppression and afflictions. And as was the case with Jesus, every deliverance and healing we engage in today pushes back the kingdom of darkness and points to a coming kingdom in which there will be no more spiritual oppression, sickness, disease, or disability.

Recently a number of issues have arisen around this aspect of spiritual warfare, and I'd like to conclude this essay by briefly addressing the three issues that strike me as the most pressing. First, there has been significant debate over whether or not Christians can be "demon possessed." On the one hand, many point out that Christians are owned by God and cannot therefore be possessed by Satan or demons (e.g., 2 Cor. 6:14–16). On the other hand are others who point out that both history and contemporary experience provide numerous examples of sincere Christians being "demon possessed" and benefiting from deliverance prayers. It seems to me this controversy can be largely resolved simply by observing that the New Testament term that is often translated "demon possessed" (*demonizomai*) literally means "to be acted on by a demon" and does not in any way suggest the person has become the owned property

---

66. Adolf von Harnack captures the importance of exorcism in the early postapostolic church when he notes that "it was as exorcists that Christians went out into the great world, and exorcism formed one very powerful method of their mission and propaganda." *The Mission and Expansion of Christianity in the First Three Centuries* (New York: Putnam's Sons, 1908), 131.

of demons or of Satan.[67] While all kingdom people belong to God, it s nevertheless possible for them to have "strongholds" of demonic influence in their mind (2 Cor. 10:3–5). And the experience of multitudes throughout history and still today demonstrates that, in the course of freeing Christians from demonic strongholds, demonic resistance can sometimes become so intense it results in the demonized believer exhibiting some of the earlier discussed behaviors that are typically associated with "demon possession."

Second, there's been a good deal of discussion and disagreement over the relationship between a deliverance approach to demonization and a therapeutic approach to mental disorders, especially in light of many mental disorders that manifest in ways that resemble demonized people.[68] The most balanced approach, it seems to me, is to avoid the extreme of assuming that everything that looks like demonization is actually caused by demons, or the extreme of assuming that everything that looks like demonization is merely a psychological disorder. Since we are usually not certain in advance about what is actually going on, the approach we take in the counseling and deliverance ministry of the church I pastor is to "shoot in both directions." We pray warfare prayers *and* engage in counseling with everyone who comes in, regardless of whether they believe they're in need of deliverance or counseling. We usually discover the extent to which a person is demonized or psychologically wounded by how they respond to each approach. In fact, we have found that there are usually psychological wounds that rendered a demonized person vulnerable to demonic influence and that need to be addressed through counseling even after the person is freed from their oppression.

Finally, a word should be said about the controversy surrounding the appropriateness of praying for the deliverance not only of individuals but of entire geographical regions. There are some who contend that "territorial"

67. For this reason I prefer the transliteration "demonization" over the phrase "demon possessed," and the term "deliverance" over "exorcism."

68. The *Journal of Psychology and Theology*, for instance, has offered a context for discussion and debate on these topics over the last few decades. See, for example, the exchange between Sall and Bach: Millard J. Sall, "Demon Possession or Psychopathology? A Clinical Differentiation," *Journal of Psychology and Theology* 4 (1976): 286–90; Paul J. Bach, "Demon Possession and Psychopathology: A Theological Relationship," *Journal of Psychology and Theology* 7 (1979): 22–26; Sall, "A Response to Demon Possession and Psychopathology: A Theological Relationship," *Journal of Psychology and Theology* 7 (1979): 27–30. See also Rodger K. Bufford, "Demonic Influence and Mental Disorders," *Journal of Psychology and Theology* 18 (1989): 35–47; J. Thomas Miegs, "Pastoral Care Methods and Demonology in Selected Writings," *Journal of Psychology and Theology* 5 (Summer 1977): 234–46; Sydney H. T. Page, "The Role of Exorcism in Clinical Practice and Pastoral Care," *Journal of Psychology and Theology* 17 (1989): 121–31; and Henry A. Virkler and Mary B. Virkler, "Demonic Involvement in Human Life and Illness," *Journal of Psychology and Theology* 5 (1977): 95–102.

powers sometimes hold entire regions in bondage and that the work of the gospel will be hindered until these powers are cast down.[69] People who believe this sometimes spend extraordinary amounts of time, money, and energy mobilizing believers to collectively take authority over these spirits.

I think there are compelling arguments supporting this concept of "territorial spirits" and even some precedent for the practice of coming against them. First, the frequent references to "the gods of the nations" throughout Scripture as well as the reference in Daniel 10 (discussed above) to the "prince of Persia" and "prince of Greece" who fought with Michael (vv. 13, 20) clearly suggests that particular powers can exercise an oppressive influence over particular geographical regions. Second, the earlier discussed apocalyptic view of the powers as associated with people groups, institutions, systemic aspects of society, and particular nations arguably supports this conclusion. Third, that we are called to revolt against the powers by cultivating a kingdom lifestyle, as well as Paul's explicit teaching to "struggle" or "wrestle" (*palē*) against the powers (Eph. 6:12), gives some biblical support to the claim that believers should pray against territorial spirits. Fourth, we find some precedent in the early church for praying against territorial spirits. And finally, while the evidence is entirely anecdotal, some argue that the practice of coming against territorial powers actually works.[70] For these reasons I cannot, as a matter of principle, object to the practice of Christians praying against territorial powers.

However, there is no example in Scripture of God's people engaging in this type of spiritual warfare, and this must surely be considered relevant. The angel in Daniel 10 said he had to return to the battle "in the spiritual realm" to join Michael against the "prince of Persia" and "the prince of Greece," but *he never solicited Daniel's help in this battle*. Given the complete lack of biblical precedent, it seems unwise for disciples to ever make praying against territorial powers a centerpiece of their ministry or to invest large amounts of time, money, and energy in this endeavor.

Conclusion

In this essay I've attempted to demonstrate that the concept of cosmic conflict runs throughout Scripture and lies at the heart of the New Testament. To live

69. See, e.g., John Dawson, *Taking Our Cities for God: How to Break Spiritual Strongholds* (Altamonte Springs, FL: Creation House, 1989); George Otis Jr., *The Last of the Giants* (Tarrytown, NY: Chosen, 1991); and C. Paul Wagner, *Engaging the Enemy: How to Fight and Defeat Territorial Spirits* (Ventura, CA: Regal, 1991).

70. George Otis Jr. has produced two documentaries to this effect. *Transformations I* (1999) and *Transformations II: The Glory Spreads* (2001).

as a disciple of Jesus and therefore under the reign of God is to live in revolt against the powers and demons. I've further argued that, while all conceptions of the powers, angels, and demons have a mythic dimension to them, there is no compelling reason to conclude that the entities themselves are mythic, but there are many biblical, theological, and even empirical reasons for concluding they are real. And, finally, I've fleshed out three practical aspects of the warfare that I believe followers of Jesus are called to engage in. It's my deep conviction that all disciples need to wake up to the reality of the cosmic conflict that engulfs them, they need to live a kingdom-centered lifestyle that revolts against the powers, and they need to manifest divine authority against demonization and infirmities whenever possible. To be a disciple of Jesus is to be involved in spiritual warfare.

RESPONSE TO GREGORY BOYD

WALTER WINK AND MICHAEL HARDIN

There are many things to take note of and appreciate in Greg Boyd's essay. However, from our perspective much of the benefit of Boyd's argument is nullified by his insistence on the existence of a "personal" devil. This is perhaps the most significant difference between Boyd's and our understanding of the satan. We developed this theory of the myth of redemptive violence using René Girard's theory of religion.[71] The mimetic theory or the victimage mechanism (it can go by either in the literature) offers an anthropological understanding of the satan. It is this interpretive matrix that we will utilize in our responses.

Before we turn to the issue of a personal satan, we note several areas of felicitous agreement with Boyd. First is his insistence that Jesus's lifestyle was one of "warfare." Boyd notes Jesus's care for the poor and oppressed, empowerment of women, antinationalist stance, and pacifism. Each of these is a crucial aspect of the systemic battle Jesus engages in his conflict with the principalities and powers. Second, Boyd has rightly defined the four major problems of a naturalistic worldview.[72] Third, Boyd's wake-up call at the end

71. Walter Wink, *Engaging the Powers: Discernment and Resistance in a World of Domination* (Minneapolis: Fortress, 1992). In the book, I say: "There is, however, a hypothesis, still being tested, but possessed of such heuristic power that it deserves serious consideration. It is René Girard's theory of the scapegoat" (144).

72. See also Wink, "The New Worldview: Spirit at the Core of Everything," in *Transforming the Powers: Peace, Justice, and the Domination System*, ed. Ray Gingerich and Ted Grimsrud (Minneapolis: Fortress, 2006). See also Wink, *Naming the Powers: The Language of Power in the New Testament* (Minneapolis: Fortress Press, 1984); Wink, *Unmasking the Powers: The Invisible Forces that Determine Human Existence* (Minneapolis: Fortress, 1986); Wink, *Engaging the Powers*; Wink, *When the Powers Fall: Reconciliation in the Healing of Nations* (Minneapolis:

of his essay is indeed a "call to arms" but to a war fought not with worldly weapons but with the weapons of the Spirit: love, peace, nonviolence, and forgiveness.[73]

While it is true that spiritual warfare is an element in the Bible, it is not the central theme. The Bible does not announce a dualism between good and evil but is the redemptive story of the overcoming of evil (John 1:5). In the Bible, redemption has many motifs and metaphors, and the battle with Satan is just one among many. Even though the Christus Victor theory of the atonement dominated the horizon of the Christian church for its first thousand years, the concept of the devil underwent many changes. A belief in a "personal" satan is not required for Christian theology. No Christian creed ever enshrined confession of a personal devil or an ontological satan. One does not need to believe in a "conscious, volitional" satan in order to be a Christian or in order to believe that Jesus does battle with "the dark side" in his life, death, and resurrection, and as our high priest at the right hand of God.

It may be the case that some elements of the Jewish tradition perceived the satan as a personal being. The oldest strata place the satan in the heavenly council as the divine chief of police turned attorney general who seeks to identify those who do not obey the divine will, as in Job and Zechariah. Following the exile and under the influence of the dualism of Persian Zoroastrianism, the satan leads an army of angels to do battle with the almighty and loses. According to some pseudepigraphal accounts, the satan begs for a small portion of his army to be allowed to remain behind to torment the followers of YHWH. Some Second Temple Jews also psychologized the satan as the "evil yetzer" or impulse, popularized by the fiction of a devil on one shoulder whispering in one ear while an angel from heaven is on the other, counseling obedience to God.[74] It is as if the very concept of evil personified goes from

Fortress, 1998); Wink, *Cracking the Gnostic Code: The Powers in Gnosticism* (Atlanta: Scholars Press, 1993); and Wink, *The Powers That Be: Theology for a New Millennium* (New York: Doubleday, 1999).

73. See also Michael Hardin, *The Jesus Driven Life* (Lancaster, PA: JDL Press, 2010).

74. The development of the idea of the satan has been researched by Jeffrey Burton Russell in *The Devil* (Ithaca, NY: Cornell University Press, 1977); Russell, *Satan* (Ithaca, NY: Cornell University Press, 1981); Russell, *Lucifer* (Ithaca, NY: Cornell University Press, 1984); and Russell, *Mephistopheles* (Ithaca, NY: Cornell University Press, 1986), as well as in a summary of these books in Russell, *The Prince of Darkness* (Ithaca, NY: Cornell University Press, 1988). Four other helpful books are Henry Ansgar Kelly, *Satan: A Biography* (New York: Cambridge University Press, 2006); Elaine Pagels, *The Origin of Satan* (New York: Random House, 1995); T. J. Wray and Gregory Mobley, *The Birth of Satan* (New York: Palgrave Macmillan, 2005); and Gerald Messadie, *A History of the Devil* (New York: Kodansha International, 1996). Alan E. Bernstein, *The Formation of Hell: Death and Retribution in the Ancient and Early Christian Worlds* (Ithaca, NY: Cornell University Press, 1993) contains helpful information. Raymund

the satan as an aspect or part of the council of God, to an entity with powers like God, to that which is human. In other words, in Judaism the concept of the devil goes from being a theological concept to an anthropological one. Girard argues that this is the very notion that lies behind Jesus saying "I saw satan fall like lightning from heaven" (Luke 10:18).

These mixed and varied accounts indicate that the idea of the satan undergoes continual transformation and thus is not a fixed idea. So we should not be surprised to see the satan undergo a later development in medieval Christianity and then after the Enlightenment. The devil, as the embodiment of evil, is an idea or concept that continually undergoes the process of interpretation.

But the devil is not the only concept that needs reinterpretation. One might also question Boyd's understanding of "person" as a conscious, volitional creature, which sounds more like Aristotle than Paul. The concept of the autonomous subject or person of modernism has come under withering and fatal fire in the twentieth century. Philosophers from Heidegger to Derrida have deconstructed the notion of subject (not always for the better), but the autonomous self or what is known as "faculty psychology" has also been indicted. The problematic idea of the "conscious, volitional human" inherited from Thomas Aquinas provoked what F. LeRon Shults calls the "turn to relationality" in psychology and anthropology.[75] It is now recognized that persons do not exist in isolated vacuums but that our personhood can be described as the net sum of our relationships. I am in relationships, therefore I am.

The idea of persons as constituted by their relationships lies behind Girard's neologism that we are *interdividual*. The implications of this shift to relationality suggest that conceiving of the satan and of humans as volitional, conscious (or free, moral) agents is antiquated and no longer very useful. What Boyd would attribute to the satan (consciousness, will) is, from the perspective of mimetic theory, the satanic ambivalence of order and disorder. The satan, as mimetically engaged violence transferred onto a random victim, both disorders and reorders human culture and thus human life. Satan is that element of humanity that reckons with the problem of unrestrained violence. Or as Girard says, "Satan can therefore always put enough order back into the world to prevent the total destruction of what he possesses without depriving himself for too long of his favorite pastime, which is to sow disorder, violence,

---

Schwager and James G. Williams interpret the devil anthropologically in *Banished from Eden* (Leominster, UK: Gracewing, 2006), 143–65. On the rabbinic understanding of the satan, see Ephraim E. Urbach, *The Sages: The World and Wisdom of the Rabbis of the Talmud* (Cambridge, MA: Harvard University Press, 2001), 135–83.

75. F. LeRon Shults, *Reforming Theological Anthropology* (Grand Rapids: Eerdmans, 2003).

and misfortune among his subjects."[76] The satan, as a mechanism of violence controlling violence, is the generative matrix of human culture and religion.

How might this shift affect the idea of the satan? For that, we can profitably turn to the phenomenon of possession. Boyd contends, "Whatever else we make of them, [incidents of perceived demonic possession] provide empirical support for the New Testament view that spirits and 'demon possession' are real." Boyd (as well as Wagner and Greenwood) would have us believe that disembodied evil spirits go around looking for habitation in humans.

Now it is true that certain persons demonstrate behaviors that for a long time were attributed to possession by evil spirits. Since Freud, however, such phenomena have been understood and treated interpersonally. Like the idea of the satan, demonic possession has been anthropologized. Jean-Michel Oughourlian, associate professor of psychology at the Sorbonne, has examined the phenomenon of possession in light of Girard's mimetic theory and concludes that possession is a phenomenon of a person whose desires are an imitation of the social group around them. The multiplicity of these, often conflicting, imitated desires is manifested as a form of hysteria. That is, the possessed is in the thrall of an alien Other(s); this Other(s) is not supernatural but psychosocial.[77] This is precisely the same definition I (Walter) have given to the satanic Other. This scientific model also explains a phenomenon we will explore in our response to Wagner and Greenwood: the power of the mob.

The Girardian model, upon which we build, provides, for the first time, an adequate understanding of the satan from the viewpoint of the human sciences. That it does so not in a reductionist manner, nor in a materialistic fashion, but by taking the Bible seriously is perhaps its greatest strength. Contemporary Christians need no longer be enchanted with a belief that supernatural alien demons somehow circulate throughout their world seeking habitation; rather, we can look to the crooked, broken, and evil contagion of human desire mediated through the Other as the source of our woes.

In a volume honoring René Girard, I (Michael) noted,

> René's development of mimetic theory has removed the Satan from the realms of our mythologizing, from the false transcendence that we have given to evil. Satan is no longer to be perceived as an abstraction, as something akin to God,

---

76. The principal text in which Girard accomplishes the demystification of the satan is *I See Satan Fall Like Lightning* (Maryknoll, NY: Orbis, 2001), esp. 96.

77. Jean-Michel Oughourlian, *The Puppet of Desire: The Psychology of Hysteria, Possession and Hypnosis* (Stanford: Stanford University Press, 1991), esp. 98–144. See also Stephen Morris, "The Nature of Mimetic Desire: Interdividuation as Phantom Community" (unpublished paper presented to the Colloquium on Violence and Religion, 2002), who uses the work of criminologist Lonnie Athens to understand the "voices" that violent predators hear.

but as one whose disguise is removed. Satan is an anthropological category. Evil arises from within, not without, the human species. Evil does not exist prior to the generative power of imitated desire. Thus there is no transcendental dualism that has to be posited prior to the advent of humanity's mythmaking.

Questions of theodicy become unnecessary from this perspective. History is seen to be less of a battle between good and evil than it is to be seen as full of the promise of redemption. This redemption does not take place as the false redemption of myth, but it does take place within myth, at its very center. In becoming the center of myth as the persecuted victim, Jesus transforms that center by seeking forgiveness for us and thus brings about not only the transformation of desire but also the transformation of myth and its structures and systems, and our history as well.[78]

Yes, we can still pray "Deliver us from the evil one," but now we know that we have met the enemy. It is us. Jesus has come to deliver us from our own satanic propensities, and it is to him that we give all honor and glory.

---

78. Michael Hardin, "Mimetic Theory and Christian Theology in the Twenty-First Century," in *For René Girard* (East Lansing: Michigan State University Press, 2009), 265.

RESPONSE TO GREGORY BOYD

DAVID POWLISON

Gregory Boyd's three main points are well taken. I will briefly elaborate each of his broad insights and in each case will raise a question. I will then raise one larger question about how he conceptualizes the relationship between God and the powers of darkness.

One Great War

First, heaven and earth are full of contention. From Genesis through Revelation, cosmic conflict is a ground motif. It touches the heart of what it means to be human—and Christian. Our earthly struggles and the heavenly battle intertwine in one great war between truth and lie, good and evil, beauty and squalor. Life and death hang in the balance.

But Boyd's argument shows significant omissions. He never mentions the role *our* sinfulness plays (except to deprecate overemphasis on the forgiveness of sins). In the Bible's portrayal, spiritual warfare is momentous not only because of cosmic powers and social injustices but also because each of us participates (and is continually tempted to participate) in evil. Devil, world, and flesh cooperate—and our choices are the flashpoint. This is why neither evil spirits nor social activism is the focal point for spiritual warfare.

Consistent with his omission of sinfulness, Boyd does not mention that Jesus set aside his divine prerogatives in order to identify with *sinful* men and women. He died in our place—whether poor or rich, white or black, female or male, American or Iraqi, powerless or powerful. All of us are "wretched, pitiable, poor, blind, and naked" (Rev. 3:17 NRSV), though self-delusion anesthetizes self-awareness of need. Surely "the blood of the covenant poured out for many for the forgiveness of sins" is not just an exaggerated preoccupation of some "American evangelicals." It is the center of Christian faith, whether evangelical, Reformed, Lutheran, Anglican, Roman Catholic, or Orthodox.

In the end, Boyd's Jesus sounds more like a social activist hero than the Lamb of God. Boyd is right that Christ humbles the powerful and dignifies the weak. But Jesus does this through the counterintuitive "foolishness of God," a dynamic of reckoning with our sin by his grace. The Bible's approach to social activism is the only approach that actively looks out for the interests of the lowly and victimized without creating a victim identity, without making excuses for reactive sins, without promoting self-righteousness. Whatever your status or condition in life, you learn to be truly evenhanded. Love for neighbor is without bias, neither partial to the poor nor deferential to the great (Lev. 19:15–18). The wise wish on themselves neither poverty nor riches, recognizing that each occasions characteristic sins (Prov. 30:8–9). There is no partiality with God, whether you are a master (Eph. 6:9) or a slave (Col. 3:25).

Second, to be educated, modern, and Western is no barrier to believing that the evil one and his servants exist. If God's enemies exist, it is no stretch to recognize that they are intelligent, purposeful, and morally accountable. Gregory Boyd and I both happen to be educated, modern, Western people who take the powers of darkness as realities. Of course, many people with the same outward characteristics anchor themselves in disbelief—"Unless I see and touch I will never believe." Their commitment to a rationalist, empiricist, and materialist worldview excludes belief in the Apostles' Creed no less than belief that Satan exists as a malice worker. Boyd's critique of Walter Wink's view is on target.

But Boyd cites examples from animist cultures as a significant component in his argument for the existence of demons. This is at best a secondary and ambiguous argument. Such phenomena might make the existence of a generic dark side possible or even plausible. But since Satan's essential character is as liar, we should not be surprised that animistic phenomena mislead about the actual nature and purposes of evil spirits. It may be interesting that some secular scholars have opened their minds to spiritist phenomena, but it adds little to the Christian contention that Satan holds sway within the normal as much as the bizarre. The bizarre, in fact, may be a sleight of hand that creates fear and excitement, reinforcing the animist worldview. It distracts everyone, whether scholars or strugglers, from attending to the strong grip of evil and the foolishness of human hearts.

Third, Jesus enlists us as the boots on the ground in his cosmic conflict. We who were evil and accursed have switched sides by the redeeming grace of God our Savior. We are called to a "Jesus-looking way of living," becoming disciples who are like the master, obeying all he has commanded. Boyd's critique of Wagner and Greenwood's view, noting the misdirection of energies toward territorial spirits, is on target.

But Boyd's deprecation of faith in Jesus as our Savior undermines his call to imitate Jesus as our Lord. Boyd is right that "popular American Christianity" often forgets the imitation of Christ (ending up in ineffectual pietism). But the bus can run off the road in the other direction too. Church history offers abundant examples of what happens when active imitation of Christ is not grounded in the gift of Christ's mercies. It slides into strenuous moralism, whether heroic or depressive. Ephesians offers a healthy corrective to both pietism and moralism.

God's Will and Unruly Wills

The second half of this response essay raises the more fundamental question of how Boyd conceptualizes God's relationship to the powers of evil. The *greater* part of wisdom consists in understanding the *relationship between* complementary truths. Boyd makes a number of valuable points in a way that pits one biblical truth against another biblical truth. He presents us with an either/or choice rather than doing justice to the complex relationship between complementary truths. In particular, how do powerful, godless, unruly wills relate to God's sovereign rule over all things?

Boyd notes, "Much of what comes to pass in history does not reflect God's benevolent will but rather reflects the wills of agents working at cross-purposes with God. The world we live in looks like a war zone because the world *is* a war zone." This is true, as far as it goes, and eloquently stated. The sum total of contra-God thoughts and actions is incalculable: "Every thought of the intentions of [mankind's] heart was only evil continually" (Gen. 6:5 ESV). And that doesn't even include the purposes and actions of invisible hosts of evil wholly dedicated to malice and mendacity. The givens of fallen natures have not changed since Genesis 6 was written.

This emphasis on fallen natures is important pastorally. In many ministry situations, it needs to come early in the queue of relevant truths. For example, some people (both Christian and Muslim) reflexively cut and run to "the sovereignty of God," effectively anesthetizing sensitivity to pain, perplexity, need, injustice, and the significance of our choices. God's purported control of all things—"If God wills"/*insha'Allah*—is used to rationalize a shrug of stoic detachment and passivity. And other people (both believing and unbelieving) blame and curse a God who could have made life turn out differently. They vault over the reality that willful agents work at cross-purposes with God (and skip over their own willfulness too). God's control is acknowledged only as an accusation, and only when events thwart the individual's will. Both stoicism and hostility need to appreciate how evil wills actively work.

But Boyd denies God's sovereign control over evil. He quotes Augustine's phrase—"The will of the Omnipotent is always undefeated"—disapprovingly, asserting that centuries of theological reflection used God's sovereignty to deny the reality of cosmic conflict. In this section of his *Enchiridion*, however, Augustine carefully works with *three* complementary biblical realities.

First, the wills of fallen people and angels actively work evil. Much of what happens is dark and destructive. Augustine saw the same evils that Boyd sees.

Second, the Bible consistently uses the phrase "God's will" (and its many equivalents) in two different ways. One focuses on his kingly power, the other on his prophetic authority. Sometimes God's will refers to his providential, purposeful rule over all events. This "will of control" describes what *he* does:

> Instead, you ought to say, "*If the Lord wills*, we will live and do this or that" (James 4:15 ESV, emphasis added);
>
> But on taking leave of them he said, "I will return to you *if God wills*," and he set sail from Ephesus (Acts 18:21 ESV, emphasis added).

Other times God's will refers to our call to obedience. This "will of command" describes what he calls *us* to do:

> [Jesus said,] "For whoever does *the will of My Father* in heaven is my brother and sister and mother" (Matt. 12:50 ESV, emphasis added);
>
> Rejoice always, pray without ceasing, give thanks in all circumstances; for this is *the will of God* in Christ Jesus for you (1 Thess. 5:16–18 ESV, emphasis added).

God's good will of control is omnipotent over events but is unknown to us except in retrospect. Trust him. He reveals his good will of command. Obey him.

Third, a deep question arises where cosmic conflict intersects the double meaning of "God's will." How do violators of God's will of command operate within God's will of control? The Bible often portrays contrary, hostile wills as in some way subject to God. Despite culpably destructive intentions, evildoers unwittingly and unintentionally serve larger purposes of salvation and judgment.

As for you, you meant evil against me, but God meant it for good (Gen. 50:20 ESV);

For this purpose I have raised you [Pharaoh] up, to show you my power, so that my name may be proclaimed in all the earth (Exod. 9:16 ESV);

Now the Spirit of the LORD departed from Saul, and a harmful [lit., "evil, bad"] spirit from the LORD tormented him (1 Sam. 16:14 ESV);

Truly in this city there were gathered together against your holy servant Jesus, whom you anointed, both Herod and Pontius Pilate, along with the Gentiles and the peoples of Israel, to do whatever your hand and your plan had predestined to take place (Acts 4:27–28 ESV);

So to keep me from becoming conceited because of the surpassing greatness of the revelations, a thorn was given me in the flesh, a messenger of Satan to harass me, to keep me from becoming conceited (2 Cor. 12:7 ESV);

What if God, desiring to show his wrath and to make known his power, has endured with much patience vessels of wrath prepared for destruction? (Rom. 9:22 ESV).

Evil intends and does evil, but good runs incomprehensibly deeper.

Augustine held these three complementary truths in relationship rather than excising any one of them because it was inconvenient. Boyd quoted only the final clause of a rich assertion: "God achieves some of his purposes—which are, of course, all good—through the evil wills of bad men. But, however strong the wills either of angels or of men, whether good or evil, whether they will what God wills or will something else, the will of the Omnipotent is always undefeated."[79]

That is not aloof determinism minimizing the power of evil. It is part of wisdom.

Boyd is half right that the hostile-to-God motif "does not reflect God's benevolent will." This is true—on the surface of our experience. But what appears transparently benevolent to us does not exhaust Scripture's portrayal of God's ways. Augustine, following Scripture, sought to do justice both to mercy (exceedingly benevolent to his children of grace) and to justice (malevolent to sons of disobedience, benevolent to the victims of evildoing, painfully benevolent to God's straying, forgetful children).

Jesus's crucifixion expresses a complex benevolence. The iniquitous malevolence of contrary and culpable wills engineered judicial murder: Judas's

79. Augustine, *Enchiridion on Faith, Hope, and Love*, trans. Albert C. Outler, 43, available at http://www.ccel.org/a/augustine/enchiridion/formats/enchiridion1.0.pdf.

treachery, Satan's hatred, a hostile sense of entitlement in the Sanhedrin, callous Roman power. Simultaneously, Jesus's death expressed God's holy malevolence against sin—*our* sins. And simultaneously, the cross expresses God's will for our salvation. By the inestimable love of the Father of Mercies the cross thus expresses God's holy benevolence to sinful human beings.

All Scripture bears witness that God is glorified both in his mercy and his justice. Evil is the dark foil against which both mercy and justice shine as light in darkness. God's higher, deeper purposes are at work in and through evil and suffering. Like the reality of our conflict with evil, this truth is a part of wise pastoral encouragement.[80]

80. Job; Ps. 119:67, 71; Rom. 8:18–39; 2 Cor. 1:3–9; and 1 Peter are starting points for probing this vast theme.

Response to Gregory Boyd

C. Peter Wagner and Rebecca Greenwood

Those who identify with our stream are indebted to Gregory Boyd for providing an indispensable theological foundation for our spiritual warfare activities. His two books *God at War* and *Satan and the Problem of Evil* are unrivaled in the literature on theodicy. In fact, when *God at War* first came out and I (Peter) read it, I immediately wrote this endorsement: "*God at War* raises the current discussion of spiritual warfare to a new and unanticipated level of scholarly investigation. I am ecstatic with the integrity with which Gregory Boyd develops his convincing argument for a biblical worldview. This is an extremely important work for all who wish to advance God's kingdom today." The publisher liked it so much that the endorsement has been highlighted in every printing since.[81]

Boyd's essay in this volume leaves little for us to criticize or contradict. However, there are some areas where he might have connected a few more dots for the reader or where we would urge him to go further.

Satan's Power and Authority

In his brief section, "The Battle against Satan," Boyd eloquently describes the far-reaching power and authority attributed to our enemy Satan. While Jesus and his followers believed that Yahweh was the *ultimate* Lord over creation, by using the term "the prince of this world," Jesus was acknowledging that Satan

---

81. Gregory A. Boyd, *God at War: The Bible and Spiritual Conflict* (Downers Grove, IL: InterVarsity, 1997), interior flyleaf.

was the *functional* lord of earth at the present time. Satan had gathered all the kingdoms of the world into a single kingdom of darkness under his rule (Rev. 11:15). John sees the whole world "under the power of the evil one" (1 John 5:19 NRSV), and Paul labels Satan "the god of this world" (2 Cor. 4:4 NRSV).

With all this, Boyd does not stop to explain how Satan attained the power and authority to rule the world in the first place. At the risk of redundancy (because we have raised this point elsewhere), we believe this issue is an essential component of the discussion and should not be omitted. Satan, or Lucifer, was created by God as a powerful angelic being and given authority to use this power in the heavenly realm. However, when he rebelled, he was cast from heaven. He retained his inherent power, but God withdrew his authority. From then on, it would be Satan's greatest desire to regain the authority he had lost.

His opportunity came when God finished his creation of the earth by creating Adam and Eve in his own image and offering them dominion over all the rest of creation in the earthly realm (see Gen. 1:28). Satan knew that Adam had the option of taking dominion or of giving dominion away. Unfortunately he chose the latter, and Satan succeeded in usurping Adam's authority over the earth. From that point on, Satan had both the power and authority to fit the descriptions of our enemy that Gregory Boyd displays in his essay.

Personal Holiness as Spiritual Warfare

We will direct our remaining comments toward Boyd's part 3, "Engaging in Spiritual Warfare." We need to note that Greg Boyd personifies the extremely rare combination of a respected, prolific academic theologian and a practicing pastor (at Woodland Hills Church in St. Paul). He shows his pastoral side when he personalizes engaging in spiritual warfare by characterizing it as "living a revolting lifestyle." The more we as individuals live a lifestyle reflecting Jesus, the more we defeat the devil. What does this mean? It means identifying with the poor, coming against greed, rejecting racism, advocating gender equality, rejecting oppressive and dehumanizing forms of religion, avoiding idolatrous patriotism, and so on.

He summarizes his point of view by saying, "In short, to imitate Jesus is to manifest the beauty of God's reign by living a countercultural life that revolts against everything on earth and 'the spiritual realm' that stands against this reign. This is the primary way we wage war against the powers and thereby bring about God's will 'on earth as it is in heaven.'"

While we applaud the lifestyle characteristics that Boyd highlights, we are not convinced that Christian people, living good, holy lives, can be regarded as "the primary way" to engage in spiritual warfare. If exhibiting Christlike lifestyles is seen as the *primary* methodology of spiritual warfare, then all other methods must, in some sense, be *secondary*. To the contrary, we feel that living a godly life, which could be closely related to putting on the armor of God in Ephesians 6, is a prerequisite for entering the battle, not the engagement in battle itself. As a matter of fact, we would not consider cultivating holiness as much a direct encounter with the devil or his agents as some would like to think. We are afflicted by the world, the flesh, and the devil, and we believe that the struggle for a godly lifestyle usually involves more confrontation with the world and the flesh than the devil.

However, when the devil or his demons do enter the picture, deliverance is needed. Boyd acknowledges this and even describes how his church has a deliverance ministry, combined with psychological counseling. We call this ground-level spiritual warfare, and we consider it closer to the primary way of doing spiritual warfare than just living good individual lifestyles.

Concerns about Strategic-Level Spiritual Warfare

We have no quarrel with Boyd on issues of ground-level spiritual warfare, but we do when he deals with strategic-level spiritual warfare, which he mostly characterizes as coming against territorial spirits. After a brief discussion, Boyd concludes that he "cannot, as a matter of principle, object to the practice of Christians praying against territorial powers." So far so good. However, in the next paragraph, he shows this was a reluctant conclusion by scoffing at those who "invest large amounts of time, money, and energy is this endeavor." We, and the fairly large circle of colleagues we work with, happen to be among those who do actually invest heavily in strategic-level spiritual warfare. While we agree with Boyd that it should never be a "centerpiece" of our ministry, we definitely do consider it one of the central strategies in our attempt to see God's kingdom come to earth as it is in heaven.

Let's focus on Boyd's chief argument for being tentative at best or negative at worst on strategic-level spiritual warfare. He says, "There is no example in Scripture of God's people engaging in this type of spiritual warfare, and this must surely be considered relevant." He goes on to speak of "this complete lack of biblical precedent." It goes without saying that, if Boyd's observations are correct, our case for engaging the enemy in strategic-level spiritual warfare would be seriously weakened. However, we do not feel that Boyd is correct.

To begin with, Paul in Ephesians—which contains proportionately more power language than any of Paul's other epistles—commands the church (i.e.,

God's people) to make known (this sounds like direct engagement) to the principalities and powers in the heavenly places (including territorial spirits?) the wisdom of God (Eph. 3:10). We see this as a mandate for strategic-level spiritual warfare.

But beyond that, the book of Acts is a good field manual for us to examine. As I (Peter) wrote my commentary on Acts, I did so with a paradigm that included a mandate for spiritual warfare including confronting territorial spirits when necessary.[82] As I did, I believe I found five examples of events in Acts that could be interpreted as strategic-level spiritual warfare:

Peter versus Simon Magus (Acts 8:13–24)

Peter versus Herod (Acts 12:3–19)

Paul versus Bar-Jesus (or Elymas) (Acts 13:6–13)

Paul versus the Python spirit (Acts 16:16–24)

Paul versus Diana (or Artemis) of the Ephesians (Acts 19:23–41)

Granted, the classical commentaries on Acts do not address the issue of possible strategic-level spiritual warfare in these passages. The existence of such things as "territorial spirits" had not entered the minds of many of those biblical scholars. When I exegeted the passages, however, I brought a set of questions to the table that would not ordinarily appear on the agendas of others. That would explain why we might have come to some different conclusions. I will not hesitate to admit that I do not have airtight arguments for my thoughts on these matters. At the same time, I think I have given reasonably good answers to the questions raised in the texts, at least from our (Peter's and Rebecca's) point of view.

Space will not permit exegetical discussions of these five passages of Scripture; however, the details can be found in these three books: *The Book of Acts*, *Spiritual Warfare Strategy*, and *Authority to Tread*.[83] In these books we try to establish strong biblical precedents for strategic-level spiritual warfare, and hopefully we adequately address the concerns that Boyd expresses toward the conclusion of his essay.

---

82. See C. Peter Wagner, *The Book of Acts: A Commentary* (Ventura, CA: Regal, 2008).

83. See Wagner, *The Book of Acts*; C. Peter Wagner, *Spiritual Warfare Strategy: Confronting Spiritual Powers* (Shippensburg, PA: Destiny Image, 1996), chaps. 7–9; and Rebecca Greenwood, *Authority to Tread: An Intercessor's Guide to Strategic-Level Spiritual Warfare* (Grand Rapids: Chosen, 2005), 26–28.

4

The Strategic-Level Deliverance Model

C. PETER WAGNER AND REBECCA GREENWOOD

A Personal Note (C. Peter Wagner)

When the word first came that Baker Academic was prepared to publish a symposium on the subject of spiritual warfare, I was overjoyed. When I later received word that my counterparts would include no less than Walter Wink, David Powlison, and Gregory Boyd, I was elated. I would anticipate that this document will enjoy quite a long shelf life as an aid to those who endeavor to teach the theology of the kingdom of God to the Christian leaders of tomorrow.

Initially I was reluctant to agree to participate because I did not feel that, over the past few years, I had kept myself sufficiently up to date on the subject. I am currently giving my primary attention to other pursuits. After some discussion, however, the editors suggested that I might bring in a coauthor who had kept abreast of developments in the arena of spiritual warfare. I immediately suggested that I approach Rebecca "Becca" Greenwood, author of *Authority to Tread: An Intercessor's Guide to Strategic-Level Spiritual Warfare*, and they agreed. Becca accepted and we formed a team.

Subsequently we agreed on our division of labor. We did not want to produce a text in which either of us would be inhibited from writing in the first person because of being coauthors. So we decided that I would write some introductory material, sketching out the foundations and historical development of the subject, then Becca, who brings the enviable combination of being a keen theoretician and a passionate field practitioner, would carry on and, with my input along the way, complete the essay.

Let me introduce the subject of strategic-level spiritual warfare with a personal anecdote. By 1990 I had taught at Fuller Theological Seminary for twenty years in the School of World Mission (now School of Intercultural Studies). My career as professor of church growth was progressing satisfactorily. However, a memorable bump in the road occurred when I received an unexpected invitation to meet with the Fuller faculty senate for what would be at best a theological reprimand or at worst a heresy trial. The issue? Strategic-level spiritual warfare.

I must explain. One of my major missiological responsibilities was to research, analyze, and accurately report the growth and development of churches worldwide. As I was visiting up to fifteen nations per year, a phenomenon began coming to my attention that stretched the boundaries of my (then) noncharismatic evangelical tradition. I discovered that some of the major leaders of the expansion of Christianity worldwide, especially in what we now term the "Global South," were developing part of their strategies for church growth around successfully combating territorial spirits. They postulated that certain demonic beings on the level of principalities and powers were responsible for organizing the forces of darkness in a given geographical region around the purpose of thwarting the advance of the kingdom of God.

For ten years or so, I chose not to publicize what I had been learning. I then broke my silence and made brief mention of the territorial-spirits phenomenon in two books, both written in 1987 and published in 1988.[1] At the same time, interest in the supernatural and power evangelism was growing among certain faculty members of evangelical seminaries due to the ripple effect of John Wimber's landmark courses at Fuller, so I convened an "Academic Symposium on Power Evangelism" at Fuller in 1988, bringing together forty scholars representing Christian institutions of higher learning. For my plenary session, I chose to address the issue of territorial spirits.[2] Following that, at

1. See C. Peter Wagner, *The Third Wave of the Holy Spirit* (Ann Arbor, MI: Servant, 1988), 60; and Wagner, *How to Have a Healing Ministry without Making Your Church Sick* (Ventura, CA: Regal, 1988), 201.

2. C. Peter Wagner, "Territorial Spirits," in *Wrestling with Dark Angels*, ed. C. Peter Wagner and F. Douglas Pennoyer (Ventura, CA: Regal, 1990), 73–91.

the great Lausanne II Congress on World Evangelization, held in Manila in 1989, no fewer than five speakers chose topics related to territorial spirits for their addresses.

The research for my address on territorial spirits uncovered seventeen authors who had previously addressed the phenomenon, so I published a compilation of excerpts from their writings in 1991 titled *Engaging the Enemy: How to Fight and Defeat Territorial Spirits*.[3] Some of the more recognizable names included Oscar Cullmann, Jack Hayford, Ed Silvoso, Michael Green, Jacob Lowen, Yonggi Cho, and John Dawson. I hoped that this publication would help alleviate theological controversy when the subject of strategic-level spiritual warfare became more widely known. Unfortunately, this did not happen.

Also in 1990 I organized a roundtable of about twenty leaders from across the nation, most of whom had attended Lausanne II in Manila, to begin to meet on a regular basis in order to discuss and refine theological and phenomenological issues related to strategic-level spiritual warfare. We called it the Spiritual Warfare Network (SWN), and it continued functioning for several years. It was the first meeting of SWN that precipitated the controversy at Fuller Seminary.

It so happened that John Dart, then religion editor of the *Los Angeles Times*, published a feature article on the first SWN meeting, held in Pasadena, California, only blocks away from Fuller Seminary. The article naturally featured some of the discussions we had of demons, territorial spirits, and supernatural phenomena, for which part of the Christian public was not prepared. The topics discussed made many of the Fuller theologians uncomfortable. And who was the organizer of this bizarre meeting? None other than Fuller professor Peter Wagner! Fears arose that this nonsense might even alienate some financial supporters. Thus the summons to the faculty senate meeting.

A good number of irate theologians entered into a heated, two-hour cross-examination of my thinking on the subject of strategic-level spiritual warfare. I was at a distinct disadvantage because I was still in the beginning stages of learning about the subject. I think they perceived that I had crossed the boundary into the theological lunatic fringe. Some wanted to accuse me of heresy because they knew that if I were guilty my tenure would be jeopardized. I was fortunate, however, because the Fuller statement of faith, which I signed every year, made no mention of the existence or activities of demons, principalities, powers, or supernatural phenomena.

3. C. Peter Wagner, *Engaging the Enemy: How to Fight and Defeat Territorial Spirits* (Ventura, CA: Regal, 1991).

Two months later, I received a letter from the president and the provost suggesting that I had not yet grasped the intensity of the concern of the faculty senate on issues revolving around my ideas of spiritual warfare. As I read it, I felt that the faculty senate had not yet grasped the intensity of *my* concern. In an attempt to probe the underlying causes of this difference of opinion, I responded with this paragraph, which I believe is very apropos to this present book. As you read it, keep in mind that I am a missiologist from the School of World Mission writing to theologians from the School of Theology:

> It seems to me that the most fundamental issue we have before us relates to research methodology. Much of our failure to hear each other stems from this. What is the relationship between theology and experience? Between the exegetical and the phenomenological? Between philosophy and social science? Between the ought and the is? Between library research and field research? Between systematic theology and contextualized theology? Between orthodoxy and orthopraxis? Between static theology and dynamic theology? Between concern for the ethical and concern for the pragmatic? Between Western worldviews and Third World worldviews? What are the underlying values of our respective schools?

The situation in Fuller eventually calmed down, but this did not end the controversy surrounding strategic-level spiritual warfare and territorial spirits. Since I was a chief proponent of these ideas, I became a lightning rod for critics. I have thick files of documents from people who were upset with me. One book referenced, footnoted, and refuted my writings no fewer than 167 times![4] My response to this rather volatile discussion was to avoid citing and refuting individual critics, and to produce a volume that would compile, classify, and address each of the predominant issues. In 1996, Regal released my definitive work on the subject, *Confronting the Powers*, which has been rereleased by Destiny Image, under the new title *Spiritual Warfare Strategy*.[5]

With this, I think it is time to hear from Becca Greenwood.

Spiritual Warfare (Rebecca Greenwood)

My portion of this discussion will be addressed from years of personal experience as a field practitioner and years of studying the Word of God as well as a library of books concerning spiritual warfare. As we begin, let me share

---

4. See Chuck Lowe, *Territorial Spirits and World Evangelization* (Ross-shire, UK: OMF International, 1998).

5. C. Peter Wagner, *Spiritual Warfare Strategy: Confronting Spiritual Powers* (Shippensburg, PA: Destiny Image, 2011).

more about myself. I am a prophetic warfare intercessor and have actively and consistently engaged in strategic-level spiritual warfare, addressing territorial spirits since 1991. To date I have contended for breakthrough in nations such as Egypt, Italy, Turkey, Korea, China, Russia, Germany, Ukraine, Spain, Nepal, and many others. During this time of engaging in warfare prayer and contending against dark rulers, I have witnessed the lack of awareness concerning the enemy, especially in the Western church. In the words of Walter Wink, "Demons in polite society, are simply 'out.' "[6] Discredited through philosophers and theologians and demystified and dispelled by psychotherapists, the devil has been minimized and is no longer believed to be the primary cause behind the evil in our modern-day society.

That is, to me, the bad news. The good news is there is a growing number of believers who are prepared to acknowledge Satan's dark presence in our world. Unfortunately, a strong contingency still holds to the belief that Christians either need not or should not spend their time bothering with him. And some pastors and leaders warn their people not to talk about the devil or think about the devil but to keep their entire focus on the Lord. The problem with this thinking is that the Scriptures *do* bother with Satan. Presented as the "god of this world," the devil and his demonic cohorts figure into the New Testament nearly twice as much as the Holy Spirit.[7] And because of numerous years of experience, I am a strong advocate of being aware of and aggressively addressing the evil schemes of our enemy. As well-known University of Chicago researcher Andrew Greeley cautions in an article in the *New York Times Magazine*, "If Satan is still in business, then it behooves us to be prepared to greet him with proper respect."[8]

Jesus's Confrontation with Satanic Powers

Jesus stated, "If I cast out demons by the Spirit of God, surely the kingdom of God has come upon you" (Matt. 12:28 NKJV). A "kingdom" has a government led by a king. Jesus was the occupying king. The kingdom he waged war against also had a government; its king was Satan. Since the fall of Adam and Eve in the garden, humankind had been under the evil dominion of the prince of darkness. Basically, Satan could do anything he wanted to the peoples of the earth. He was up to no good. Satan has never nor will

---

6. Quoted in George Otis Jr., *Twilight Labyrinth: Why Does Spiritual Darkness Linger Where It Does?* (Grand Rapids: Chosen, 1997), 70.

7. Ibid., 71. In the second appendix in his book *The Prince of Darkness*, Jeffrey Burton Russell lists 106 New Testament passages providing either the name of, or general references to, the devil.

8. Quoted in Otis, *Twilight Labyrinth*, 71.

he ever play fair. He is complete evil, our adversary, the great deceiver, the enemy of our souls, the prince of the power of air, and the mocking, prideful, rebellious foe of our Lord. But things radically changed when God sent his Son.

The Word of God describes the many power encounters Jesus had with Satan and his army of darkness. The very first encounter happened after God audibly announced in Matthew 3:17, "This is My beloved son, in whom I am well pleased." Then "Jesus was led up . . . into the wilderness to be tempted by the devil" (Matt. 4:1 NKJV). Wagner pointedly states: "Jesus's public ministry began with an eyeball to eyeball power encounter with Satan himself!"[9] Michael Green observes that Jesus "has more to say about Satan than anyone else in the Bible. . . . The Gospels are full of his actual conflict with Satan, which reached its climax on the cross."[10] In the real world, Jesus regularly talked about, taught about, and personally confronted the devil and his demons.[11] When the apostle John looked back at the ministry of Jesus, he characterized it this way, "For this purpose the Son of God was manifested, that He might destroy the works of the devil" (1 John 3:8 NKJV). From the time of Jesus until now, the battle has intensified and continues to intensify. Satan's fury is raging because he knows his time is short and that there is an army of spiritual warriors God is raising up to defeat him and his kingdom of darkness.

Spiritual Warfare Defined

"Spiritual warfare" is an invisible battle in the spiritual realm involving a power confrontation between the kingdom of God and the kingdom of darkness. Spiritual warfare occurs on three different levels: ground level, occult level, and strategic level. I appreciate what Wagner says in *Confronting the Powers*: "It is helpful to remind ourselves from time to time that the technical terms we have been using for the last few years—ground-level, occult-level, and strategic (or cosmic)-level spiritual warfare—are somewhat artificial. Although they are helpful terms for teaching and comprehension, they are not three separate worlds, but only one invisible world of darkness."[12] Therefore, as we continue this discussion we should remember that we are dealing with one kingdom of darkness with different, interrelated levels.

---

9. C. Peter Wagner, *Confronting the Powers: How the New Testament Church Experienced the Power of Strategic-Level Spiritual Warfare* (Ventura, CA: Regal, 1996), 121.

10. Michael Green, *I Believe in Satan's Downfall* (Grand Rapids: Eerdmans, 1981), 26–27.

11. Wagner, *Confronting the Powers*, 122.

12. Ibid., 135–36.

GROUND-LEVEL SPIRITUAL WARFARE

Ground-level spiritual warfare is the practice of deliverance ministry that involves breaking demonic influences in an individual. It occurs on a personal level. This ministry was practiced by Jesus and has been a part of many Christian churches throughout the centuries. As one who operates as a deliverance minister, I have seen incredible breakthroughs occur in individuals' lives though the casting out of demons. I have also witnessed obvious, definite freedom in individuals as I have engaged in warfare prayer over life situations. I elaborate quite extensively on these concepts in *Breaking the Bonds of Evil*.[13]

OCCULT-LEVEL SPIRITUAL WARFARE

Occult-level spiritual warfare involves resistance to a more ordered level of demonic authority. Warfare at this level deals with witchcraft, Satanism, freemasonry, New Age beliefs, Eastern religions, and many other forms of spiritual practices that glorify Satan and his dark army. This obviously calls for a higher dimension of warfare prayer.[14]

STRATEGIC-LEVEL SPIRITUAL WARFARE

Strategic-level spiritual warfare requires power confrontations with high-ranking principalities and powers as described by Paul in Ephesians 6:12. These demonic entities are assigned to geographical territories and social networks. They are also referred to as territorial spirits. Their assignment is to keep large numbers of humans—networked through cities, neighborhoods, regions, nations, people groups, industries, governments, businesses, education systems, religious alliances, media, or any other form of social institutions—in spiritual captivity. Results of this oppression include but are not limited to the rampant injustice, oppression, misery, hunger, disease, natural disasters, racism, human trafficking, economic greed, wars, and the like now plaguing our world. Let's look at a scriptural example of contending with darkness at this level.

According to Greek legend, the Grecian god Apollo killed Python, the wicked earth serpent who dwelled in the caves of Parnassus in Delphi. He defeated Python in revenge for tormenting his mother as she was searching for a location to deliver her twins. Because of his act, Apollo is at times denoted as Pythian or a soothsayer of future events.

---

13. Rebecca Greenwood, *Breaking the Bonds of Evil: How to Set People Free from Demonic Oppression* (Grand Rapids: Chosen, 2006). See also Doris M. Wagner, *How to Cast Out Demons: A Guide to the Basics* (Ventura, CA: Regal, 2000).

14. For further information, see Cindy Jacobs, *Deliver Us from Evil* (Ventura, CA: Regal, 2001).

During Paul's day, the citizens in the region of Philippi thought Apollo, also referred to as Apollo Pythian, personified the influencer of events. The term "Python" designated those through whom the python spirit uttered his prophetic revelations. We learn in the book of Acts that Paul moved into spiritual warfare by casting out this Python or divination spirit from a slave girl (see Acts 16:18). This induced a great tumult in the city of Philippi. It is my belief that the reactions and activities that took place as a result of Paul's authoritative command affirm that the spirit working through this young woman was indeed a territorial spirit. Allow me to explain what I mean.

Acts 16:19 articulates that once the proprietors of the slave girl recognized what had happened, they became greatly agitated. Paul's casting out of this spirit destroyed their chance to gain wealth from those searching for information about the future. They sequestered Paul and Silas and brought them in front of the authorities in the marketplace. In verse 20 the slave owners declare, "These men are Jews, and are *throwing our city* into an uproar" (emphasis added). I find this accusation extremely informative. Paul addressed a demonic spirit functioning through a young girl. Next he was accused of throwing an entire city into an uproar. I personally have prayed deliverance prayers over numerous persons, but never has my deliverance ministry resulted in a city tumult.

What happened? "The crowd joined in the attack against Paul and Silas" (Acts 16:22). Not only was the total metropolis in an uproar, but right away a crowd united in the assault against Paul and Silas. Why would banishing a demon from one girl induce a city uproar and incite a hostile crowd against Paul and Silas? A reasonable explanation would be that the python spirit operating through this slave girl was a territorial spirit that had transfixed the region of Philippi.

The magistrates dictated that Paul and Silas be beaten, flogged, and cast into prison. Locked away in an inner cell with their feet fixed in stocks, Paul and Silas started to pray and worship God. "*Suddenly* there was such a *violent earthquake* that the foundations of the prison were shaken. At once *all the prison doors flew open, and everyone's chains came loose*" (Acts 16:26 emphasis added). One amazing outcome of casting out this demonic spirit in a slave girl was a fierce earthquake across the region. Not only were Paul's and Silas's chains freed, but *everybody's* chains came unleashed.

When effectual spiritual warfare prayer has transpired, a reflection of what has taken place in the spiritual realm will frequently be evident in the physical realm; hence, the earthquake. Apparently, God was shaking the foundational worship of Apollo in that region. The earthquake led to the breaking of *everybody's* chains.

The most substantial manifestation of effective spiritual warfare prayer is the liberation of people who have been immobilized in spiritual wickedness by a territorial spirit. They are then loosed to see and receive the truth and love of God. Seeing lost souls rescued out of darkness into the kingdom of God is among the chief focuses of combating territorial spirits. Take note of the breakthrough that came about in this spiritual warfare confrontation in Philippi:

> The jailer called for lights, rushed in and fell trembling before Paul and Silas. He then brought them out and asked, "Sirs, what must I do to be saved?" They replied, "Believe in the Lord Jesus, and you will be saved—you and your household." Then they spoke the word of the Lord to him and to all the others in his house. At that hour of the night the jailer took them and washed their wounds; then immediately he and all his household were baptized. The jailer brought them into his house and set a meal before them; he was filled with joy because he had come to believe in God—he and his whole household. (Acts 16:29–34)

Let's recap this dramatic face-off. Paul did not back off from this power encounter, but with boldness cast out a python spirit, also named a spirit of divination, from a slave girl. The resultant actions incited a city uproar, a raging gang, the incarceration of Paul and Silas, a violent earthquake that broke everybody's chains, and the salvation of the prison guard and his household. A fairly inescapable conclusion would be that the demonic spirit in this young woman was indeed a territorial spirit or principality that had maintained this region in darkness.

Weapons of Warfare

The 1990s were a season when those of us engaging in spiritual warfare were learning, refining, and polishing our weapons of warfare. It was a time of gaining understanding of what weapons have been made available to us from the Word of God and, through intercession and prophecy, speaking forth in agreement with the voice of God to see amazing answers to prayer and breakthroughs. As a result, a new language began to emerge in the body of Christ. Terms such as "spiritual warfare," "spiritual mapping," and "identificational repentance" were coined. For me personally during this decade, I began to "cut my teeth" in warfare intercession and learned to lead warfare prayer assignments in cities, our nation, and nations of the world, an experience I share extensively in my book *Authority to Tread*.[15] And the results of using the following weapons have repeatedly been tangible outcomes that actually cause desired changes.

15. Rebecca Greenwood, *Authority to Tread: An Intercessor's Guide to Strategic-Level Spiritual Warfare* (Grand Rapids: Chosen, 2005).

Spiritual Mapping

Spiritual mapping and spiritual warfare work together. While spiritual mapping is not a solution in itself, it provides us with a means to a solution. In fact, as I have visibly witnessed, spiritual warfare prayer is much less likely to be effective without the indispensable tool of spiritual mapping. George Otis explains: "Fortunately, God has not left us to fight blind. Meaningful intelligence on our communities is readily obtainable through spiritual mapping. As we absorb the benefits of this Spirit-led research, it becomes easier to abandon our primitive hit-and-miss approach to spiritual warfare (sometimes called the piñata method). Fresh insight and understanding release us to economic and effective action."[16]

Moses, under the direction of God, dispatched spies into the nation of Canaan to "see what the land is like" (Num. 13:18 NASB). This mapping/ investigative expedition lasted forty days and included detailed research assignments. I appreciate George Otis's assessment: "The fact that God was already well acquainted with Canaanite challenges testifies to the importance He places on human interaction with spiritual strongholds."[17] This case carried implications for an entire nation.

God can certainly ordain breakthroughs over regions when we pray, but it is informed intercession—having the necessary facts and revelations as the groundwork of our prayers—that seems to empower us for the most effective regional and societal transformations. In my experience it would be a fair evaluation to say that God does not reveal territorial strongholds just for the sake of information but also for the sake of action. The more we pray and delve into research, the more warfare strategies for social transformation are revealed and confirmed. Spiritual mapping provides scholarly answers and spiritual insight to identify root causes of social issues such as systemic poverty, human trafficking, sexually perverse societies, human genocide, racism, economic downfalls, and immoral governmental structures, therefore giving us a map on how to battle in spiritual warfare with precise accuracy to hit the mark in the Spirit. I agree with Gary Kinnaman: "Orthodoxy is necessary, but it is not enough. If it is true that our battle is not against flesh and blood, then we need spiritual insight and power of our own to make a fight of it."[18]

Spiritual mapping is the practice of identifying the spiritual conditions at work in a given community, city, or nation. By gathering objective information

16. George Otis Jr., *Informed Intercession: Transforming Your Community through Spiritual Mapping and Strategic Prayer* (Ventura, CA: Renew, 1999), 85.

17. Ibid., 91.

18. Quoted in George Otis Jr., *The Last of the Giants: Lifting the Veil of Islam and the End Times* (Tarrytown, NY: Chosen, 1991), 84.

(including key historical facts such as foundational history, locations of blood-shed, idolatrous practices, key historical leaders, broken covenants, and sexual immorality) and combining it with spiritual impressions (prophecy, revelation, words of knowledge, dreams, and visions), believers can prayerfully combine all of this information and draw a map that identifies the open doors between the spirit world and the material world. These open doors help determine our response as we enter into warfare prayer. In the discussion below about land issues, allow to me explain further how historical issues and spiritual practices provide direction in spiritual mapping.

LAND ISSUES

As the Word of God unmistakably expresses: "The earth is the LORD's, and everything in it" (Ps. 24:1–2). He set the nations in order. He established an inheritance and boundaries for all humankind (Deut. 32:8). The Lord is concerned about the cities in which we exist (Prov. 11:10–11). The word "land" is mentioned over two thousand times in the Word of God. Since the creation, God intended an ongoing relationship between humankind and the land. I appreciate the following statements of Watchman Nee from his book *Changed into His Likeness*:

> All of God's work for His people is connected with a land. If they were faithful, they possessed it; if not, they lost it. From that land all enemies would be cast out, and they were to occupy it for God. "The land" is the central thought of the Old Testament. God wants a land for His own.
>
> Thus the land is not an end in itself; it stands for the whole earth. God is thinking ultimately in large terms. "Blessed are the meek," says Jesus, "for they shall inherit the earth." This earth of ours, which will come back to God in fullness at the end of this age, is being won back now by the meek. . . . God wants us not only to preach the Gospel and to edify and build up His Church, He wants us especially to stand on this earth for Him.[19]

It is safe to conclude that God clearly created the earth with precise intentions in mind. However, throughout the world Satan has unleashed consummate authority over people and the land. This raises the question, if God is so concerned with the land, then why are so many people and lands transfixed in darkness?

Through Satan's perverted need to grip regions and territories, he and his demonic army invade lands, illegally gaining possession of what is not theirs. Jim Chosa, an enrolled member of the Keweenaw Bay Chippewa Indian Tribe, expressly states:

---

19. Watchman Nee, *Changed into His Likeness* (Wheaton: Tyndale House, 1978), 28–29.

Remember, Satan has expressed his desire to be god. He knows the importance of the Earth as part of God's plan to make His sons truly like Himself as they righteously rule their spots in His name. Satan is already a god over all of his demonic hordes; however, his continual lust for more power drives him to be like god over all the Earth and its inhabitants as well. Therefore, he has deviously driven the nations of the Earth from their spots, causing them to pursue a false inheritance through false religions, greed, covetousness, war and lusts of all kinds, and to defile their spots making them unfit for God to dwell in.[20]

In his plot to skillfully fulfill his role as "the ruler of the world," Satan acts as an illegal squatter and pulls humankind into partnering with him to ensure his further success. Unfortunately in the history of our own nation, as we will discuss further, this has become one of the deciding causes of darkness resulting in the unrighteous treatment of the host people of our nation, our Native American brothers and sisters.

So how does land become defiled? Put simply, defilement comes from irresponsible stewardship. In his book *Releasing Heaven on Earth*, Alistair Petrie explains stewardship of the land:

> This is one of the very first directives given to man by God: "The Lord God took the man and put him in the Garden of Eden to work it and take care of it" (Gen. 2:15). The Hebrew word *shamar* used in this verse has many meanings: to hedge around something, to keep, to guard, to watch as a watchman, to protect. That is our stewardship responsibility—nothing less than *to keep the land*. Stewardship, then, is a divine principle emphasizing our accepting responsibility for possessions entrusted to us by somebody else. . . . This is our personal and corporate call to be stewards of the Kingdom of God. Putting it simply, stewardship speaks of management.[21]

As Petrie's summation explains, God has purposed the church to manage the land. Therefore, throughout history, as humankind has fallen into unrighteous, sinful practices and aligned with Satan in his schemes of defilement, a sinful allegiance of mis-stewardship has occurred and demonic authority has been established.

Let's look at Satan's four key tactics of defilement that have become the primary focus in the spiritual mapping of regions.

20. Jim Chosa and Faith Chosa, *Thy Kingdom Come Thy Will Be Done in Earth: A First Nation Perspective on Strategic Keys for Territorial Deliverance and Transformation* (n.p.: Day Chief Ministries, 2004), 125.

21. Alistair Petrie, *Releasing Heaven on Earth: God's Principles for Restoring the Land*, (Grand Rapids: Chosen, 2000), 22.

BLOODSHED

Shedding of innocent blood contaminates the land, particularly when the bloodletting demands the worship of demonic deities. God's command in Numbers 35:33–34 is clear: "Do not pollute the land where you are. Bloodshed pollutes the land, and atonement cannot be made for the land on which blood has been shed, except the blood of the one who shed it. Do not defile the land where you live and where I dwell, for I, the LORD, dwell among the Israelites." Bloodshed includes the taking of innocent life and the untimely slaughter of suppressed people groups. As the blood of the guiltless is shed on the earth for satanic purposes, Satan then takes the bloodstained land as his possession. As a scriptural example, Molech was the pagan deity idolized by the Ammonites. The ritual killing of children was a demand for his followers (see Lev. 20:1–5). It was through the bloodshed of innocent children that Satan claimed their territory. Through spiritual discernment and historical research, it has been proved that bloodshed of any type, from the past or in the present, affects humankind in many ways. And often we can testify that the result is death-gripped regions, high suicide rates, murder, violence, and gang activity, as well as the nursing of criticism, anger, jealousy, bitterness, division, and rage over succeeding generations and regions.

IDOLATRY

As Wagner states in his book *Hard-Core Idolatry*, "Idolatry is worshiping, serving, pledging allegiance to, doing acts of obeisance to, paying homage to, forming alliances with, making covenants with, seeking power from, or in any other way exalting any supernatural being other than God. The supernatural beings refer to angels, cherubim, seraphim, Satan, principalities, powers, deities, territorial spirits, goddesses, and demonic beings on any level."[22]

The Lord abhors idol worship. I believe that the first two commandments are listed first because they are the sins that God hates the most. Evidence throughout other parts of Scripture suggests this very strongly. As expressed in the first and second commandments in Exodus 20:3–6, God makes clear we are to have no other gods before him and that we are not to make "an image in the form of anything in heaven above or on earth beneath or in the waters below" that may take up a position of importance in our lives. In verse 5 he goes on to express his position as a "jealous God" and that idolatry can lead to the punishment of the children "for the sin of the parents to the third and fourth generations." As a covenantal God, he expects us to maintain and

---

22. C. Peter Wagner, *Hard-Core Idolatry: Facing the Facts* (Colorado Springs: Wagner Institute for Practical Ministry, 1999), 11–12.

honor our covenantal relationship with him. When this is done he promises his love shown "to a thousand generations of those who love me and keep my commandments" (v. 6).

Jeremiah 3:6–10 is one of the many passages in the Word of God that reveals the sin of idolatry. In verse 9 we learn that through Israel's immorality "she *defiled* the land and committed adultery with stone and wood" (emphasis added).

Sexual Immorality

Those who practice idolatry are often led into immoral lifestyles because they are influenced by the territorial spirits behind idolatry and therefore have no sense of accountability before God. Many times those trapped in sexual immorality have made themselves and their immoral sexual desires the point of idolatry in their lives. Leviticus 18:1–23 defines unlawful sexual relations. Verses 24–25 explain the results of sexual immorality: "Do not defile yourselves in any of these ways, because this is how the nations that I am going to drive out before you became defiled. Even the land was defiled; so I punished it for its sin, and the land vomited out its inhabitants." God makes it clear that as ungodly sexual practices are perpetuated in a city and region, the land is defiled.

Broken Covenants

In the Scriptures it is evident that our God is covenantal and has entered into relationship with his people. For the Christian a nonnegotiable belief is that God renewed his covenant with the human race through the death and resurrection of Jesus Christ. Therefore, it is a fair assumption to say that since Jesus is covenantal, we too are to be covenantal.

Anytime a covenant is established with God, Satan will endeavor to destroy the treaty. And when a person, church, government, business, people group, nation, and so on violates the principle of covenant, vulnerability to the consequences of broken promises at personal, family, church, community, and national levels are welcomed. Isaiah 24:5–6 states: "The earth is defiled by its people; they have disobeyed the laws, violated the statutes and broken the everlasting covenant. Therefore a curse consumes the earth; its people must bear their guilt."

Unfortunately in our nation, broken covenants with the host people of our land has released a great curse. As Jim Chosa reveals:

> Because the United States of America gained possession of the natural landscape through fraudulent means of 371 broken treaties with the Native Americans, the Native Americans still retain in the Court of God the host-stewardship of

the spiritual landscape. . . . These 371 [treaties] were forcefully imposed on the tribes by the USA, ratified by the US Senate and became, by US Constitutional language the supreme law of the land. These are the ones which severely defile the land, and through the spiritual law of sowing and reaping have opened the whole landscape up to curses of widespread lawlessness because they were broken by the very government charged with enforcing the laws of the Constitution.[23]

Identificational Repentance

Keeping in mind the historic information contained in Chosa's statement, we are guided into our next weapon of warfare, namely identificational repentance. Responsible spiritual mapping will frequently unveil sins of a people, city, nation, or government that have been perpetrated in the past, often generations ago. These uncovered iniquities have become strongholds of the powers of darkness, maintaining multitudes in physical desolation and spiritual enslavement. Therefore, those of us who contend with territorial spirits on a professional level believe that no expression of spiritual warfare prayer is more significant than identificational repentance. As George Otis defines it, "Identificational repentance is a two stage intercessory action that involves: (1) an acknowledgement that one's affinity group (clan, city, nation or organization) has been guilty of specific corporate sin before God and man, and (2) a prayerful petition that God will use personal repudiation of this sin as a redemptive beachhead from which to move into the larger community."[24]

Nehemiah models for us how identificational repentance can release forgiveness and set things in motion to turn an entire nation from devastation to redemption. Let's look at his prayer in Nehemiah 1:5-9: "LORD, the God of heaven, . . . let your ear be attentive . . . to hear the prayer your servant is praying before you day and night. . . . I confess the sins we Israelites, including myself and my father's family, have committed against you. We have acted very wickedly toward you. We have not obeyed the commands, decrees and laws you gave your servant Moses." Notice that Nehemiah confessed sins that his father committed but that he did not commit personally. Thus the concept "identificational." Scripture reveals the outcome of this prayer initiated the plans and rebuilding of the walls of Jerusalem and the redemption of the children of Israel.

Allow me to pose a question. What would happen if, in the manner of Nehemiah, white Americans repented of all 371 broken treaties along with all the unjust treatment and killings unleashed on the host people of this

23. Chosa and Chosa, *Thy Kingdom Come*, 138.
24. Otis, *Informed Intercession*, 251.

nation? If there were then effective war strategies against the spirits behind these broken treaties and steps made toward restitution, could our nation experience a new measure of freedom, breakthrough, and transformation? Just as Nehemiah's prayer birthed transformation to his nation, I personally have witnessed firsthand prayers of repentance from the white man to the host nations birth miraculous changes in our land.

One strong example is the south central region of Kansas. The Lord impressed upon pastors and leaders of the region to repent to members of the Cheyenne tribe. Not only did they repent, but they also felt led to do an act of restitution in which they presented a buffalo as a gift. Once repentance and the act of restitution was made, healing began to be realized in the natural resources of the land. They have seen oil and gas production increase greatly, to the extent of its being the topic of focus in newspaper articles. Farmers in the region are now able to pay off debts and are no longer in need of bank loans.[25]

Prophetic Decrees

A prophetic decree is an announcement or proclamation given with the authority of a prophet. Ephesians 3:10, 20 states: "So that the manifold wisdom of God might now be made known through the church to the ruler and authorities in the heavenly places. . . . Now to Him who is able to do far more abundantly beyond all that we ask or think, according to the power that works within us" (NASB). According to Ephesians, God is going to make known his wisdom through the church. As I investigate this verse further, the Greek word for "known" comes from the verb *gnōrizō*. It means "to certify, to declare, to make known." Therefore, God is going to use the church to make known or to make prophetic declarations to demonic rulers and authorities.

Jesus said in John 15:15: "No longer do I call you slaves, . . . but I have called you friends, for all things that I have heard from My Father I have made known to you" (NASB). What does this mean to us? Jesus has made us friends, and he says he will make known or declare (*gnōrizō*) to us everything he has heard from the Father.

Barbara Wentroble clearly lays out the process in *Prophetic Intercession*:

> Jesus is going to make known to us the things He has heard from the Father. Intercessors then make known to the evil powers through prophetic proclamations

25. See Chris Frank, "Oil Boom Could Revitalize South Central Kansas," *KAKeland*, September 21, 2011, http://www.kake.com/home/headlines/Oil_Boom_Could_Revitalize_South_Central_Kansas_130318078.html, accessed March 14, 2012.

the information received from Jesus. We are not just giving a random outcry, but we are participating in a process released from heaven.

- God the Father makes known (*gnoridzo*) His intentions to Jesus.
- Jesus makes known (*gnoridzo*) the Father's intentions to the Church.
- The Church makes known (*gnoridzo*) the intentions of God to the evil powers through proclamation (*kerusso*).
- The result? Breakthrough![26]

Prophetic Acts

A prophetic act is defined as a thing or deed done, having the powers of a prophet, or an action or decree that foreshadows what is to come. Steve Hawthorne and Graham Kendrick discuss the significance of obedience to these actions in their book *Prayerwalking*: "As you become comfortable with some of the standard physical dimensions of prayer, you will find yourself at ease with the other order of prophetic symbols, the *special prayer actions* that God prompts from time to time. God may use these *prophetic symbols* more than we may even know. Even if they make little sense to us, obedience to the Spirit is what is required. A little bit of faith goes a long way when reinforced with the total concentration of spirit, mind and body."[27]

We witness in Joshua 6:3–5 Joshua and the children of Israel facing a well-fortified, walled city full of idolatry and occultic power. "You shall march around the city, all the men of war circling the city once. You shall do so for six days. Also seven priests shall carry seven trumpets of rams' horns before the ark; then on the seventh day you shall march around the city seven times, and the priests shall blow the trumpets. It shall be that when they make a long blast with the ram's horn, and when you hear the sound of the trumpet, all the people shall shout with a great shout; and the wall of the city will fall down flat, and the people will go up every man straight ahead" (NASB).

Joshua's part was not to be stronger than the occultic leaders of the city—his part was to be obedient to the Lord. As we have learned in performing prophetic acts, the Lord often requires obedience many times before we see the manifestation of God's power. The result: "The people shouted, and priests blew the trumpets; and when the people heard the sound of the trumpet, the people shouted with a great shout and the wall fell down flat, so that the people went up into the city, every man straight ahead, and they took the city (Josh. 6:20 NASB).

26. Barbara Wentroble, *Prophetic Intercession* (Ventura, CA: Regal, 1999), 100.

27. Steve Hawthorne and Graham Kendrick, *Prayerwalking* (Orlando, FL: Creation House, 1993), 97–98, emphasis added.

Power Encounters

A power encounter is defined "as a visible, practical demonstration that Jesus Christ is more powerful than the spirits, powers or false gods worshiped or feared by the members of a given people group."[28] Just as we witness power encounters in the New Testament church and into the first few centuries, they can be an important key in effective warfare and evangelism today in cities and regions around the world.

Ramsay MacMullen, a historian specializing in the Roman Empire, describes in his book *Christianizing the Roman Empire A.D. 100–400* the historical phenomenon of how the completely pagan Roman Empire became Christian over a period of about three hundred years. In a section in his book relating to Paul and John's ministry in confronting Diana of the Ephesians, he explains that the power of Christianity was confirmed in Ephesus and "demonstrated head-on in the riven altar [of Diana]."[29] He further explains: "Driving all competition from the field head-on was crucial. The world, after all, held many dozens and hundreds of gods. Choice was open to everybody. It could thus be only a most exceptional force that would actually displace alternatives and compel allegiance; it could only be the most probative demonstrations that would work. We should therefore assign as much weight to this, the chief instrument of conversion, as the best, earlier reporters do."[30] I agree with MacMullen's assessment. Power encounters with the demonic army are a chief instrument or weapon of warfare for conversions. And as I will share in the closing portion of this essay, power encounters with territorial spirits can often result in awesome, supernatural, radical breakthroughs.

Prayerwalking and Prayer Journeys

Prayerwalking is just what it sounds like: walking while praying. And it is defined as "praying on-site with insight."[31] This form of praying has been widely participated in and practiced since the 1990s. Believers pray persistently while walking their cities, street by street. Some use well-thought-out plans; others are led by more spontaneous prompts from the Holy Spirit. These prayers are filled with fervor and expectancy that God will release dramatic breakthroughs of love, that souls will receive the truth of salvation, and that righteousness will penetrate a segment of society. Prayerwalking is not a personal devotional time

28. Wagner, *How to Have a Healing Ministry in Any Church*, 150.
29. Ramsay MacMullen, *Christianizing the Roman Empire A.D. 100–400* (New Haven: Yale University Press, 1984), 27.
30. Ibid.
31. Hawthorne and Kendrick, *Prayerwalking*, 12.

of prayer; rather, it provides a means of focused intentional intercessory prayers on cities, neighborhoods, homes, and people within our nation and abroad. Prayer journeys constitute spiritual warfare and mapping assignments where praying on-site through informed intercession and prophetic revelation brings transformation throughout the cities and nations of the world. As the walking provides a connection with these places, every step becomes an acted prayer.

As Steve Hawthorne and Graham Kendrick explain in *Prayerwalking*: "Insight for prayer can come in three ways: responsive insight, researched insight and revealed insight.

1. Responsive Insight. Prayer walkers do their work with their eyes open, allowing the sights of people, objects, events and entire communities to flood their prayers with significance.
2. Researched Insight. Examining the history of what has taken place at select settings often directs prayerwalkers to significant spots and informs potent prayers. . . . When research uncovers sources of persistent crime, injustice or occult practices, prayerwalkers can often find a useful direction for their praying.
3. Revealed Insight. Prayer walkers find that God seems to draw their attention to certain people or homes or places. Prayerwalkers find themselves in a position to meet divine appointments, in which the timing of encounters or events points toward a direction for prayer.[32]

What Authority Has Been Given to the Church?

One of the truths I strongly adhere to is that once we receive salvation we have enrolled in the most powerful army of the universe. In this army there is no way to avoid conflict with the enemy. Ed Murphy says it well: "While our enemies are already defeated, they are not dead, not even sickly."[33] The war is not over, and we cannot naively underestimate or overlook the power of Satan and his schemes in the earth. God mandated humankind since the foundation of creation to have dominion, to rule and reign in a position of authority in the earth.

The first thing God stated to Adam and Eve was: "Be fruitful and multiply, and fill the earth, and subdue it; and rule over [all the creation]" (Gen. 1:28 NASB). We must recognize the importance of this statement. God not only created the earth but also founded a government for the earth with humankind, positioning Adam and Eve as the authority. Adam and Eve were handed

32. Ibid., 18–20.
33. Ed Murphy, *The Handbook of Spiritual Warfare* (Nashville: Nelson, 1992), 290.

total authority to take dominion in the Lord's name. However, they also still had a choice. They had been entrusted with the position of authority to take dominion, but they also had the authority to give their dominion away. Satan, lusting for authority that was stripped from him when he was banished from heaven, sought to steal and acquire the dominion afforded to Adam and Eve. As Adam disobeyed God, history abruptly shifted. Adam rendered to Satan the authority to take dominion over God's creation. Sadly, Adam positioned himself and humanity under the authority of Satan.

To reverse this tragedy, God sent Jesus in genuine human flesh to accomplish what Adam failed to do. Colossians 1:19–20 gives a clear understanding of why the Lord sent Jesus: "For it was the Father's good pleasure for all the fullness to dwell in Him, and through Him to reconcile all things to Himself, having made peace through the blood of His cross; through Him, I say, whether things on earth or things in heaven" (NASB). As the second Adam he was the only human who ever lived who qualified to take back the dominion that Adam handed over to Satan. "The Son of God appeared for this purpose, to destroy the works of the devil" (1 John 3:8 NASB). Here is the crux of what we need to understand: Jesus died to revoke the evil, tyrannical reign of Satan in the earth and to completely reverse history. Jesus successfully accomplished his mission that he testifies about in Matthew 28:18, "All authority has been given to me in heaven and on earth" (NASB).

What does this mean for us? "God . . . gave us the ministry of reconciliation" (2 Cor. 5:18 NASB). Therefore, for those of us who are committed to doing God's will, this now becomes our identity, purpose, calling, and responsibility. Steve Thompson says: "Jesus having won back the authority on earth, could now mediate and rule in the affairs of earth. However, Jesus did not stay on the earth to rule it. He ascended to the Father and is seated at His right hand. So who is now responsible to rule and reign in the earth? Believe it or not, the church, which is the Body of Christ."[34] This ministry also becomes a mandate for social transformation. Joe Mattera agrees and explains: "When Jesus was crowned Lord of all, it was over God's entire jurisdiction—not just the church—and this includes 'all things.' All 'things' includes the land, the environment, politics, education, science, medicine, healthcare, the arts, space, economics, social justice and all the humanities."[35]

Strategic-level spiritual warfare is not the only means of accomplishing transformation, but it is one of the main weapons in the church's arsenal to realize change. The truth is, those who are called to the frontline battle

34. Steve Thompson, "Your Authority in Christ," *Morning Star Journal* (Summer 2006): 22.
35. Joseph Mattera, *Ruling in the Gates* (Lake Mary, FL: Creation House, 2003), 49.

of contending with Satan's army will need the same spiritual weapons that Jesus used. Our Lord confirmed this: "He who believes in Me, the works that I do, he will do also; and greater works than these he will do, because I go to the Father" (John 14:12 NASB). As Wagner succinctly explains, "The Holy Spirit was the source of all of Jesus's power during His earthly ministry. Jesus exercised no power of or by Himself. We can do the same or greater things than Jesus did because we have access to the same power source."[36]

Jesus said in Luke 10:19, "Behold, I give unto you power to tread on serpents and scorpions, and over all the power of the enemy: and nothing shall by any means hurt you" (KJV). The Greek word for "tread" is *pateō*. The *Enhanced Strong's Lexicon* gives the following definitions: "to trample, crush with the feet, to advance by setting foot upon, to tread upon; to encounter successfully the greatest perils from the machinations and persecutions with which Satan would fain thwart the preaching of the Gospel."[37] Because we are members of the army of God, we have the legal right to wield power over the enemy in the name of Jesus. We have territorial rights as well. In truth, legal power involves a certain jurisdiction, and jurisdiction implies the ability to administer justice in a certain area. I agree with Francis Frangipane: "I believe the Scriptures are clear: Not only do Christians have the authority to war against these powers of darkness, but we have the responsibility to as well. If we do not pray against our spiritual enemies, they will, indeed, prey upon us."[38]

Contending against the Spirits behind Abortion

Up to now, this essay has focused mostly on the biblical, theological, and theoretical aspects of strategic-level spiritual warfare. However, it would not be complete without at least one case study of the operation of intentional spiritual warfare methodologies as I have described them and the resulting visible and measurable outcomes. Over the years I have been personally involved in quite a number of such ventures in various parts of the world. But in order to make this case study more relevant to what will largely be an American audience, I felt that I should choose one that would be recognizable to many readers, partly because of the media coverage that emerged from it.

Unfortunately the chief incident that the media picked up lends itself to a spectrum of interpretations and therefore invites controversy. First of all,

36. Wagner, *Confronting the Powers*, 129.
37. J. Strong, *Enhanced Strong's Lexicon* (Ontario: Woodside Bible Fellowship, 1995), Libronix Digital Library System.
38. Francis Frangipane, "Our Authority in Christ," *Charisma*, July 1993, 40.

the moral issue involved, namely abortion, is one of the more controversial public issues in America today. Second, the tragic murder of Dr. George Tiller of Wichita, Kansas, an outspoken abortionist, on May 31, 2009, greatly complicates the matter. I need to affirm up front that Tiller's untimely death shocked and appalled all of those of us who were dealing with the sanctity of life in Kansas. For us, advocating the sanctity of life most assuredly included the sanctity of Dr. Tiller's life. It is a sad fact, as you will see, that he died after our spiritual warfare initiative, but this was not my desire nor the desire of anyone else on our team. Our prayers were focused on a much more benign closure to the high-profile advocacy of abortion in Kansas.

A word about abortion. As a charismatically inclined evangelical, my paradigm dictates that human life begins with conception. Consequently, I disagree with those whose paradigm tells them that a fetus is simply organic tissue without life that may be removed like an appendix, without guilt. My view is that terminating unborn life is as morally reprehensible as terminating life after birth. To put it more bluntly, I think abortion is a form of murder and thus not the will of God. As I shared above, bloodshed, the killing of the innocent, is among the primary weapons that the enemy applies in his scheme to corrupt lands. This will give us a moral and spiritual rationale for our field application of spiritual warfare in Kansas.

My first trip to Kansas was in 2005. I was invited by recognized apostles of the state Sandy Newman and DeeAnn Ward. They asked me to teach a group of hungry and attentive intercessors, pastors, and leaders who were fully prepared to study the importance of spiritual mapping and spiritual warfare. To my delight, in the first teaching session I found that the Lord had placed me with a passionate army of believers who were prepared to begin this journey of spiritual mapping. They welcomed prophetic revelation from the throne room and were passionate about setting into actions warfare strategies to see social transformation realized.

Dr. George Tiller ran an abortion clinic in Wichita; he was considered America's most prolific abortionist. In his lifetime, he aborted no less than sixty thousand unborn infants.[39] Abortions, including late-term abortions, were the only medical procedures he executed in his practice. Sandy, DeeAnn, and others whom I was training felt strongly that the Lord was guiding them to contend with this death structure in their state.

Since the initial training, I returned to Kansas repeatedly. A trip in the fall of 2007 proved to be a divinely appointed and engineered strategic-level spiritual

39. Scott. P. Riechert, "Late-Term Abortionist George Tiller Murdered," May 31, 2009, http://catholicism.about.com/b/2009/05/31/late-term-abortionist-george-tiller-murdered.htm.

warfare assignment. For months, believers in the state had been aggressively researching and praying that the spiritual root or demonic principality behind the notorious abortion clinic would be exposed, so strategic prayer could defeat it. Another organization, Operation Rescue, held three prayer initiatives in front of Tiller's clinic throughout 2007. There was much focused prayer, but we knew that the principality itself needed to be uncovered and defeated in order to ensure the closing of this clinic.

In preparation for our prophetic act, Sandy, DeeAnn, and I met with Stephanie Norton, their lead intercessor and researcher, and we prayed, asking the Lord to disclose the stronghold. At that moment, the Lord remarkably brought back to my memory a dream I had in 1994 in which he revealed to me the demonic spiritual entity Lilith. She is cited in Isaiah 34:14 as the night monster. The Hebrew word is *lilim* or *Lilith*, which means the night monster, night hag, or screeching owl. In the dream the Lord expressly showed me this territorial deity to be one of the principal forces behind death and abortion. After further research, I understood why.

Lilith is an ancient deity, depicted as a nocturnal great-winged goddess with bird-clawed feet. She carries a ring or rod of power signifying that she is among the first-ranked gods. She is a seductress and replete with destruction, known as the Goddess of Death or Hades. "The Talmud says that Lilith was formed by the Lord in response to Adam's request for a mate. According to the patriarchs, God used filth and sediment to create her, rather than the pure dust he had used for Adam. The children of Lilith were demons."[40] Eventually, Lilith objected and refused to lie submissively beneath Adam as he wanted. She left and fled to the Red Sea, where daily she gave birth to more than one hundred demons. Angels were sent to assure her she would die if she did not return to Adam. Lilith reasoned that it was not possible for her to die since she had charge of all newborn infants. So God penalized her by killing one hundred of her babies each day.

As I shared this revelation we all felt strongly that this was the principality perpetuating death through this abortion clinic. The next day they drove me to the airport for my return flight home. We decided to stop in front of the clinic to pray. A few minutes into the prayer, I heard the voice of the Lord, "Becca, bind the territorial spirit operating behind the killings of this clinic." At the same exact time Sandy and DeeAnn heard the Lord speaking this as well. With all three of us in agreement, I spoke out, "In the name of Jesus I bind the territorial spirit of death, I bind you, Lilith, and say you no longer will be able

40. Buffie Johnson, *Lady of the Beasts: The Goddess and Her Sacred Animals* (Rochester, VT: Inner Traditions International, 1994), 83.

to execute bloodshed of the innocent and unborn from this location. You will no longer advance in your demonic strategies and agendas. You are bound!"

After my flight departed and as Sandy and DeeAnn made their journey home, a fierce windstorm blew across the state of Kansas. Two days later Sandy and her staff returned to the church offices only to come upon an amazing surprise. In the only tree on the church property an owl was bound with fishing line used to hang decorations. They called a wildlife ranger to the church to free the owl. The key point to remember is that Lilith is characterized as the screeching owl!

Upon freeing the owl and examining it, the ranger told Sandy, "Based on the level of dehydration and the amount of bird waste below the tree, I can establish a fair estimate of how long the owl has been here. Do you recall the windstorm that blew across the state two days ago? I believe the wind made it impossible for the owl to fly and forcefully blew it into the tree where the fishing line bound it." Sandy immediately called and exclaimed, "Becca, one hour after you prayed and bound Lilith, who is the screeching owl demonic entity of death, the Lord sent a sign. Through a fierce windstorm, an owl was blown into our tree and bound by fishing line!" We both rejoiced and then prayed to receive the next part of the prayer strategy.

For the next twenty-one days, believers across the state of Kansas and the nation began a period of fasting and prayer in the night hours, since Lilith is a nocturnal god. The idea behind this was to pray and war in the night hours when the demonic activity of Lilith is the strongest in order to counter and defeat her diabolical strategies. It was an amazing twenty-one-day focus. During this time, new legal cases were instituted against Dr. Tiller and his practice on top of the already existing ones. They focused on his repeated pattern of illegal late-term abortions. "Tiller now faces two Board of Healing Arts investigations that could cost him his license. He faces 19 criminal counts of illegal late-term abortions that could cost him huge fines, and he faces a grand jury investigation that could net literally hundreds of additional counts of illegal abortions from the past five years that could cost him his freedom," said Operation Rescue president Troy Newman.[41] Even patients began to come forward and give shocking revelations of all the illegal reasons and actions surrounding their abortions in Tiller's clinic, Women's Health Care Services.[42]

From 2007 on, things continually intensified for Dr. Tiller. He was perpetually involved in court hearings, and repeated accounts of illegal activities within

---

41. Operation Rescue, "Tiller's License at Stake as KSBHA Launches New Abortion Investigation," October 4, 2007, http://www.operationrescue.org/archives/tiller%E2%80%99s-license-at-stake-as-ksbha-launches-new-abortion-investigation/, accessed July 15, 2010.
    42. Ibid.

his medical practices were being exposed. Statistics show that the abortion rate of postviability abortions performed at Tiller's clinic dropped 23 percent in 2007 and the following years. A report from 2009 by Troy Newman, president of Operation Rescue, whose ministry was housed next door to the Tiller clinic, says:

> During the first part of this year, our focus was on efforts to try late-term abortionist George Tiller for criminal charges that we discovered and exposed. Unfortunately, Tiller was acquitted of performing illegal late-term abortions in March. But minutes after the verdict was read, the Kansas State Board of Healing Arts released a statement indicating that they had filed an 11-count petition against Tiller on those same charges, and that the burden of proof was different than in a criminal case. They assured us that the case was progressing. Those counts were based on a complaint filed by Operation Rescue staff. We expected to see discipline, perhaps even the revocation of Tiller's license, within six months.[43]

This, obviously, is what we had prayed for, and we felt that the hand of God was working to put a stop to Dr. Tiller's activities. At the risk of being repetitious, let me say very emphatically that in the midst of our praying, not one time did we pray or even consider praying for Tiller's demise. Our hearts' cry was for his spirit to soften and turn from this practice of aborting babies. We prayed for his salvation and God's subsequent blessing on him. The news that he had been gunned down in his home church was appalling, sad, and repulsive to those of us who had been praying. The abortion clinic, of course, was closed, and now the largest city in Kansas remains abortion free.

In Closing

After twenty years of praying in cities, states, our nation, and the nations of the world, I could provide many similar accounts of breakthrough as a result of strategic-level spiritual warfare. We have seen laws shift for righteousness and gentleman's clubs shut down in the city of Houston. In Spain we have witnessed governmental elections in which unrighteous rulers attempted to attain power, but suddenly after warfare prayer the election outcome turned in favor of righteous leaders. In Italy we engaged in spiritual combat in a temple dedicated to the demonic god the Queen of Heaven and immediately following had unbelievers on-site approach us inquiring how to receive salvation.

43. Operation Rescue, "Operation Rescue's Top Ten Stories of 2009," December 3, 2009, http://www.operationrescue.org/page/7/?s=Tiller+Archives, accessed July 15, 2010.

Repeatedly we have contended against principalities and rulers and observed the land liberated from drought and famine. In Ukraine we contended to see a region set free from idolatry and witchcraft in which Christianity was almost nonexistent except for one Christian married couple. There was not even one church. Since the time of focused warfare prayer, the majority of the villagers were saved, there are now nine established churches, and the region is experiencing transformation for the glory of God. Strategic-level spiritual warfare holds great potential for defeating the powers of darkness and seeing people freed and society transformed toward the model of God's kingdom.

Response to C. Peter Wagner and Rebecca Greenwood

Walter Wink and Michael Hardin

It is difficult to respond to an essay that does not offer a clear or sustained exegetical argument and relies so heavily on personal anecdotes. We will confine our remarks to Rebecca Greenwood's section of the essay.

First we applaud Greenwood's observations on the atrocities that the United States government has committed against Native Americans. Not only has this government committed horrid atrocities and held the nation's first people hostage on reservations, but they also engaged in mass genocide by using weapons of mass destruction: it was the US Cavalry that gave smallpox-infected blankets to the native peoples to wipe them out. If there ever was a country that engaged in mythmaking from the perspective of mimetic theory it is the United States of America. Howard Zinn's *A People's History of the United States* documents the numerous people groups that have been scapegoated in order to build American civilization.[44]

Our concern, however, is the tendency within evangelicalism to do something dangerously similar toward Muslims, homosexuals, and other groups that have a different social agenda than they do. The brand of spiritual warfare advocated by Wagner and Greenwood is actually the warfare of a minority social, religious, and political base against those outside this circle. Our response will focus on the hermeneutic used in the appropriation of Scripture

44. Howard Zinn, *A People's History of the United States* (New York: Harper, 1980).

and offers another interpretation of the events that took place in Kansas described by Greenwood.

The evangelical myth of redemptive violence begins with a theory of inspiration that the Bible is God's Word. All passages in the Bible are read from a flat perspective and given equal credibility. Because God is perfect and God wrote the Bible, the Bible is perfect. This Platonic view of Scripture does not mesh with the way Jesus, Paul, the writer of the Fourth Gospel, and the author of the Epistle to the Hebrews understand Scripture, nor is it consonant with the many diverse views of Scripture in Second Temple Judaism.[45]

Greenwood's exegesis is not only flawed by hermeneutical considerations, but also her use of only conservative resources mitigates her historical analysis. For example, she asserts the identity of Apollo and Pythia. Eminent Greek religious historian Walter Burkert notes that it was only later Christian literature that made this identification; thus it is anachronistic for Greenwood to make this a historical assertion about Acts 16.[46]

Greenwood argues that "territorial spirits" (like her alleged spirit of Apollo/ Python) use four strategies: bloodshed, idolatry, sexual immorality, and broken covenants. But Greenwood's understanding of what constitutes bloodshed, idolatry, and so on is problematic. Shouldn't one consider the death penalty as bloodshed? One only need look at the many death penalty cases where the accused are later proved innocent with DNA analysis or where false charges are made by the legal authorities or the disproportionate number of African American males on death row. What about torture? Surveys done in 2009 and 2010 indicate that a high percentage of conservative evangelicals support the use of torture as an interrogation technique. And what shall we say about war? Jesus was a pacifist. No scholar we are aware of, except S. G. F. Brandon, would make Jesus out to be a zealot.

Idolatry has always been an issue for the people of God, and this Greenwood rightly notices. What is striking here is less the examples she mentions and more the ones she does not. For example, is not the American fixation

45. For a discussion of these issues see Michael Hardin, *The Jesus Driven Life* (Lancaster, PA: JDL Press, 2010); and Craig D. Allert, *A High View of Scripture? The Authority of the Bible and the Formation of the New Testament Canon* (Grand Rapids: Baker Academic, 2007). The excellent survey by Kern Robert Trembath, *Evangelical Theories of Biblical Inspiration: A Review and Proposal* (New York: Oxford University Press, 1987), demonstrates the logical fallacies of locating inspiration in the biblical text and concludes with: "The phrase 'biblical inspiration' initially points not to the Bible but to Christian believers who have experienced salvation from God through the Bible" (114). On biblical authority in Second Temple Judaism see Martin Jan Mulder, ed., *Mikra* (Philadelphia: Fortress, 1988), esp. 39–86.

46. Walter Burkert, *Greek Religion* (London: Blackwell, 1985), 116. No critical commentary we consulted made this identification.

with wealth and material possessions idolatrous? What is left unsaid is that the Jesus portrayed by some charismatic evangelicals is a caricature of the Jesus of the Gospels. Their Jesus justifies violence (see their use of the temple narrative), which goes against the grain of his entire ethical program.[47] In *The Jesus Driven Life*, I (Michael) contend that the American fundamentalist/conservative evangelical Jesus is an idol, an anti-Christ. This Jesus is rightly rejected by a growing numbers of Christians, including evangelicals.

Greenwood turns to Leviticus 18 to mention proscribed sexual relationships but does not mention that Leviticus 20:13 requires that persons who engage in same-sex relations are to be killed. And she does not engage the difficult task of justifying why these texts are taken to be "for today" when she and many other conservative Christians ignore large chunks of the Levitical law.

Finally, Greenwood's use of federal theology raises many questions. Unless one is Mormon, we know of no covenant God has made with the American people. That covenant is an important category in biblical thought cannot be denied, but it cannot be transferred to any national body. Furthermore, the notion that America is a "nation chosen by God" is not only wrong but also dangerous. If such were true, and it isn't, then one would think that American history would be replete with salvation-historical acts of God (and it isn't).

Citing Barbara Wentroble, Greenwood argues that God is giving new revelation to the church today. A christocentric view of revelation as one finds in my (Walter's) *Powers* trilogy or the New Testament would argue that God has completely revealed God's self in Jesus (John 1:1–18; Col. 1:15–20; 2:9; Heb. 1:1–3). In Scripture God's revelation upsets the status quo, challenges inherited assumptions, and reorients one's thinking and values. It is striking that the "revelation" received by the so-called apostles and leaders of charismatic evangelicalism justifies their social, political, and theological beliefs. One is tempted to say they are naively experiencing little more than religious projection.

It is also troublesome that Greenwood lumps together "witchcraft, . . . freemasonry, New Age beliefs, Eastern religions, and many other forms of spiritual practices" as a glorification of Satan. There is no attempt to engage each of these religious or spiritual traditions, no attempt to note the varieties within these practices, no attempt to critically discern what exactly is satanic about them. They are simply decried satanic—lock, stock, and barrel. This labeling of groups and persons within these groups as satanic or under the

---

47. On this, see the work of John Howard Yoder, Stanley Hauerwas, Richard Hays, N. T. Wright, David Flusser, and Willard Swartley, just to name a few.

power of darkness suggests a sectarian mentality, "us against them." It is also a manifestation of the accusatory process labeled as satanic by René Girard.

It is this "us against them" position that Greenwood exposes in her lengthy narrative under the heading "Contending against the Spirits behind Abortion." Her story tells of the ministry she and others in Kansas engaged in against the abortion clinic of Dr. George Tiller. Twice she laments the death of Dr. Tiller, who was murdered by a pro-life advocate. In her attempt to distance herself and the movement from Dr. Tiller's death, Greenwood asserts, "Let me say very emphatically that in the midst of our praying, not one time did we pray or even consider praying for Tiller's demise." The end result of this demonic expulsion is seen as a victory enabled by Jesus.

We offer an alternative explanation of this event from the perspective of mimetic theory and the myth of redemptive violence. Several phenomena suggest that such an interpretation is warranted. First, there is a social crisis, in this case a crisis between those who are pro-life and those who are pro-choice. Second, the gathering of a group allows for mimetic contagion to spread among a "mob." Third, this contagion is cast in terms of a Manichean good versus evil metaphysic.[48] Fourth, there is a labeling or accusatory process whereby those "possessed" are named (as was Dr. Tiller, amazingly not only at the Kansas rally but also in Congress, by Republican Robert K. Dornan). Fifth, there is an expulsion, in this case the metaphoric demon. Sixth, the resolution to the crisis was cathartic and brought a sense of peace (or this case, victory) to the group. Seventh, there are manifest the pillars of culture: ritual, prohibition, myth. The ritual process enacted in these casting out of "territorial demons" is very specific and precise and includes the use of certain sacred words or phrases. The prohibition—namely, "Thou shalt not commit abortion"—is reinforced as the problem of the crisis. Finally, the story of the expulsion is told in such a way that a random or innocent scapegoat is reckoned as truly guilty, whose death or expulsion creates group unanimity. Every single sign of the victimage process described by Girard in the mimetic theory is present in the narrative offered by Greenwood.[49]

Two other comments are in order. The first is that Greenwood names the territorial spirit as Lilith. Greenwood's evidence is the coincidental appearance

---

48. A devastating critique of this dualism in conservative evangelical Christianity can be found in Phillip Lee, *Against the Protestant Gnostics* (London: Oxford University Press, 1987).

49. The mimetic process is described by René Girard in his *Deceit, Desire and the Novel* (Baltimore: Johns Hopkins University Press, 1965); Girard, *Violence and the Sacred* (Baltimore: Johns Hopkins University Press, 1977); Girard, *Things Hidden from the Foundation of the World* (Stanford: Stanford University Press, 1987); and Girard, *The Scapegoat* (Baltimore: Johns Hopkins University Press, 1986).

of an owl. She equates the owl with Lilith with no evidence, just an unwarranted assertion. In certain Native American cultures (the Aztec, the Hopi, the Maya) the owl is a symbol of death. And in this case a real death occurred, that of George Tiller.

Twice in her essay Greenwood seeks to distance her work and those of the Kansas mob from the death of Dr. Tiller. However, given the mimetic character of those involved and the conjuring of sacred violence, it is evident that this resolution would eventuate in a real death, just like the mob scene in the Passion Narrative of Jesus. Tiller's death by assassination by antiabortion activist Scott Roeder was the cathartic death sought by the Kansas prayer rally, Greenwood's pleas to the contrary. Only death could bring a resolution to the crisis fomented by the antiabortion activists outside Tiller's clinic. While we do not doubt Greenwood's sincerity that she nor others desired the death of Dr. Tiller, their activity set in motion a ritual process as old as human culture itself, which required a scapegoat. For this reason we would contend that not only were there no demons "cast out" during the prayer rallies and vigils but also that one (Roeder) may have been encouraged and supported, even if unintentionally, by their actions.

From our perspective of the myth of redemptive violence, one can only marvel at Christian groups that fail to see the importance of Jesus's death as the unmasking and disempowering of the mechanism of sacred violence. Worse yet is that it is possible to do a study of the actions and rhetoric of these groups and find that the old satanic victimage mechanism is in full operation. Truly this is a case where satan casts out satan. This is not spiritual warfare but archaic pagan religion dressed up as Christianity. All of the *notae* are there for those with eyes to see and ears to hear.

RESPONSE TO C. PETER WAGNER AND REBECCA GREENWOOD

DAVID POWLISON

We share the same Bible, so there is much outside of the topic at hand that I share with Wagner and Greenwood. I expect we would find significant agreement on the contours of positive Christian truth about God, sin, the person and work of Christ, the way of salvation, church, the fruit of the Spirit, the Lord's Prayer, and so forth. Our differences arise in places where I think they step off that foundation and build their practical theology from ingredients incompatible with our shared Christian faith.

We agree on the real existence of diabolical agents operating within the fog of war and behind the scenes in human affairs. I trust that we also share a conviction in principle that our battle with evil has three interweaving and cooperative components—flesh, world, and devil—and that none of these reduces to or cancels out the others. But the devil drowns out both flesh and world in what Wagner and Greenwood have written. They do not capture the interplay of all three, the place where every human lives, the place where spiritual warfare actually happens.

Wagner's letter to his colleagues raises good and abiding questions. These are questions that practical theology must always ask and answer for ministry to bring God's revelation to life lived. But I would change his final question, "What is the relationship between Western worldviews and Third World worldviews?" Significantly, this is the only one of his ten questions that names a particular. It's a different kind of question from the previous nine. The better question to ask is this: "What is the relationship of the *biblical worldview* both to Western rationalism and to Third World animism?" Just criticism of the effects of Western rationalism on Christian thought and practice is often used to legitimate importing categories from non-Western animism into Christian thought and practice. The alternative to rationalism-with-Christian-flavoring is not animism-with-Christian-flavoring. I find the charismatically inclined view incautiously animistic in what it accepts, proclaims, and does—not on the surface, which remains zealously Christian in orientation, but in the deeper structure of thought and practice.

I agree with Wagner and Greenwood that evil spirits might well be localized and territorial—though our certainty levels on this differ, and our assessments of the significance and implications are poles apart. Territoriality is plausible for several reasons. First, only God is omnipresent (and omniscient, omnipotent, and self-existent). His creatures are always localized (and limited in knowledge, limited in power, and dependent on God for their continued existence). Demons are only creatures, however rebellious and pretentious. Second, the reality of supernaturally evil powers standing behind earthly powers that be is hinted at in Isaiah 24:21 and is one of the major themes in Revelation: the counterfeit trinity of Satan, the beast, and the false prophet work in and through the prostitute Babylon, who embodies kingdoms of institutional evil. Third, Daniel's apocalyptic vision (10:13, 20–21) sets up a parallelism between Michael (an archangel in some manner responsible for the people of God) and the "princes" of Persia and Greece (presumably archdemons in some manner responsible for idolatrous earthly regimes that threaten God's people). These are not open-and-shut arguments, but localization seems to me to be a reasonable inference.[50]

The possibility of territoriality "backstage" does not mean we are called to expend effort in scoping out such spirits. "Spiritual mapping" has no biblical precedent or warrant—the Bible is a ministry book, and it simply doesn't go there. For example, when Paul spoke in Athens (Acts 17:16–32), he had obviously done thoughtful research and audience analysis—all his speeches and letters are exquisite in this regard. But, equally evident, he made no attempt to psych out invisible powers that might lurk in the background. This is because ministry operates in the foreground and addresses people. The examples of spiritual mapping that Greenwood gives strike me as highly speculative and as poor substitutes for gaining a thoughtful understanding of the human audience. It seems to me no accident that Greenwood must rely on such things as Greek mythology, Talmudic fantasy, and a vivid dream she once had.

50. Regarding this paragraph, I am indebted to Vern Poythress, "Territorial Spirits: Some Biblical Perspectives," *Urban Mission* 13, no. 2 (December 1995): 37–49, available at http://www.frame-poythress.org/poythress_articles/1995Territorial.htm.

Similarly, territoriality backstage does not mean we are called to directly address such spirits, seeking to drive them out. Strategic-level spiritual warfare has no biblical precedent or warrant—the Bible simply does not go there. Greenwood puts forth Acts 16:11–34 as her exegetical foundation. Let's look at this passage more closely.

1. Fruitful evangelism was already occurring before the incident with the slave girl (16:11–15 ESV): "The Lord opened [Lydia's] heart to pay attention to what was said by Paul." The attentiveness of other women and the baptism of Lydia's household are also mentioned. Philippi is already good soil for the Word of life. A church is planted, presumably in Lydia's house (see 16:40). There is no indication that a territorial spirit had power to transfix the region in unbelief. On the contrary, faith was blossoming.

2. Paul commanded a fortune-telling spirit to leave a particular slave girl who had been earning money for her owners (16:16). There is no indication that a behind-the-scenes territorial principality was being cast out in this pointedly individual encounter.

3. Paul's reasons for taking this action are stated. He finally got irked. In fact, he was "greatly annoyed." That is a rather unusual ministry motive. The girl had been following them around and crying out—saying things that were true (!) but distracting from their ministry. She was pestering them. So Paul turned around—he hadn't even been looking at her—and ordered the spirit to leave, silencing her and negating her money-making potential (16:17–18). Addressing supposed territorial spirits was so far from being either a ministry goal or a standard operating procedure that Paul had ignored the girl's actions until she became a bother. Even an individual exorcism of this sort of spirit was no ministry priority for Paul. Far from being a dramatic face-off between Paul and a territorial spirit, the deliverance was a minor, almost matter-of-fact demonstration of Jesus's divine power. It simply rids Paul of a distraction to his ministry.

4. Paul and Silas were then manhandled to the marketplace to appear before the local authorities. There they were verbally accused by the owners and the crowd and then formally stripped, beaten, and jailed. Two reasons for this reaction are clearly stated. First, the owners had suffered financial loss. Second, and the basis of the actual charges made, the gospel's anti-imperial implications were causing trouble in this privileged Roman city (16:19–24).[51] The notion that a territorial spirit might be agitating the townspeople is neither mentioned nor implied. Normal human evil is enough of an explanation. After all, moral

51. In Thessalonica (Acts 17:1–9) an even bigger uproar occurred, further illumining the political issues involved and illustrating how religious jealousy could also be a motive.

bondage to Satan's lies and lusts is the real issue in spiritual warfare. In Scripture, moral bondage is *never* dealt with by casting out demons, whether at "ground level," "occult level," or "strategic level." That methodology typically addressed suffering individuals and never addressed their sins.

5. That night while Paul and Silas were worshiping in jail, a strong earthquake freed those who were incarcerated (16:26). This earthquake, like all earthquakes, expressed God's providential purposes. But the passage contains no hint that we ought to see more arcane connections, no hint that the quake was an outcome of "effectual spiritual warfare prayer," no hint of Greenwood's generalization that the effects of such praying "will frequently be evidenced in the physical realm." After all, there is no strategic-level spiritual warfare praying in Acts 16—or anywhere else in Scripture.

6. Fruitful evangelism continued because many people in Philippi continued to be receptive. The other prisoners had apparently been so transfixed by hearing God worshiped that they chose not to go on the lam. The jailer was saved from suicide, and he and his household came to joyous faith (16:27–34). There is no indication that the people of Philippi had been "immobilized in spiritual wickedness by a territorial spirit" until a power encounter set them free. Furthermore, there is no hint that God was overthrowing "the worship of Apollo in that region." Apollo was irrelevant to what happened. Scripture shows that money, Roman citizenship, and Roman law were highly relevant.

7. Paul, a Roman citizen, was doing nothing contrary to Roman law, and was vindicated legally the next day. He insisted the magistrates come and apologize (16:35–39). This touches a significant theme in the book of Acts. Paul pointedly engaged the visible powers that be—but there is no hint that his ministry sought to directly address invisible powers.

Greenwood's interpretation of Acts 16 did not arise from the text. She has offered a string of exegetical conjectures based on her preexisting theory. Though mysteries remain about the slave girl's paranormal ability, the passage is crystal clear about many things. It offers a striking refutation of the premises and procedures of strategic-level spiritual warfare.

The Wichita, Kansas, Case Study

Charismatically inclined spiritual warfare predicates crucial parts of both theory and methodology on anecdotes. But anecdotes are not authoritative, nor is their meaning self-evident. Anecdotes need to be subjected to critical reflection. Interpretive conclusions need to be cautious.

I appreciate that Greenwood begins her case study by mentioning the interpretive ambiguity that attends her Wichita story. I believe she speaks honestly of how shocked and appalled she was at George Tiller's murder, and how contrary that crime was to her ministry desires. I believe she sincerely desired a benign closure to Tiller's abortion practice, not the violent ending of his life. I believe she prayed for his spirit to soften, that he might willingly turn, that he might be saved and blessed by God.

But having begun cautiously and caringly, she proceeds incautiously. This anecdote strikes me as more unfortunate than persuasive. It demonstrates an overactive imagination more than wisdom from above. Here are elements that seem particularly volatile:

a preoccupation with identifying the background diabolical agency presumed responsible for the existence of Tiller's abortion business;

the supposed presence of "recognized apostles";

an army of passionate people engaged in spiritual mapping, expecting prophetic revelations, and anticipating decisive social transformation through the overthrow of the territorial demon holding Wichita in thrall;

the credulity of attaching significance to an ancient Talmudic fantasy about a fictional being named "Lilith";

the credulity of attaching revelational significance to a dream about Lilith;

the credulity of attaching revelational significance to the bedraggled owl deposited in a tree;

the credulity that animated twenty-one nights of fasting and prayer "since Lilith is a nocturnal God. The idea behind this was to pray and war in the night hours when the demonic activity of Lilith is the strongest"; and

the heightened sense that spiritual conflict and hostilities were coming to a head and that the imminent defeat of Lilith would lead to the closing of the clinic.

That's a heady combination. But Lilith is a *fictional literary character*. She is in the same category as the White Witch of Narnia, Sauron, Darth Vader, and Lord Voldemort. The biblical reference being pressed into unwilling service is Isaiah 34:14. This passage portrays the desolation of Edom by listing the desert creatures that come to live in the ruins (Isa. 34:11–17). As with many biblical names for flora and fauna, we don't know the exact creature that Isaiah's contemporaries called a *lilith* (34:14). This unidentified desert creature is most likely one of the seven owl species still native to Jordan. Seizing on this homely bit of our collective ignorance, a florid Lilith mythology has arisen over the centuries. The anecdote fixates on a bit of occult mythology, not the wisdom of Scripture.

Jonathan Edwards once noted that "there is nothing that belongs to Christian experience that is more liable to corrupt mixture than zeal."[52] The zeal of the spiritual warriors in Wichita was unmistakable. But was it wise?

52. Jonathan Edwards, *Some Thoughts Concerning the Revival*, in *The Works of Jonathan Edwards*, ed. C. C. Goen, vol. 4, *The Great Awakening* (New Haven: Yale University Press, 1972), 460.

Response to C. Peter Wagner
and Rebecca Greenwood

Gregory Boyd

I want to thank Peter Wagner and his colleague Rebecca Greenwood for participating in this important discussion on the nature of spiritual warfare. I have always had a deep respect for Wagner's pioneering work in this area. Few have done as much as he to address the "lack of awareness concerning the enemy" in the Western church. Given that my understanding of the purpose of multi-viewpoint books such as this one is to flesh out *differences* among thinkers on a given topic, I must forgo commenting on the many areas where I fundamentally agree with Wagner and Greenwood and instead focus my response on three aspects of their essay that concern me.

Centralizing a Biblically Unprecedented Practice

The first concern I have is with the central role Wagner, Greenwood, and others who adopt their perspective assign to what they call "strategic-level spiritual warfare"—engaging in battle against principalities and powers through various activities such as spiritual mapping, receiving personal revelations, prayer, prophetic acts, and prophetic pronouncements. Not only is there no support for this in Scripture, but one *could* even argue that the fact that the angel didn't invite Daniel to join in his battle against the "prince of Persia" provides a *counterexample* to this movement (Dan. 10:20). Now, I personally don't feel we are bound in a legalistic fashion to the precedent of Scripture, which is why I am not opposed to people praying against demonic, territorial-level powers if they feel so led. I grow concerned, however, when practices for which there are no biblical precedents take *center stage* in anyone's theology and ministry.

The response that is typically given whenever this objection is raised is that this approach is proven to work, as is evidenced by a litany of anecdotal accounts, such as is provided in the two *Transformations* videos.[53] Since I wasn't personally involved in any of these accounts, I'm in a poor position to deny their accuracy. At the same time, I don't see that these reports justify centralizing the strategic-level spiritual warfare approach. I readily grant that God sometimes uses these sincere and hardworking Christians to advance his kingdom, sometimes in miraculous ways. But this hardly proves that God endorses these practices, let alone that he approves of people placing them at the heart of their theology and ministry.

On top of this, we need to be aware of just how subjective our perspectives are when it comes to assessing whether or not a ministry strategy "works," especially when we are already committed to the strategy in question. Psychological studies confirm what most of us know from common sense: when we believe something passionately, we tend to place great significance on things that *confirm* our views and to minimize the significance, if not totally ignore, things that might *count against* our views.[54]

To illustrate, for Greenwood and those she ministered with in Kansas, the fact that the abortion rate in Kansas dropped 23 percent in two years after they "bound Lilith" undoubtedly helped confirm that their dreams, impressions, and research about Lilith were accurate and that their strategic-level spiritual warfare "worked." What did not register as significant, however, was the multitude of other factors that could potentially explain this fortunate drop. In fact, the time-consuming legal issues Tiller was enveloped in and the negative press this generated would alone suffice to explain this.

Along the same lines, for Greenwood and those she ministered with, the Talmudic legend she discovered about Lilith, and the owl they discovered trapped in a tree confirmed for them that their strategic-level spiritual warfare had "worked." What was not considered significant, however, was the fact that scholars uniformly consider this fanciful story to be a piece of medieval rabbinic folklore and that the legendary association of Lilith with an owl in Isaiah 34:14–15 has no basis in fact.

My concern here is not with this episode in particular, still less to deny that God used Greenwood and her friends to help lower the abortion rate in Kansas.

53. George Otis Jr., *Transformations I* (1999) and *Transformations II: The Glory Spreads* (2001).
54. For an overview of research on the "confirmation bias" (sometimes called the "verification bias"), see "Confirmation Bias" at http://en.wikipedia.org/wiki/Confirmation_bias.

I don't know. I'm rather simply pointing out how subjective our assessments of ministry strategies can be when we're already committed to them. My concern about the central role that Wagner and Greenwood give to strategic-level spiritual warfare is thus not alleviated by the stories they and others offer in support of it.

Remembering Our Myopia

My second concern is also related to the importance the strategic-level spiritual warfare movement gives to their approach and to our need to remember how subjective our perspectives tend to be. I want to say at the start that I passionately agree with Wagner and Greenwood in believing that God speaks to us today. In my own pastoral ministry, I consistently teach people to be open to receiving personal revelations, prophetic words and pictures, words of knowledge, and the like. However, given how myopic, sin-tainted, and culturally conditioned our perspectives tend to be, and given how prone to error we are in distinguishing our own inner voice from the voice of God, I also teach that we need to take great care not to leverage too much on what we *believe* God may be saying to us. Regardless of how strong our impressions may be, we must never forget the myopic, sin-tainted, and error-prone nature of our perspectives. My concern is that the authority and importance given to subjective impressions in the strategic-level spiritual warfare movement inclines people to minimize, or ignore altogether, this all-important fact. And this, in turn, can lead to a host of other potential problems.

For one thing, placing too much authority and importance on our subjective impressions while focusing on what may be going on in the spiritual realm can lead people to become so preoccupied with fighting invisible forces that they minimize the significance of other important factors that pertain to an issue. For example, if a person called to address the abortion issue is part of a ministry that is centered on confronting the invisible forces behind abortion on the basis of information someone believes they've received from God, they can easily minimize the significance of the multitude of more earthly factors that affect abortion and that need to be addressed.[55] They can easily believe that the most important thing needed to bring an end to abortion is to bind the demonic power behind abortion in the particular way they believe God told them to.

While I'm all for people receiving revelations, and while I'm not against giving a place to praying against spiritual forces, I believe our approach to

55. I want it to be clear that I am here offering an observation about a *general tendency* among strategic-level warriors. I am in no way commenting on Greenwood's particular activity in Kansas, for I know nothing about this activity beyond what she reported in her chapter.

abortion and every other social issue we may feel called to address needs to be more balanced. If abortion is the issue an individual or community feels called to address, it seems to me their focus should be on more practical, and generally more challenging, questions, such as: How can we individually and collectively sacrifice our time and resources to make it practically feasible for mothers with unwanted pregnancies to go full term with their unborn babies, since studies show a high percentage of women who have abortions do so because they feel they have no viable alternative?[56] How can we sacrifice our time and resources to alleviate poverty, since studies suggest there is a strong correlation between poverty and abortion? How can we sacrifice our time and resources to befriend and serve young people who come from tragically broken homes, since studies suggest there is a correlation between broken homes and abortion? And how can we individually and collectively sacrifice our time and resources to demonstrate Christlike love to the abortion practitioners, since loving and serving "enemies" lies at the heart of the kingdom Jesus brought?

Without commenting on any particular strategic-level spiritual warrior or ministry, it's been my impression that this movement tends to spend much less energy addressing these sorts of issues than it does engaging in biblically unprecedented activities that pertain to confronting invisible forces. And this, I submit, is because they tend to place too much confidence in, and too much importance on, personal revelations and on confronting invisible powers.

Lifestyle Warfare

Closely related to this is a third and final concern I have with Wagner and Greenwood's essay. I wholeheartedly agree with Greenwood when she says the church is called to bring an end to the oppressive reign of the fallen powers and to reclaim the authority God originally gave humans to rule the earth. This is an essential aspect of what it means to manifest Jesus's lordship over all things. The question is, *how* are we to go about doing this? The answer provided in Wagner and Greenwood's essay concerns me deeply.

Because of the authority we've been given, writes Greenwood, "God has purposed the church to manage the land." Similarly, Greenwood asks, "Who

56. On reasons why women choose abortion, see Lawrence B. Finer, Lori F. Frohwirth, Lindsay A. Dauphinee, Susheela Singh, and Ann M. Moore, "Reasons U.S. Women Have Abortions: Quantitative and Qualitative Perspectives," in *Perspectives on Sexual and Reproductive Health* 37, no. 3 (2005):110–18; Akinrinola Bankole, Susheela Singh, and Taylor Haas, "Reasons Why Women Have Induced Abortions: Evidence from 27 Countries," *International Family Planning Perspectives* 24, no. 3 (September 1998): 117–27, 152.

is now responsible to rule and reign in the earth?" "Believe it or not," she replies, "the church, which is the Body of Christ."[57] What this entails is made clear a bit later when she argues that, since Jesus is Lord over "all things," it is the church's job to seek to rule and reign over all things, including "the land, the environment, politics, education, science, medicine, healthcare, the arts, space, economics, social justice, and all the humanities."[58] This, it turns out, is the ultimate objective of strategic-level spiritual warfare, according to Wagner and Greenwood, as it is for many in the strategic-level spiritual warfare movement.

With all due respect, this triumphant theology strikes me as little more than a new twist on the old Constantinian paradigm the church has been afflicted with for the last fifteen hundred years. In contrast to Christians in the first three centuries, who generally understood that their calling was simply to imitate and proclaim Jesus as they sacrificially served the world, Christians after Constantine began to imagine it was the calling of the church to "rule and reign" over the world. Though Jesus rejected the opportunity to acquire the power and authority of the world's governments as a temptation *from the devil* (Luke 4:5–7), theologians such as Eusebius and Augustine tragically welcomed the political power that Constantine granted them as a gift *from God*.

Once the church embraced the notion that they were to "manage the land," the all-important mandate of the New Testament to imitate Jesus by humbly serving the world tragically began to fade. The church of the crucified savior became the church "militant and triumphant." While there have always been countermovements within the church that continued to live out the calling of the gospel, the church as a whole looked less and less like a corporate Jesus and more and more like a corporate Caesar.

If the example of Jesus and the teachings of the New Testament are not enough to convince us to shun the aspiration to "rule and reign in the earth" as a temptation of the devil, the tragic history of the church that for fifteen hundred years has tried to do this should be. If history teaches us anything, it should be that it is disastrous for the church, as well as for the state, to have Christians "rule and reign." In the name of Jesus, the church began to rely on power *over* others to achieve its objectives rather than power *under* others—the power of self-sacrificial love.[59] Indeed, all too often the church "militant and

---

57. Greenwood is here quoting with approval Steve Thompson, "Your Authority in Christ," *Morning Star Journal* (Summer 2006): 22.

58. Greenwood is here quoting with approval Mattera, *Ruling in the Gates*, 49.

59. For a fuller discussion of the distinction between "power over" and "power under," see Gregory Boyd, *The Myth of a Christian Nation: How the Quest for Political Power Is Destroying the Church* (Grand Rapids: Zondervan, 2005).

triumphant" coerced conversions, persecuted heretics, tortured dissidents, and slaughtered enemies.[60]

I of course am not in any way suggesting that Wagner and Greenwood would want anything to do with the violence displayed by the Constantinian church as it sought to maintain and advance its "rule and reign." They rightly see that our battle is "not against flesh and blood, but against principalities, against powers" (Eph 6:12 KJV). Yet their mind-set, as reflected in this essay, is nevertheless thoroughly Constantinian. By engaging in strategic-level spiritual warfare and other means, they aspire to have Christians *take over* and *win*.

I submit that our only call is to *serve*, not take over, and to even appear to *lose* when necessary, not win. To be sure, with Wagner and Greenwood, I believe that someday, when Christ returns, we will "rule and reign" with him (2 Tim. 2:12; Rev. 5:10; 20:6; 22:5). This has been humanity's destiny and calling from the start (Gen. 1:26–28). But until that time comes, our call is to humbly follow Jesus on the way to the cross. He manifested God's reign and waged war against the fallen powers by shunning all the ungodly and dehumanizing aspects of society that fuel them and by living a life of self-sacrificial service, even toward his enemies, and even to the point of death. Our most fundamental call is to simply imitate this example while trusting God to rule over this fallen world until Christ returns.

Adopting the God-trusting, self-sacrificial, and always countercultural lifestyle of Jesus is the primary way we wage war against the fallen powers and express the unique authority we have in Christ. There's nothing wrong with praying against the powers, but our all-consuming focus should be on manifesting Jesus's victory over the fallen powers by living the way he lived.

---

60. Several works recounting some of the atrocities committed by the church "militant and triumphant" throughout history are James A. Haught, *Holy Horrors* (Buffalo: Prometheus, 1990); Henry Charles Lea, *The Inquisition of the Middle Ages*, abr. Margaret Nicholson (New York: Macmillan); W. Sumner Davis, *Heretics: The Bloody History of the Church* (La Verne, TN: Lightning Source, 2002); and Helen Ellerbe, *The Dark Side of Christian History* (Orlando, FL: Morningstar and Lark, 1995).

Contributors

James Beilby is professor of systematic and philosophical theology at Bethel University, St. Paul, MN. He has coedited several multiple-views books (with Paul Eddy), most recently *The Historical Jesus: Five Views* (Downers Grove, IL: IVP Academic, 2009) and *Justification: Five Views* (Downers Grove, IL: IVP Academic, 2011). He is also the author of *Epistemology as Theology* (Burlington, VT: Ashgate 2005) and *Thinking about Christian Apologetics* (Downers Grove, IL: IVP Academic, 2011).

Gregory Boyd is senior pastor of Woodland Hills Church (St. Paul, MN) and president of ReKnew. He has written a wide range of books, essays, and articles, including *Letters from a Skeptic: A Son Wrestles with His Father's Questions about Christianity* (with Ed Boyd) (Wheaton: Victor, 1994); *God at War: The Bible and Spiritual Conflict* (Downers Grove, IL: InterVarsity, 1997); *Satan and the Problem of Evil: Constructing a Trinitarian Warfare Theodicy* (Downers Grove, IL: InterVarsity, 2001); and *The Myth of a Christian Nation: How the Quest for Political Power Is Destroying the Church* (Grand Rapids: Zondervan, 2006).

Paul Rhodes Eddy is professor of biblical and theological studies at Bethel University, St. Paul, MN. He has coedited several multiple-views books (with James Beilby) and has authored and coauthored a number of other books, including *John Hick's Pluralist Philosophy of World Religions* (Burlington, VT: Ashgate, 2002); *The Jesus Legend* (Grand Rapids: Baker Academic, 2007); and *Across the Spectrum*, 2nd ed. (Grand Rapids: Baker Academic, 2009).

Rebecca Greenwood is the founding president of Christian Harvest International. She served on staff at Global Harvest Ministries, she is a core faculty member of Wagner Leadership Institute, and she sits on the Founder's Circle of the International Society of Deliverance Ministers. She has authored a number of books, including *Authority to Tread: An Intercessor's Guide to Strategic-Level Spiritual Warfare* (Grand Rapids: Chosen, 2006); *Breaking the Bonds of Evil: How to Set People Free from Demonic Oppression* (Grand Rapids: Chosen, 2006); and *Let Our Children Go: Steps to Free Your Child from Evil Influences and Demonic Harassment* (Lake Mary, FL: Charisma House, 2011).

Michael Hardin is the executive director of Preaching Peace in Lancaster, PA (www.preachingpeace.org), a nonprofit committed to "Educating the Church and the World in Jesus' Vision of Peace." Michael is the author of the acclaimed *The Jesus Driven Life* (Lancaster, PA: JDL Press, 2010); coeditor of *Compassionate Eschatology* (Eugene, OR: Cascade, 2011); *Peace Be With You* (Scottdale, PA: Cascadia, 2010); and *Stricken by God?* (Grand Rapids: Eerdmans, 2007); and editor of *Reading the Bible with René Girard* (2012).

Gareth Higgins is executive director of the Wild Goose Festival, a national gathering at the intersection of spirituality, justice, and art. He has taught reconciliation studies at Trinity College Dublin and founded the zero28 Project, a postsectarian peace-building initiative in his birthplace, Northern Ireland. He is author or coauthor of *Anti-Catholicism in Northern Ireland* (New York: St. Martin's Press, 1998); *How Movies Helped Save My Soul* (Lake Mary, FL: Relevant Books, 2003); and *Religion, Civil Society, and Peace Building in Northern Ireland* (New York: Oxford University Press, 2011).

David Powlison teaches pastoral counseling at CCEF (Christian Counseling and Educational Foundation) and Westminster Seminary, and he edits and writes for the *Journal of Biblical Counseling*. His books include *Seeing with New Eyes* (Phillipsburg, NJ: P&R, 2003); *Speaking Truth in Love* (Winston-Salem, NC: Punch Press, 2005); and *The Biblical Counseling Movement* (Greensboro, NC: New Growth Press, 2010). He has contributed essays in *Psychology & Christianity: Five Views* (Downers Grove, IL: IVP Academic, 2010) and to tribute volumes honoring John Piper and John Frame.

C. Peter Wagner is vice president of Global Spheres, Inc., served as a missionary to Bolivia for sixteen years (1956–71), and was professor of church growth at Fuller Theological Seminary for thirty years (1971–2001). He founded Global Harvest Ministries (now Global Spheres, Inc.), as well as Wagner Leadership Institute. He has authored or edited over seventy books, including *Spiritual Warfare Strategy* (Shippensburg, PA: Destiny Image, 2011); *Warfare Prayer* (Ventura, CA: Regal, 1992); *Territorial Spirits* (Ventura, CA:

Regal, 1991); *Wrestling with Dark Angels* (Ventura, CA: Regal, 1991); and *The Book of Acts: A Commentary* (Ventura, CA: Regal, 2008).

Walter Wink (1935–2012) a groundbreaking figure in the field of New Testament theology, died on May 10th in Sandisfield, MA, at the age of 76. At the time of his death he was professor emeritus of biblical interpretation at Auburn Theological Seminary in New York City. Previously, he was a parish minister and taught at Union Theological Seminary in New York City. From 1989 to 1990 he was a peace fellow at the United States Institute of Peace. He authored the award-winning *Engaging the Powers* (Minneapolis: Fortress, 1992) and *The Human Being* (Minneapolis: Fortress, 2001).

Index of Authors and Subjects

Index of Scripture